r

# THE EPISTLE OF
# JAMES

# THE EPISTLE OF
# JAMES

## C. LESLIE MITTON

### B.A., M.Th., Ph.D., D.D.

Formerly Principal of Handsworth College, Birmingham
and Editor of The Expository Times

MARSHALL, MORGAN & SCOTT
*London*

MARSHALL, MORGAN & SCOTT
*A member of the Pentos Group*
I BATH STREET
LONDON ECIV 9LB

PRINTED IN GREAT BRITAIN BY
HOLLEN STREET PRESS LTD AT SLOUGH
772022L20

# CONTENTS

# PREFACE

The commentary is based on the Revised Standard Version of the Bible, and I should like to express gratitude to the National Council of the Churches of Christ in the United States of America for permission to use it.

In the comments themselves, however, the Revised Version (as it is known in Great Britain) is used occasionally, since its practice of normally translating a Greek word consistently by the same English word makes similarities between passages more easily recognizable.

Since the book was written with American readers in mind, what in Great Britain is normally known as the Authorised Version (A.V.) is usually referred to as King James' Version (K.J.V.).

I wish to acknowledge very gratefully the most valuable help in proof-reading given by the Rev. David J. T. Matthews, M.A., and also the encouragement of Professor G. A. Turner of Wilmore, Kentucky, who in the first place urged me to write an "Evangelical Commentary" on James.

C. L. MITTON

# ABBREVIATIONS

A.V.   Authorised Version—King James' Version (1611)
K.J.V.  King James' Version of the Bible (=A.V.)
LXX    Septuagint, the official translation of the Hebrew Old Testament into Greek
MSS    Manuscripts
N.E.B.  New English Bible (1961)
R.V.   Revised Version of Bible (1881)
R.S.V.  American Revised Standard Version of Bible (1946)

# INTRODUCTION

This commentary has two main aims: One is to expound the teaching of James in this epistle, to show its importance for Christian people, and its continuing relevance to our own day. The second is to show how James's teaching is an integral part of the total message of the New Testament, and that what he has to say is wholly in accord both with the recorded teaching of Jesus, and with the writings of the other apostles.

Among Christians who value the evangelical tradition in the Church, this epistle has come to be viewed with a measure of suspicion. There are even doubts among them whether it can be regarded as basically true to the central message of the New Testament. Perhaps Martin Luther more than any other single person is responsible for this attitude of doubt and misgiving. It was he who branded the epistle as "an epistle of straw" (in comparison, that is, with Romans), and also pronounced upon it the damning sentence, that it "contains nothing evangelical".

If we ask why Luther spoke so sharply about it, we have to admit that, superficially at any rate, there are reasons, perhaps good reasons, for it. For instance, in the whole epistle the name of Christ is mentioned only twice; there is no reference at all to the Cross or the Resurrection or the Holy Spirit; moreover, it actually includes words whose express purpose seems to be to contradict one of the most precious of the Apostle Paul's great evangelical affirmations: "A man is not justified by works of the law but through faith in Christ" (Gal. 2: 16). In contrast James explicitly says: "A man is justified by works and not by faith alone" (2: 24). So James has been adjudged guilty by some of sins both of omission and of commission.

In spite of these apparent shortcomings and the censure to which he has been subjected, we confidently uphold the wisdom of the Church in according to James a place in the Canon of the New Testament. It is true that James was not written with the primary purpose of converting unbelievers, nor yet of confirming the wavering Christian in his faith. It was written for those who had no doubt that they were Christians, but needed to have their understanding of the word "Christian" greatly deepened and widened. They assumed that the essence of being a Christian was the willingness to make a verbal confession of Christ, and a readiness to worship Him in the community of the Church. James, however, saw very clearly that a true Christian, once converted, must set himself the goal of true holiness. The author therefore longs to awaken in those who have been won into the Christian life the kind of robust faith which is not content merely with orthodoxy of belief, but fills a man with passionate longing to have his life in every part brought into perfect obedience to the will of God as made known through Jesus Christ.

In this, James is entirely at one with Paul. Paul declared, as he emphasized the fundamental importance of faith, that true faith is "faith working through love" (Gal. 5: 6). This Pauline phrase could well stand as the title of the epistle of James. If Paul wanted in his converts the kind of faith which produces love, James longed to find in them that true love which springs from faith and proves beyond question the reality of faith. In his letter, with its somewhat stern teaching on practical holiness, he is seeking to show how Christian love would express itself in a variety of actual situations. If then true faith is not only faith that justifies but also faith which leads on to true holiness of life (or perfect love, as John Wesley preferred to call it in the phrase of 1 John 4: 17–21), then James undoubtedly takes his rightful place in the Book of the Faith.

James would claim that love for God cannot be separated from love for one's fellowman. In this he merely follows the teaching of Jesus who selected the two great commands of "Love God" and "Love your neighbour" as the perfect summary of God's will for man. It is an emphasis which also links James with John, who wrote: "He that loves God should love his brother also" (1 John 4: 21).

James, however, knew how easily the human heart avoids the implications of the Gospel by sentimentalizing both faith and love. Faith comes to be understood as fine words of orthodox belief, and love as fine feelings, and both stop short of the stern requirement of conduct. James, however, will not allow love to remain as merely kindly feelings. True love is an unselfish concern for the welfare of others, which issues in action, if need be in costly action, in actual deeds of justice and of mercy. This is James's emphasis: true faith produces love, and true love issues in practical action.

The epistle is, therefore, largely a series of exhortations to true Christian holiness of life, that is to perfect love towards God and man. The writer takes for granted the great basic truths of the evangelical faith, because they are not at all in question. Both readers and writer are agreed on those. It is the outworkings of that faith which he is concerned to stress, because his readers are showing themselves curiously indifferent in this respect. Either they do not realise how Christian love should work out in practice or they have become very careless about it.

Our main concern in this commentary is with the exposition of its message, not with what are commonly called matters of Introduction. Questions about the authorship of the epistle, its date, provenance, destination and history will not be the focus of attention at all, though they will be dealt with in the appendix to the commentary. We shall seek primarily to understand its contents, and try to see how these fit easily into the wider message of the New Testament as a whole.

The epistle claims to be by James. No other description, however, apart from the name, is added, to enable us to identify this James. It may be one of the Jameses named elsewhere in the New Testament, or else a James not otherwise mentioned in the New Testament. But in the tradition of the Church this James has in fact been identified with the brother of our Lord who bore that name (Gal. 1: 19) and who became the leader of the Church in Jerusalem (Acts 15:13; cf. Gal. 2: 9), who also was one of the first to see Christ after His resurrection (1 Cor. 15: 7). For the purposes of this commentary we shall accept this tradition, though in fact it makes little difference to an exposition of the contents of the Epistle whether the tradition is actually true or not.

Since, however, the reputation of this epistle has suffered from depreciatory comments, and Luther, besides speaking slightingly of it, actually relegated it to a subordinate position at the end of his translation of the New Testament, as though it hardly deserved to stand in the same company as the other books, I wish, as a secondary purpose, to draw attention to the constant similarities of teaching that are to be found between James on the one hand, and on the other the teaching of our Lord, and also the writings of Paul, and John and Peter. It is my hope that readers of this commentary will at the end of it feel that they have not only come to understand the message of James more fully, but through it have also found themselves being led into many other important parts of the New Testament. The result, I hope, will be a recognition that James stands firmly within the message of the New Testament as a whole, and himself expounds one aspect of it with great faithfulness.

We proceed, therefore, with the commentary on the assumption that the epistle was written by James the brother of our Lord, and that it was written for the benefit of Jewish Christian visitors to Jerusalem who wished to have some record of James's characteristic teaching to take back with them for the benefit of the Christians in their home towns.

Where other commentaries on James are referred to and no page reference is given, it may be assumed that the reference will be found where that particular commentary is dealing with the passage under discussion.

# CHAPTER ONE

*1: 1. James, a servant of God and of the Lord Jesus Christ, to the twelve tribes in the dispersion: greeting.*

The letter begins with a conventional opening: the name of the writer, the people to whom the letter is addressed, and a word of greeting. Paul frequently elaborated the brief customary formula into quite a long paragraph, but James, who appears to be a man of few words, is content with this very simple form of introduction.

**1: 1** The writer introduces himself modestly by his name only. He does not indicate who he is, or what his status in the Church is. Paul often added the word "apostle" to his own name, as if to give authority to what he wrote. This writer simply calls himself *"James"*, but the very lack of titles suggests that he was a well-known figure, whose right to send a letter of this kind would not be questioned.

Since the writer uses only the name James, a common name among the Jews, and since several men of that name appear in the pages of the New Testament, there has from earliest times been some doubt as to the precise identity of the writer. He may, of course, have been some man called James, of whom we know nothing more than that he wrote this epistle. Usually, however, it has been assumed that he is one of the Christian leaders of that name, of whom we hear elsewhere in the New Testament. Two of the twelve disciples, in the list recorded in Mark 3: 16–19, are called James, one the son of Zebedee, the other the son of Alphaeus. There is also James, the brother of the Lord, who came to be the recognized leader of the Church in Jerusalem, to whom Paul refers in Galatians (1: 19; 2: 9–12).

One early manuscript does in fact identify our author with James, the son of Zebedee, whose call to be a disciple, along with his brother John, is described in Mark 1: 19, and whose death as a martyr at the hands of Herod Agrippa is recorded in Acts 12: 2. This suggestion, however, has found little support either in the early Church or since. The common tradition of the Church affirmed that the writer of this epistle was "the Lord's brother", mentioned by Paul in Galatians, and also referred to in Acts 15: 13 and 21: 18, as an important figure in the Church at Jerusalem. This tradition cannot be traced back further than the early part of the third century, but from that time it was commonly accepted throughout the Church. Only at the time of the

Reformation was this tradition questioned by some of the Reformers, and in reply the Roman Catholic Church at the Council of Trent explicitly pronounced the tradition to be correct.

The identification of the author with James of Jerusalem cannot be fully proved. Many scholars have raised arguments against it; but any alternative theory raises as many difficulties as it solves. Since our primary concern in the commentary is with the contents of the epistle, we shall be content to assume the traditional authorship.

Those who wish to study the question of authorship in greater detail will find the subject discussed in the Appendix on pages 222–232.

James describes himself as "SERVANT OF GOD AND OF THE LORD JESUS CHRIST", a description which associates him with all other Christians who would wish to use the same words of themselves. He does not claim to speak from a position of special authority but as one with those to whom he addresses himself. What he has to say they will accept as true not merely because he personally says it, but because their own consciences, illumined with the light of Christ, will recognize its truth.

Our English word "SERVANT" does not quite tally with the word James actually uses. The word (Greek *doulos*) really means "slave", a common word in the ancient world, because slavery was a common institution. It indicates one who belongs to a master. An ordinary servant, in our normal sense of that word, hires out his labour to anyone who will pay him well, and feels himself at liberty to change his employer if he thinks a change will be to his advantage. But a slave is the property of his master; he belongs to him, and is not at liberty to leave him; even any property the slave may acquire belongs to the master. It is this utterly self-effacing word which James applies to himself. He is the property of God, utterly and without condition at God's disposal. God has the right to command and to use him just as He will.

We can hardly use the word "slave" in modern English because it has today humiliating and sordid associations, which it did not necessarily have in the ancient world. Today we use it in connection only with evil masters. A man may be the slave of his passions, a slave to drink or to gambling, because he has no power to disobey these tyrants. But in the ancient world, though no one wanted to be a slave, some fine men were slaves, men of great ability and intellect. They had become slaves not through their own failures, but as the result of military conquest. In such cases the word was not wholly a shameful word. Moreover, there could be a certain pride in it if your owner was a great man. A slave, particularly if he was a trusted slave in the service of a great man, could come to feel pride through his relationship to his master. Some indeed found such satisfaction in the service of a great family that when freedom was offered to them, as a reward for faithfulness, they preferred to remain in the household they were proud to belong to. So when James calls himself "the property of God", there is a clear note of humble abasement before God, since God has undisputed right to all that he has or is. There is, however, a note of pride as well. If one has to be a "slave", the property of another, what could be finer than to be the property not just of some splendid king, but of the King of kings?

James, of course, was not the only one so to describe himself. In the Greek version of the Old Testament Moses is called "the slave of God" (1 Kings 8: 53), and Paul too sometimes uses it of himself (Rom. 1: 1; Phil. 1: 1). The utter devotion implicit in this word, and also the pride and joy of belonging to such a Master, find expression in some of our hymns:

> Our souls and bodies we resign;
>     With joy we render Thee
> Our all, no longer ours, but Thine
>     To all eternity.

Perhaps we should note in passing that, though Christians should think of themselves as the "slaves" of God, God in His mercy does not think of us in that way. Our Lord in John 15: 15 says to his followers: "No longer do I call you servants . . . but I have called you friends". And in Rom. 8: 16 Paul assures us that "The Spirit Himself beareth witness with our spirit that we are children of God". God treats us as His "friends", His "children", and we accept the privilege with wondering gratitude. God confers it; but it is not our own by any natural right. We dare not claim it as something which is our due. Our highest claim, when we think and speak of ourselves (apart from God's incredible generosity), is that we belong to God, we are His property. Our Lord Himself taught us: "When you have done all that is commanded you, say, 'We are unworthy servants (i.e. slaves); we have only done what was our duty' " (Luke 17: 10).

James describes himself as "servant OF GOD AND OF OUR LORD JESUS CHRIST". Our Lord Himself warned us: "No man can serve two masters". But, of course, God and Jesus Christ are not two masters, but one. For the Christian they are One in purpose and authority. "I and the Father are One," said Jesus. He is God's Word to man. Through Him we know the Father. It is in Him that God has chosen to confront man in his sin and need. "God was in Christ", testifies the apostle Paul.

It is indeed possible to translate the Greek words used here as: "servant of Jesus Christ, who is God and Lord", but it is very doubtful whether James meant us to understand the words in this way. Only very rarely in the New Testament is Jesus explicitly called "God", though that is the confession to which all the New Testament is leading, and which finds explicit affirmation in the words of Thomas: "My Lord and my God" (John 20: 28). But even if Jesus is not here identified with God, He and the Father are clearly associated together in what is in effect a unity. One who becomes a servant of Christ thereby becomes a servant of God. A servant of God comes to understand both God and his service of God better when he is also a servant of Jesus Christ.

James refers to Jesus as THE LORD JESUS CHRIST. The two words "Lord" and "Christ" became, in combination, the way in which the early Church confessed its faith. They, more than any others, served to gather up in one simple phrase what Jesus had come to mean in their lives. It was the way Peter gave expression to their faith on the Day of Pentecost: "God has made him both Lord and Christ, this Jesus whom you crucified".

Understandably enough the disciples of Jesus did not reach this fulness of faith all at once. They did not recognize Jesus immediately as the unique Person we believe Him to be, though they were well aware that He was someone very much out of the ordinary. In the gospels we find them applying to Him at first the names they were accustomed to accord to the men they most greatly honoured: Rabbi, teacher, prophet, Son of David. None of these, however,—nor all in combination—was felt to be adequate, and all soon dropped out of use among Christians. Mark in his gospel helps us to realise what an outstanding moment it was in the earthly life of Jesus and in the experience of His disciples, when Peter, acting, as so often, as their spokesman, at Caesarea Philippi declared Jesus to be the Christ. For the Jews there was no higher category in which Jesus could have been placed. Peter must have felt almost shocked at his own audacity when he first dared to speak this confession of faith aloud. His ability to do so was ascribed by our Lord to a special insight given to Peter by God Himself (Matt. 16: 17). This name for Jesus came to be accepted by all Christians, for though no name was wholly adequate for Jesus (there was needed "a name which is above every name", Phil. 2: 9) this at any rate was not so inadequate as most others.

The word "Christ" is the Greek translation for the Hebrew word "Messiah", which meant "anointed one". It was first used of someone marked out by God with special dignity for the fulfilment of some high purpose. It had been applied in earlier days to kings and prophets. By the time of Jesus, however, there had not been a real Israelite king for very many years. The people of Israel lived under foreign rule. Moreover there had been no prophet for many generations, and it was believed that the line of the prophets had ended. The nation was oppressed and the wicked flourished, and God did not seem to be doing much about it. But hope was not extinguished. It was believed by many that God would, in His own time, perhaps very soon, take action to set all wrongs right; and the one through whom He would act for the good of His people would be His "Messiah", His anointed one, God's representative, God's special messenger, equipped with God's authority. It was this that Peter meant when he confessed Jesus to be the Christ, the Messiah. This was a word which carried deep significance for those of Jewish background; but it had not the same meaning among the Gentiles. To them it seems to have been little more than a kind of second name for Jesus, a way in which He could be distinguished from others who might be called Jesus. They had to avail themselves of another title which had been ascribed to Jesus, and which was as meaningful for Gentiles as for Jews, in order to ascribe to Him the authority and majesty which the word "Christ" implied among Jews, and which Gentile Christians had found in Christ no less than those of the Jewish race.

It was the word LORD which fitted their need, and this name too was able to stand the test of time. In its simplest use it means "owner" and is the counterpart of the word "slave" though it could be applied in a more general sense to anyone of high standing. It had its special use, however, in the sphere of religion. Many of the heathen gods were addressed as "Lord". Indeed some scholars have argued from this that it was in the heathen world that this name "Lord" came first to be applied to Jesus, and that it denoted for the Gentiles what "Christ" did for the Jews. This, however, is unlikely. The Gentiles did not invent this way of speaking of Jesus, but took it over readily from the Jewish Christians. We know the Jewish Christians did use it of Jesus, because the Aramaic words quoted by Paul in 1 Cor. 16: 22, "Maranatha", mean "Our Lord, come". They are a simple prayer as it was used by Aramaic-speaking Jewish Christians in Palestine, and carried over into the Gentile mission.

It was very significant that Jewish Christians spoke of Jesus as "Lord", because this is one of the commonest titles for God in the Old Testament. The name they had been accustomed to ascribe to God, they now ascribed to Jesus; and the Gentiles readily accepted it, because it was a word they too were familiar with in the sphere of worship. Indeed it is probable that the earliest creed of the early Gentile Church was "Jesus is Lord" (cf. Rom. 10: 9) and for them this meant very much what Peter's confession had meant for the first disciples: "Thou art the Christ".

It is easily understandable, therefore, that "the Lord Jesus Christ" came to be the way in which the Church first confessed and worshipped Jesus.

James addresses his letter TO THE TWELVE TRIBES IN THE DISPERSION. The "Dispersion", or "Diaspora", as it is sometimes more technically called, was the name given to all Jews living outside Palestine. The history of the Jewish people had been full of disasters. Often they had been defeated and overrun by powerful, aggressive nations; and by the merciless practices of those days Jews were carried off in their thousands, and either sold as slaves in foreign lands, or else made to settle in some distant part of their conqueror's empire. Assyria in 722 B.C., Babylon in 586 B.C., and Rome under Pompey in 63 B.C. had all carried out this ruthless treatment in some measure. Besides this, however, there was a vitality and vigour in the Jewish people for which there was not sufficient scope within their own borders, and constantly they were setting off in their hundreds to make their fortunes overseas, settling in some distant land, and raising their families there. Indeed it is probable that in the first century A.D. a far greater number of Jews lived outside Palestine than within it. Mommsen, the historian of the Roman Empire, was not exaggerating when he wrote: "The inhabitants of Palestine were only a portion, and not the most important portion of the Jews; the Jewish communities of Babylonia, Syria, Asia Minor and Egypt were far superior to those of Palestine". From Philo (*In Flaccam* 6: 8) we learn that there were a million resident Jews in Alexandria at this time. Josephus, the Jewish historian, records: "There is no city, no tribe, whether Greek or Barbarian in which Jewish law and Jewish customs have not taken root"; and Strabo, the Greek writer, claimed: "It is hard to find a spot in the whole world which is not occupied and dominated by the Jews". Even if some of these statements may be exaggerated, they nevertheless bear testimony to the presence of Jews in almost every known land. This was the Dispersion. It was characteristic of the Jews that wherever they were they retained their identity as Jews, and were doggedly loyal to their national customs and allegiances.

The Acts of the Apostles also bears witness to the Dispersion, because it is made clear that wherever Paul went, he could rely on finding a Jewish community there, to whom he could make his first appeal, and from whom he normally won enough converts to the Christian Faith to form the nucleus of his further appeal to the Gentiles in that area.

It is worth noting that the First Epistle of Peter is also addressed to members of the Dispersion (1 Pet. 1: 1), but whereas Peter writes only to certain specified areas, James sends his letter to *"the twelve tribes"* of the Dispersion. The people of Israel consisted of twelve "tribes", corresponding to the twelve sons of Jacob, later called Israel. It is true that some of the northern tribes had disappeared entirely from known history, but the nation in its entirety was spoken of still as "the twelve tribes". Here it is James's way of insisting that his message is an open one for *all* the people of Israel, wherever in the world they may be.

Who then are meant in this context by the twelve tribes of Israel in the Dispersion? Superficially it would appear that James is addressing his fellow Jews throughout the world, summoning them to accept a better faith, and to live according to the high standards of Christian conduct. It is difficult to reconcile such an explanation with the contents of the epistle. Others, however, have tried to maintain part of it by arguing that originally this letter was not a Christian writing, but a Jewish writing addressed to Jews, and was only later modified by the introduction of some Christian phrases to make it suitable for Christian reading. More probably, however, the fact of the matter is that the "twelve tribes" do not mean Jews at all. The phrase is used metaphorically of Christians. Christians believed that they were the true Israel of God. The Jewish people, God's chosen people, had proved themselves unworthy of their position and responsibility by their rejection of Jesus, God's Messiah; and in their place God had adopted as His own people and nation the Christian community. They were "an elect race", "a holy nation" to use the words of Peter in 1 Pet. 2: 9; and Paul, giving his blessing to those among the Christians who are faithful, describes them as "the Israel of God" (Gal. 6: 16; cf. Matt. 19: 28). The Christian Church is therefore the New Israel, the New People of God. The Twelve Tribes of the Dispersion are the whole company of Christian people everywhere throughout the world.

It is addressed to all, without any delimitation of the number for whom it is intended. That is why this epistle is classed among the general or "Catholic" epistles. It is not addressed to any particular readers, but it is a "general" letter to all who care to read it, an "open letter" to Christians everywhere. It is true that some of its counsels seem precise enough to be addressed originally to a community well known to the writer, but it may be he is deliberately applying to a much wider circle those instructions which he has reason to believe would be applicable to them also.

The contents of the letter are much more appropriate as addressed to converted Christians than to unconverted Jews. If it were to Jews that James was writing, we should expect him to put forward the central facts of the faith, the "proclamation" ("kerygma") of the early Church, which declared that God's long-intended purpose to redeem His people had been fulfilled in Jesus, who had died at the hands of wicked men and been raised from the dead by the power of God. The contents of the letter are, however, not proclamation of the essentials of the Christian faith, but rather instruction to those already Christians, what is technically called "*didache*". The writer is clearly aiming, not to win non-Christians into the faith, but to persuade those who are

Christians to let the words and Spirit of Christ rule their conduct in even the most practical concerns of daily life.

Some scholars have found still a further significance in the word "Dispersion" as used of Christians. The word implies those who are absent from their homeland, strangers in a strange country. Christians thought of themselves like that, as "strangers and pilgrims on the earth" (Heb. 11: 13; cf. 1 Pet. 2: 11). They passed through this world as if it were a foreign country through which they must travel to their own country which lies beyond the bounds of this earth. In the fine words of the Epistle to Diognetus: "They dwell in their own father-lands, but as if sojourners in them; they share all things as citizens, and suffer all things as strangers. Every foreign country is their father-land, and every fatherland is a foreign country. . . . They pass their time upon the earth, but they have their citizenship in heaven" (5: 5, 9; cf. Phil. 3: 20).

The word for "*greeting*" which James uses is the normal word used in contemporary Greek letters. He does not attempt to elaborate it into a specifically Christian salutation, as Paul and Peter do.

> 1: 2–4. *Count it all joy, my brethren, when you meet various trials,*
> 3. *for you know that the testing of your faith produces steadfastness.*
> 4. *And let steadfastness have its full effect, that you may be perfect and complete, lacking in nothing.*

James seeks to comfort and encourage his readers in their "trials" which they will have to endure, by assuring them that these very troubles may become the means by which they may advance to greater maturity in the Christian faith.

**1: 2** He addresses them as "MY BRETHREN". This mode of address is characteristic of this epistle (see 1: 16, 19; 2: 1, 5, 14; 3: 1, 10, 12; 4: 11; 5: 7, 9, 10, 12, 19). The Israelites had used this word "brother" to describe not only members of their own family, but also all their brother Israelites. For instance, in Exod. 2: 11 we read that Moses saw "an Egyptian beating a Hebrew, one of his brethren". Also in some of the religious communities among the Greeks, the members addressed one another in this way (see references in Arndt and Gingrich under *adelphos*). It was among the Christians, however, that this word attained the widest currency as the normal word by which to refer to fellow-believers.

This widespread practice would arise very naturally because they all acknowledged God, the Father of their Lord Jesus Christ, as their own Father. They were members of the family of which God was Father, and in which Jesus Christ was, as it were, the eldest brother

("first-born among many brethren" as Paul described Him in Rom.
8: 29). The growth of the practice would find encouragement from
the way in which their Lord Himself had accepted His disciples as
His real family. The ties which bound Him to them were felt to be
stronger and closer than the ties that bound Him to His own kith and
kin. When the members of His own family came to persuade Him to
return home with them, and a message was brought to Him that His
mother and brothers wished to speak to Him, Jesus replied: "Who are
my mother or my brothers?" And looking round on those who sat
about Him, He said: "Here are my mother and my brothers! Whoever
does the will of God is my brother, and sister, and mother" (Mark 3:
33-35). Even apart from this precedent which made the use of the
word "brother" so appropriate among the early Christians, the word
seemed the right one to express the warm sense of loyalty and love
which members of the early Church felt for one another.

VARIOUS TRIALS. In the Greek the word translated "trials" has a
wider meaning than this single English word. It may refer either to
inward impulses (temptations) prompting a man to evil (as it does in
1: 13-14) or to outward trouble of different kinds. It may be used, for
instance, of those disappointments, sorrows, hardships, which befall
us all; or it may indicate special suffering inflicted upon the Christians
by hostile pagan neighbours or government officials. All these may be
called "trials", and the very use of this word interprets the way in
which they were to be regarded. They were felt to be experiences
which "tried", "tested", or "proved" the faith of the Christian. As
stresses are applied to test the strength of metal, so stresses come to
test our faith. If there were no stresses to endure and withstand, we
should not know whether our faith was really robust or not, whether
or not it was the kind of faith which Jesus spoke of, as the kind which
endures to the end, and so can receive salvation (Mark 13: 13).

It seems probable that in this context James is thinking primarily
of outward afflictions which human life must face, though indeed these
quickly awaken inward temptations, since the outward trouble prompts
a man to "give up", or to tell untruths in order to avoid further distresses, or to give way to self-pity, bitterness and discontent, or to
allow fear to dictate his actions. It is in facing these adversities with
courage and cheerfulness without being in any way diverted from his
primary loyalty, that a man's Christian faith is proved to be true
faith, and Christian character is formed and strengthened.

There is nothing in the context to suggest that James is thinking
particularly of troubles brought on by persecution, though these are
by no means to be excluded. Probably, however, he has in mind those
inevitable disappointments, griefs, sorrows and annoyances which no
human life can avoid. The ordinary human response to these upsetting

experiences is anger, resentment, irritability or despondency. But James bids his fellow-Christians to welcome them rather as an occasion for joy, because, though unpleasant at the moment, they can in fact prove to be the means by which rich treasure, in the Christian sense of the word, can be added to their lives.

VARIOUS translates the Greek word *poikilos*, which means "variegated", "all kinds of", or "different kinds of". It means here "all the various sorts of troubles" that beset this human life of ours, "of whatever kind they may be".

We are bidden to COUNT it all joy. . . . The tense of the verb in the Greek is aorist, and implies a certain decisiveness of action rather than a passive attitude of mind. Perhaps we should get the feel of this in English by translating: "Make up your mind to regard adversities as something to welcome and be glad about". It is not that the readers are at the present moment in great affliction, but it is one of the certainties of life that adversities will come, and the Christian should make up his mind, before they come, how to meet them when they do come.

JOY. It is indeed most unexpected and puzzling to find "joy" recommended as the correct response to the onset of trouble. It is a complete reversal of our normal attitude in such circumstances. But then, the early Christians were described as men who did turn the world "upside down", and our Lord before them had shown the way by utterly reversing the normal standard of joy and sorrow. In the beatitudes as Luke records them in 6: 20-23, the people whom He pronounces "blessed" are the very ones whom the world pities—the poor, the hungry, the sorrowful who weep, and those who are hated and avoided by their fellowmen; it is these who are bidden "Rejoice and leap for joy; for behold your reward is great in heaven". And His pity is offered to the rich, the well-fed, the carefree, and the popular people, the ones whom most of us would be inclined to envy.

It is a most notable characteristic of this epistle that recurringly as here it reflects with marked faithfulness the teaching of our Lord. His injunction here might indeed be a summary of these four beatitudes from Luke. In the presence of adversity, James writes, "rejoice"; and if he does not actually promise a reward, he does give the assurance of great gain as an outcome of the "trials".

JOY is one of the big words of our Christian faith. There is joy with God, we read, when a sinner repents and turns to Him. Our Lord spoke of "my joy", and promised His disciples a share in it (John 15: 11). It is one of the recognizable marks of the Kingdom of God, a characteristic of the rule of God, in human life. When a man senses the wonderful privilege of entering this blessed relationship with God, he is willing *"for joy"* to go and sell all that he has to gain the treasure (Matt. 13: 44). The joyous prospect of what awaits him makes him ready to accept happily any apparent hardship involved in the transaction. With the same emphasis Paul declares of the Kingdom of God that it is righteousness, and peace, and *joy* in the Holy Spirit (Rom. 14: 17). When God really controls a human life, and by the living presence of His Holy Spirit brings a man's heart and will into full obedience to Him as King, the consequence in that life is *joy*. Part of the fruit of the Spirit (Gal. 5: 22), that which emerges where the Spirit of God rules, is love, *joy*, peace.

All this is readily understandable—that one of the gifts of God to His obedient children should be joy. But it is strange to find joy commended as a proper accompaniment of heavy trouble. It would be easier to accept if joy was named as the mark of the end of trouble, rather than its beginning. "A woman in travail hath sorrow" but the birth of the child causes it quickly to be forgotten "for joy" at its outcome (John 16: 21). So our Lord promises His disciples that their sorrow shall be turned into joy. Similarly we read of Jesus "for the joy set before Him" being ready to endure the Cross (Heb. 12: 2). This we can understand—bearing hardship patiently because beyond it lies great joy. But here it is not the ending of the grief which is to be hailed with joy, but the actual onset of "trial". As we have noted, this is exactly in line with the word of Jesus in His Beatitudes (Matt. 5: 11–12 and Luke 6: 23), and we find His early disciples radiantly obedient to it, as they rejoiced "that they were counted worthy to suffer shame for his name" (Acts 5: 41).

Count it ALL joy: that is, regard it as an occasion for "nothing but joy", for "unmixed" joy (so Paul in Col. 1: 24).

**1: 3** The reason why the Christian can be told to regard "trials" as "things of joy" is that they may become the means by which rich treasures come into his life. These, of course, are not the treasures which make us rich in worldly goods, but rich in those things which God values, "rich toward God" (Luke 12: 21). These Christian "riches" consist—in part, at any rate—of those qualities of character which cannot be acquired except through "trials", because these "try" or "test" our faith, and our faith is something less than true faith until it has been "tried" and "tested" and "proved".

The "TESTING OF YOUR FAITH" is a necessary condition of fulness of faith. Faith is not faith which dissolves in the presence of hardship. But we cannot know whether our faith is only "fair-weather" faith or real, enduring faith until hardship has proved its quality. We may think we have faith, but if "affliction or persecution arises" we may find ourselves "caused to stumble" (that is, alienated from our loyalty to Christ, cf. Mark 4: 17). There is no way of knowing whether our faith is of better quality than that except by meeting trials and surviving them, and proving that our faith does not fail.

Our Lord spoke about this faith which is tried and which does not fail. Just before His own arrest and Peter's denial he attempted to prepare Peter for the grim ordeal ahead. "Satan has asked to have you," He said, "to sift you as wheat." That is, the ordeal might have the effect of sifting the trivial and superficial in Peter from the solid good. And Christ's prayer for him is to be that his faith "shall not fail" (Luke 22: 31–32). His faith certainly trembled and faltered, but it did not utterly fail; and when he was "converted" (brought back to his loyalty to Christ), he was able—his own faith now proved and tested—to "strengthen his brethren" (Luke 22: 32).

So James speaks to his readers of "the testing of their faith" by "trials" in order that out of them their faith may come tested and proved.

Peter also uses identical phrases in giving similar counsel in 1 Pet. 1: 6–7. He too speaks about "various trials" (the very words which James here uses) and also of "the genuineness of your faith" (the same words in the Greek which in James are translated "the testing of your faith").

The word "FAITH" is one of the most important in the Christian religion. Indeed we often speak of the religion itself as "our faith". In its most comprehensive use it includes several different kinds of faith. Confusion has sometimes arisen when one kind of faith is meant but is understood as another kind.

Sometimes "faith" means the acceptance of the doctrines of the Christian Church; sometimes it represents a personal commitment to Jesus Christ in trust and obedience, a determined loyalty to Him through all kinds of difficulty and opposition; and sometimes—as predominantly in Paul—it means a full abandonment of the whole of our life to Christ for Him to heal it by His grace and equip it with His Spirit and shape and direct it by His commands. It seems probable that for James the second of these is the meaning he most commonly attaches to "faith"—a professed loyalty to Christ, which needs to be tested by adversity before it can be confidently regarded as reliable and trustworthy. The fact that for James this is the main emphasis in faith, whereas Paul's is rather different, may partly explain the apparent contradiction, which we shall later discuss, between Jas. 2: 14–26 and Rom. 3: 28.

The outcome of the adversities which test our faith, provided that it does not fail under them, is described as "patience". The testing of faith produces steadfastness.

The New Testament uses two Greek words both of which in older translations were rendered as "patience". The one in this verse is "*hypomenē*". The other one is "*makrothymia*" (and it is this second one which is listed as part of the fruit of the Spirit in Gal. 5: 22). It is probably claiming too much to insist that these two words are always clearly distinguished in the Greek, but in general they do indicate two different kinds of "patience". "*Makrothymia*" is commonly used to mean "patience" or "forbearance" with other people, and their irritating faults and foibles. By derivation it means the quality of being "long-tempered" as opposed to "short-tempered". "*Hypomenē*", on the other hand, usually indicates not so much patience towards awkward people, but steadfastness and endurance in trying circumstances. This is the word used here, and it occurs again, at 5: 11, of the "steadfastness" of Job. Job's "patience" was outstanding, not in the sense of his forbearance towards friends and acquaintances, but in his continuing steadfastness of faith in spite of the most distressing sequence of disasters. In spite of the death of all his sons and daughters, the loss of wealth and health and the esteem of friends, he could still say out of his anguish: "The Lord gave, and the Lord hath taken away; blessed be the name of the Lord" (Job 1: 21). "Shall we receive good at the hand of God, and shall we not receive evil?" (Job 2: 10). This is "steadfastness"; it is to produce this that our faith is tried in adversity.

Ellicott (commenting on 1 Thess. 1: 3) interprets its meaning as follows: "In this noble word there always appears a background of courage. It does not mark merely the endurance, but also the perseverance, the brave patience with which the Christian contends against the various hindrances, persecutions, and temptations that befall him in his conflict with the inward and outward world." "Fortitude" or "staying power" have been suggested as translations of it. It is this word which is used in the saying of Jesus: "By your *endurance* you will gain your lives" (Luke 21: 19). It is, moreover, the verb from the same Greek root which in Jas. 1: 12 is translated "endures", and is used in the word of Jesus: "He who endures to the end will be saved" (Matt. 10: 22). It is also used to describe Christian love in action in 1 Cor. 13: 7: "It endures all things".

The close similarity should be noted between these verses in James and Rom. 5: 3-5, especially verse 3: Faith and joy have already been named in verse 2, and then Paul continues: "We rejoice in our sufferings, knowing that suffering produces endurance (*hypomenē*), and endurance produces character".

Clearly James attaches the utmost importance to this Christian characteristic of "steadfastness". In what follows he seems to suggest that it is an important stage in the progress to Christian perfection.

1: 4 LET STEADFASTNESS HAVE ITS FULL EFFECT. There are two ways of interpreting this: Either (a), Let steadfastness persist until it produces perfect steadfastness. Calvin understood it in this way, as a plea for "perseverance throughout life", in contrast to "heroic greatness" at the beginning, fading off into weariness and faintheartedness later as hardships persist or increase. Or (b), Let steadfastness lead on to its proper fulfilment in the complete perfection of Christian character. The word translated "full" is the same as the one translated "perfect" in the next clause.

The second of these two, (b), has the advantage of leading on more naturally to the second half of the verse with its summons to "perfection and completeness". It also accords better with Rom. 5: 3–4, where "steadfastness produces character", and with 2 Pet. 1: 5–7, where "steadfastness" is named as a prelude which properly leads on to "godliness, brotherly affection and love".

The word "perfect" (Greek *teleios*) is a favourite one with James. Besides its repeated use in this verse, it occurs also at 1: 17, 25; 2: 22; 3: 2. Here James urges that his readers will set before them the goal of becoming PERFECT AND COMPLETE, LACKING IN NOTHING. There is no escaping, however disconcerting it may be, this lofty uncompromising summons, sounded here as elsewhere in the New Testament, to what has come to be called "Christian Perfection", as God's purpose for His Christian people. James emphasises this call to perfection by adding the word "complete" (Greek *holoklēros*) and the phrase "lacking in nothing". "Perfect" means "having reached full development". "Complete" means "with no unfinished part". It is, however, a mistake to try to differentiate the significance of the two words. Rather it is that they are used in combination to emphasize the single idea of "perfection".

No Christian can be regarded as "perfect" until he has withstood heavy trials, and in spite of distressing ordeals has maintained his faith and loyalty to Christ, and proved himself able to display continually a Christian bearing in all these distresses, and towards the people who are responsible for them. When his faith and obedience have been tested as it were by fire then he may be regarded as a perfect Christian. Indeed there seems almost to be present by implication the suggestion that the very purpose of such trials is to provide the circumstances in which a Christian may win a final victory over himself and his frailties, and prove himself a "perfect" man.

Certainly James insists that God's purpose for the Christian is that he may be "perfect and complete", and life's trials are the discipline by which alone these heights may be attained.

There is no avoiding the awkward, even frightening challenge of this word "perfect" in the New Testament. It is by no means only in James that we hear it. Indeed the reason we meet it here is probably because James knew he had behind him the greater authority of his Lord. Jesus already had said: "You therefore must be perfect, as your heavenly Father is perfect" (Matt. 5: 48).

It is true that the Greek word *teleios* sometimes carries a meaning less exacting than "perfect". In some contexts it means "mature", "fully developed". Here, however, its association with "entire, wanting nothing" shows that the full meaning of "perfect" must be accepted. Moreover in Matt. 5: 48 the word is applied to God Himself as well as to the Christian, and it would be quite impossible to translate it, when applied to God, merely as "mature" or "fully developed". So too in Heb. 6: 1 the readers are bidden to "go on to perfection" (cf. also Heb. 13: 21); and here again the word must carry its full meaning for it is also applied to Jesus who was "made perfect through sufferings", and thereby became the author of eternal salvation (Heb. 5: 9). A reduced meaning of *teleios* could not appropriately be applied to Jesus here.

Paul also uses this word of the goal towards which Christians must aspire. His work in the Church is inspired with the hope "that we may present every man perfect in Christ Jesus" (Col. 1: 28); and it is the prayer of his colleague, Epaphras, "that ye may stand perfect and complete in all the will of God" (Col. 4: 12). John too in 1 John 4: 17–18 pleads that his readers will rest content in nothing short of "perfect love".

This word "perfect" as applied to the aspiration of the Christian is not an oddity found in one writer in the New Testament, but is shared by many. It is a feature of our common faith that once a man is a Christian his aim should be to become a "perfect" Christian, and though the calling is so high as to be frightening it is not for us to try to whittle it away in order to make it easier. Perhaps, however, we should note that in all the references we have cited, the word does not describe the attainment of the Christian, but rather the aim towards which he must eagerly reach. It may be that the acutest difficulty in regard to this word comes not when it is expressed as the aim, but when it is claimed by some Christians as their attainment. John Wesley, who believed that God had laid it upon him to insist upon this aim of the Christian, and perhaps more than any other Christian leader stressed the importance of the doctrine of Christian Perfection, not only set it before his hearers and readers as their goal, but claimed that some had reached it. He never made this claim for himself, however, perhaps feeling that in his own case to have claimed it would have brought him too dangerously near to the sin of pride. Moreover he tried to avoid the phrase "sinless perfection" which some used rather glibly, preferring the Scriptural phrase "perfect love". If by perfection is meant the complete elimination of every fault, then it becomes a mocking word, because weaknesses of temperament and errors of judgement will continue with us to the end. But if by perfection we mean "loving God with all our heart, mind, soul and strength" and "loving our neighbour as ourselves" then this is undoubtedly the aim of every true Christian. If by perfection we mean the willingness, even the longing to know at every point what is the will of God for us, and the readiness to receive from God the strength to do that will, then this is what every true Christian should be aiming at. No one can ever reach this perfect obedience in such a way as to be sure that he will never slip from it, but there have been those whose lives have seemed, to those who knew them best, in perfect accord with the mind of Christ. Even if such people would shrink from claiming that their obedience is perfect, yet there are those who if pressed with the importunate and perhaps embarrassing question: "Do you ever do what you know God does not want you to do?" have to answer: "I don't think so."

If then we interpret "perfection" as the willingness to know what is for us the will of God, and to learn where we are not fully in line with it, and the willingness to receive the gift of God's Holy Spirit in such measure as to enable us to do what is commanded, then undoubtedly this should be our aim, what we "hunger and thirst after".

Some shrink from the word "perfect" because they say it will induce smugness and self-satisfaction. For most this is not so. It is a goal that beckons us, but ever lies beyond our grasp. Moreover, even if one is so cleansed and empowered by the Holy Spirit that he may not be aware of any actual disobedience to the will of God, he must always be conscious of the vast amount of good he would be able to do for others, spiritually and morally, if only he himself were a better man. He knows well what our Lord meant when He said: "We are unprofitable servants: we have done what it was our duty to do". Even if we have not consciously failed to obey God where His will was known and within our power, how can we be self-satisfied when round about us men live in spiritual peril without Christ, and thousands die physically of hunger, though perhaps in lands other than our own; and perhaps within our own circle of friends are antagonisms and hatreds we seem powerless to heal? "We are unprofitable servants." What greater good might not God do through us, if only we were better men and women, even though we may not actually be conscious of precise deeds of disobedience?

The achievement of Christian Perfection in its full, positive sense may seem infinitely remote. Nevertheless the obligation to make it our persistent and urgent aim in life is made unmistakably clear in the New Testament.

1 : 5–8. *If any of you lacks wisdom, let him ask God who gives to all men generously, and without reproaching, and it will be given him.*
*6. But let him ask in faith, with no doubting, for he who doubts is like*

*a wave of the sea that is driven and tossed by the wind. 7–8. For that person must not suppose that a double-minded man, unstable in all his ways, will receive anything from the Lord.*

In this section James turns our attention to one important element in the full equipment of the complete Christian. This is WISDOM. He insists that it is a gift from God, to be received by faith, not a quality of character to be achieved by human effort and ingenuity.

1: 5 IF ANY LACKS WISDOM. The previous verse concluded with the word "LACK"—"lacking in nothing". It has been noticed as an interesting mannerism of this writer that he likes to start a new paragraph with a word similar to one used at the end of the preceding paragraph. The word "joy", for instance, in verse 2 (*chara* in Greek) is closely related to the word "greeting" (*chairein*) at the end of verse 1.

Some commentators suggest that this mannerism is the work of an editor: that James himself left a number of brief units of teaching, and that someone else brought them together into a longer whole, using the fact of a common word to associate what originally were separate sayings. Some sayings of Jesus appear to be associated together by similar "link-words", as for instance in Mark 9: 40–50. It is, however, simpler to treat this as the mannerism of the author himself.

WISDOM plays an important part in this epistle, and occurs again at 3: 13, 15, 17. Mayor (p. 36) even claims that it may be regarded as the characteristic word of James. He writes: "To James wisdom is the principal thing, to which he gives the same prominence as St. Paul to faith, John to love, Peter to hope".

Perhaps the book in the Old Testament most akin to James in the New is the Book of Proverbs, and this is usually classed as part of the Wisdom Literature, and contains memorable descriptions of "Wisdom". Certainly it is from the Old Testament and Jewish thought rather than from Greek writers that James derives his concept of wisdom. For the Greeks wisdom came to be associated with "cleverness" and subtlety of thought and rare erudition, implying the ability to make fine verbal distinctions and follow abstruse arguments. For the devout Jew, however, wisdom was an endowment of practical usefulness. It was the power to discern right from wrong and good from evil. A "wise" decision in an emergency was one which led to the greatest possible good in the circumstances. Solomon, the exemplar of wisdom in the Old Testament, revealed his wisdom by being able to devise a test by which it could be determined which of two women claiming to be the mother of a child was in fact the real mother. It is similar to what we call "moral discernment", or, in the words of Hort, "that endowment of heart and mind which is needed for the right conduct of life". It is what Paul prayed that his readers might gain, the power to discern "what is the will of God, what is good and acceptable and perfect" (Rom. 12: 2). The beginning of wisdom is the fear of the Lord, the recognition that we are morally accountable before God for all we do in life. The fulness of wisdom is to be found in Christ, a greater than Solomon, and Himself the Wisdom of God (1 Cor. 1: 24).

The other kind of wisdom, which Paul calls "the wisdom of this world", is intellectual speculation about life and the universe, often divorced from a recognition of moral responsibility. It is this which Paul denounces in 1 Cor. 1: 18–31. This "wisdom" could only mock at the idea of God seeking to win men to Himself through the "foolish" method of the Cross. But Christian wisdom starts from an acknowledgement of God and a willingness to understand His will for man. In the context of modern Church life it is the gift specially needed by one to whom people go for counsel in their spiritual, moral and domestic dilemmas. It is the gift of being able to sense that course which is most likely to lead to Christian good for all concerned, the gift of being able to guide people to an understanding of God's will for them in the actual situation in which they find themselves. This gift may be found in those of high intellectual equipment, but it is also found in those who have had few educational advantages and are of little academic ability. It is God's gift, not an achievement of human skill or endeavour.

J. B. Phillips suggests a very practical translation of this phrase, "If any of you lacketh wisdom," which brings home its meaning to modern readers: "If anyone does not know how to meet any particular problem . . ."

We suggested that "perfection" implied the willingness to know the will of God and to do it when it is known. Wisdom is the ability to understand what the will of God is and to help others in their perplexities to understand what it is for them.

LET HIM ASK GOD. This Christian endowment of wisdom is God's gracious gift, to be received humbly and gratefully from God's hand. But that does not mean that God gives the gift indiscriminately and that no responsibility rests with the human recipient. This gift God bestows on those who long to have it, and give evidence of that longing by the persistence of their prayers for it. Indeed the Greek word here translated simply as "ask", if its full significance is to be brought out, should be rendered "keep on asking". It is the same form of the word used in the words of Jesus in the Sermon on the Mount: "Ask (keep on asking) and ye shall receive" (Matt. 7: 7). This insistence on the need to persist in prayer reminds us of the twin parables of Jesus, the Importunate Widow and the Friend at Midnight, which St. Luke (18: 1) tells us were told "to the effect that they ought always to pray and not to lose heart".

We have already noted how closely wisdom is associated with King Solomon in the thought of the Bible. This insistence on "asking" for wisdom in our prayers establishes a further link with Solomon. It recalls for us how God said to Solomon in a dream, soon after he became king, "Ask what I shall give you". Solomon requested, not long life, or riches, or power, but "an understanding mind . . . that I may discern between good and evil"; and therefore God gave him "a wise and discerning mind", and many other gifts besides. But the gift was granted because he wanted it enough to ask for it, and to ask for it first before all other blessings.

God GIVES TO ALL MEN GENEROUSLY. "Generously" probably includes both the extent of His gifts and the manner in which they are given. The generosity of God's giving is emphasized again in verse 17. It is a recurring theme in Scripture. Jesus brings it out vividly in Luke 6: 38 where He represents God, not as One who measures out gifts with niggardly exactness (nicely "calculated less or more"), but as a generous tradesman who gives "good measure, pressed down, shaken together, and running over". For many this would not be untrue of life's material blessings, but for all it is true of God's spiritual gifts. He does not give the Spirit "by measure", we are reminded in John 3: 34, and in the Old Testament Isa. 55: 1–2 proclaims the same truth.

It is not the extent only of the gift which is generous but the manner of the giving. Some gifts are spoiled by officiousness in the act of giving, a lack of courtesy and delicacy of feeling. Others are enhanced in their value by the unobtrusive kindliness with which they come to us. Real generosity of giving includes finding the happiest way of bestowing the gift as well as liberality in the gift itself. Both these qualities mark God's gifts to us, and both are outstanding in the Christmas story which tells of God's greatest gift to men, and the humble gentleness of the manner in which He bestowed it.

ALL. Many of God's gifts are bestowed broadcast upon all men. He sends his rain and sunshine on both just and unjust. Since, however, James is speaking primarily of the gift of wisdom, granted in response to earnest prayer, the word "all" here probably means "all who so ask".

WITHOUT REPROACHING. A gift can be spoiled not only by niggardliness in the gift or grudgingness in the giver, but also by continual reminders of it after the gift has been made, with reproaches that it is not sufficiently appreciated or gratitude for it not adequately shown. It is this ungracious conduct which is here referred to. In Ecclus. 41: 22 some particularly unpleasant actions are being rebuked, and included among them is the habit of "upbraiding after making a gift", of making a gift and then making sure the recipient is not allowed to forget it. This God does not do, says James. He is not like the possessive parent, who is for ever reminding his children how much he has sacrificed for them, and how appreciative they ought to be. Tyndale in the plain language of his own day translates: "God casteth no man in the teeth". The words are added, writes Calvin, "lest any-one should fear to come too often to God".

It is true that we who have received so much should constantly remind ourselves of our debt, and offer in return what we can of gratitude and obedience. But God does not petulantly keep bringing it to our notice. The well-known hymn which represents Christ as saying:

> I gave my life for thee.
> What hast thou given for me?

is usefully reminding us of how much we owe to God, but perhaps it does something less than justice to our Lord by misrepresenting Him as "reproaching" us.[1]

**1: 6** As Jesus promised that those who ask shall receive, so here the promise is clearly expressed, that a prayer for wisdom, prayed earnestly and persistently, will be granted: IT WILL BE GIVEN HIM. But some-thing more than persistence in asking is in fact required. The prayer must be made IN FAITH, with no doubting. In this too James reflects faithfully the teaching of Jesus, who insisted not only on persistence in prayer, but on the need for faith. James too here seems to use the word faith in the simple, basic meaning which we find in the teaching of Jesus in the Synoptic Gospels. Later in the story of the Christian movement, faith came to include the acceptance of certain funda-mental affirmations about the Person of Christ, and the public sub-mission of life to Him in obedience. In Paul's letters both these elements are sometimes included in "faith", but here and in the Synoptic Gospels it means primarily the simple act of coming to Jesus with some need in complete confidence that He can and will deal with it. It was this attitude of faith that seemed to release powers in Jesus that made all things possible. Often when Jesus had healed an ailing man or woman, his explanation of the healing was, "Thy faith hath saved thee".

In the same passage where He bids us ask persistently, he goes on to urge us to ask confidently. As a child asking a kindly human father for bread or a piece of fish knows he will not receive a mere stone or a scorpion, so we must ask confidently of our heavenly Father (Matt. 7: 7–11). He insists: "Whatever you ask in prayer, you receive, if you have faith" (Matt. 21: 22). And again: "All things whatsoever ye pray and ask for, believe that ye *have received* them, and ye shall have them" (Mark 11: 24; R.V.). The "faith" must be so sure that as we pray we believe, not that we *shall* receive them, but that we actually already *have received* them.

---

[1] In fact, Miss Havergal, the author, later changed it to: "Thy life was given for me. What have I given for Thee?"

Sometimes this epistle has been viewed with suspicion by evangelical Christians, because of its constant emphasis on conduct. Luther as is well known described it, in comparison with Romans, as "an epistle of straw", because it seemed to emphasize "works" rather than "faith". But John Wesley appropriately brings to our notice that "James also both begins and ends with faith" (referring to the mention of "faith" in this verse and again at 5: 15).

WITH NO DOUBTING. These words underline what is meant by the prayer of faith. The thought that his request may not be answered simply does not enter the mind of the one who prays. Misgiving has no place at all, and in consequence his attitude is totally free from hesitation. This again bears out the teaching of Jesus, who not only looked for faith in all who came to Him for help, but showed disappointment with those who came with "if" and "perhaps" on their lips, since this betokened misgiving and doubt, and misgiving and doubt hindered even His mighty powers. We read: "He could do no mighty work there because of their unbelief" (Mark 6: 5–6). When people in need came, prefacing their request for healing with the words: "If you will" (Mark 1: 40) or "If you can" (Mark 9: 22–23), He clearly regretted this indication of misgiving. "All things are possible to him who believes", He declared (Mark 9: 23), and the kind of faith which warmed His heart and made all things possible was that of the centurion who discouraged Jesus from spending time in coming to see his ailing servant, since it was unnecessary: "Only say the word and my servant will be healed" (Matt. 8: 8), he said. Jesus commended this faith as the greatest he had found, and was able to act through it to restore the sick man. This is the kind of faith which can be described as "with no doubting".

Sometimes the misgiving which undermines the effectiveness of faith springs from doubt about God, whether He is willing or perhaps whether He is able to solve our problem. Sometimes, however, the misgiving arises because of our own divided heart. Part of us is pathetically eager to receive the good gift God is ready to bestow, but another part of us does not want the gift, shrinking from the change the gift would make in our lives. That is why Jesus confronted a helpless invalid with the apparently heartless question: "Do you want to be healed?" (John 5: 6). He could see that part of the man's own nature was still clinging to some of the pleasant accompaniments of physical helplessness. The word of Jeremiah is very relevant to all our dealings with God: "You will seek me, and find me, when you seek me *with all your heart*" (Jer. 29: 13).

This "doubting man", the man who "halts between two opinions", who feels one moment that he wants something very badly, and then realizes that he also wants something quite incompatible with it, now thinks he believes in God's effective power, and then cries out, "Help my unbelief", James likens to the unsettled, unstable waves of the storm-tossed sea. Mayor adds: "Like a cork floating on the wave". The rock, however, which stands strong against the turbulent sea may remind us of the man whose "heart is fixed, trusting in the Lord" (Ps. 112: 7). The restless sea is an apt simile for the man of wavering, unsteady heart.

James is fond of introducing a simile, to awaken in the reader's mind a picture which will help him to visualize something of the spiritual truth his words have been trying to impress. Other similes are introduced at 1: 24; 3: 4, 6, 11, 12.

**1: 7** Here the confident assurance of God's generous dealings with all who come to Him in faith changes to a stern warning addressed to any who may be in danger of presuming on this merciful kindness. They argue perhaps that since God's mercy is free to all, apart from any merit in the believer, therefore all, whether good or bad, faithful or disobedient, will benefit from His merciful dealings with men. This attitude of presuming on the mercies of God, acting as though the grace of God was what has been called "cheap grace", is one that angers James greatly, as indeed it angered Paul. Paul, though continually glorying in the grace of God in Christ, nevertheless needed to pause and remind his readers of the converse truth about God: "Behold the goodness and the severity of God: toward them that fell, severity; but towards thee, God's goodness, if thou continue in His goodness: otherwise, thou also shalt be cut off" (Rom. 11: 22). So here James, having stressed God's generosity, reminds his readers that there is also severity with God. Towards the human response of faith, God's mercy is unfailing; but where there is hesitation and delay and only half-hearted commitment, the fulness of God's gifts is withheld. If we are uncertain of God's readiness to bring us the help we ask, or if we ourselves are DOUBLE-MINDED in the same kind of way that Augustine was when he prayed: "Lord, make me pure, but not yet", then, says James, we must understand that our prayer is not likely to be answered.

**1: 8** This "double-mindedness" is frequently rebuked in Scripture. James returns to rebuke it again at 4: 8. Jesus Himself clearly warned that we "cannot serve God and Mammon". A divided hesitating loyalty shuts a man out from the full blessings of the Kingdom of God. As the N.E.B. accurately translates it: "No one who sets his hand to the plough and then *keeps looking back* is fit for the Kingdom of God" (Luke 9: 62). Peter walks safely over the water towards Jesus until his eyes turn to the uncertain waves beneath him and he begins to sink. "Why did you doubt?" says Jesus. Ecclus. 1: 28 similarly insists: "Do not approach the Lord with a divided mind". Conversely "singlemindedness" is often the subject of commendation: Matt. 6: 22, Luke 11: 34, Eph. 6: 5, Col. 3: 22, Acts 2: 46.

UNSTABLE IN ALL HIS WAYS. N.E.B. renders: "never can keep a steady course".

The punctuation of the Greek in verses 7–8 is open to a variant rendering from that given in the R.S.V. Both R.V. and N.E.B. make it clear that the double-minded, unstable man is a description of the person himself, and not someone else: "A man of that kind must not expect the Lord to give him anything; he is doubleminded, and can never keep a steady course" (so N.E.B.). This is probably preferable to R.S.V., which suggests that the person "supposing" and the "double-minded man" may be different people.

> 1: 9–11. *Let the lowly brother boast in his exaltation,* 10. *and the rich in his humiliation, because like the flower of the grass he will pass away.* 11. *For the sun rises with its scorching heat and withers the grass; its flower falls, and its beauty perishes. So will the rich man fade away in the midst of his pursuits.*

In this section, as later in others also, James contrasts the rich and the poor, and gives to the rich man warning not to trust in his wealth.

**1: 9** If we are to look for a link between this paragraph and those which precede it, it may be found either in the word "BOAST" or in the thought of the "double-minded" man. "Boast" and "count it all joy" (in verse 2) are similar. Just as the Christian man, as he faces life's trials, is bidden to find in them cause for rejoicing, so here the Christian man of humble social status and small income is reminded of the grounds on which he may feel proud. Alternatively, the double-minded man who approaches God with something less than full trust and commitment (as in verse 8) has much in common with the rich Christian who is torn between his loyalty to God and his attachment to Mammon (i.e. money and worldly success) with all its pleasures and advantages.

The paragraph clearly applies to Christian people, since the word "brother" is introduced at the very beginning. It is true, as some have pointed out, that it is not actually repeated in reference to the rich man, and therefore it may be argued that the rich man is not a Christian. This point of view will be considered later, but in the exposition it will be assumed that both the poor and the rich man are members of the Christian community, though neither of them has yet fully learned to accept all the implications of his new place in the brotherhood. One is still a little ashamed of being socially a "nobody", and the other rather

B

proud that he is treated by others as "somebody", in consequence of his wealth.

The word "BROTHER" reminds all concerned that they are members of one family (see the comment on verse 2). Within the family circle there is usually, and properly, a basic equality. The successful man may be pompous and self-important among his social acquaintances, but his own brothers will not treat him with deference. Within a family there are of course differences of ability and aptitude, but so long as the family remains a true family there will be a fundamental sense of equality among its members. So it is in the family of God, the family of the Church of Christ, where God is Father, and Christ, as it were, the eldest brother, and all others children of the same Father and brothers together.

In the early Church the "LOWLY" brothers were very numerous. In his letters to the Christians at Corinth Paul writes: "Behold your calling, brethren" (we notice that Paul as well as James uses the family word) "how that not many wise after the flesh, not many mighty, not many noble are called" (1 Cor. 1: 26). Among them were some so poor that when they came with their own food to the common meal of the Christians they had not even enough to satisfy the pangs of hunger (1 Cor. 11: 21). In Col. 3: 22 (as in Eph. 6: 5) there are special instructions addressed to slaves, which implies that there were many of them among the Christians at Colossae. Similarly in 1 Pet. 2: 18 a paragraph of advice is offered to "household servants", many of whom would be slaves, and all of humble social standing.

The word "lowly" or "humble" may bear a spiritual as well as a physical meaning. "Humility" is an essential inward quality of Christian character. But here as elsewhere the word describes outward circumstances of poverty and social insignificance.

Let him BOAST in his high estate. "Boasting" in English usually refers to the spoken word, but here, while not excluding what is spoken, it includes also the whole attitude and bearing of a man. It suggests, in its bad sense, self-confidence and self-congratulation. It implies an arrogant bearing towards others, as though they were of less importance than oneself, and even complacency before God, as though he had done all that God had any right to expect of him, and perhaps even more.

Paul uses the word often, and nearly always in the bad sense. He himself, as a Pharisee, had been guilty of this sin before God, and perhaps it continued to be his besetting temptation. He had wanted to achieve by his own merits high standing with God and to outstrip his fellows in achievements. He seems to have found it difficult to the end to take second place. But he knew his fault and wrestled to overcome it. We hear him crying: "Far be it from me to *boast* save in the cross of our Lord Jesus Christ" (Gal. 6: 14). Here, of course, the word changes from a bad sense to a good one. As most men boast of what they themselves have gained or achieved, Paul now finds his joy and satisfaction and well-being in what God has done for him in Christ's self-giving of Himself on the Cross. He also "boasts" in the privileges of the Christian experience and of the Christian hope (Rom. 5: 2, 3, 11, where the same word is represented by the word "rejoice").

Here in James too the word is used in its good sense. First, the man of humble circumstances is urged to boast IN HIS EXALTATION. Poor though he is in worldly goods, as a Christian he is spiritually enriched. His life, previously insignificant, is now vested with a new importance. Outwardly he may still be a slave, or a poorly paid servant, little valued by those who use his labour, and hardly noticed by his fellow-servants; but he now knows himself to be a child of God, a joint heir with Christ, the Lord's freedman (1 Cor. 7: 22). He may not seem to matter in the world of men, but he matters to God. God values him, even to the extent of coming in Christ to die on a Cross for him. He can say with wondering incredulity at the marvel of it: "He loved *me*, and gave himself up for *me*".

Nor was this merely an inward, or emotional experience, with no counterpart in the world outside himself. He could believe in this love of God for him because he found something of the same kind of thing in the lives of those he met within the community of the Church. There he had experienced forgiveness, people accepting him in spite of all the miserable things that were true of him in the past; there he found love, as he realized that these people were really interested in him for his own sake and concerned for his welfare (and not for anything they hoped to get out of him); they watched over him, came to see him when he was absent from the church gathering, pleaded with him, if he was growing careless. The loving care for him he found in them made it easier for him to believe in God's love for him in Christ. (Is this what Jesus meant in John 20: 23 and Matt. 18: 18?) As Mayor puts it (p. 41): "If in low estate, he should glory in the Church, where all are brothers and there is no respect of persons . . . he should realise his own dignity as a member of Christ, a child of God, an heir of heaven".

In the Evangelical Revival in Great Britain under the Wesleys one of the most degraded and poverty stricken sections in the land were the miners of Kingswood, near Bristol, but as they entered into the spiritual riches of life in Christ they learned to sing and to make their own the hymn which included the lines:

On all the kings of earth
With pity I look down.

Their new privileges as Christian believers seemed far greater than the passing privileges of even the world's most privileged people.

James himself summarizes some of the privileges of this "EXALTATION" in 2: 5: "God chose them that are poor as to the world to be rich in faith and heirs of the Kingdom which He promised to them that love Him". The humble Christian is described as "rich in faith". This is similar to phrases used by Jesus, who spoke of those who are "rich towards God" (Luke 12: 21), that is, rich in those things which God treasures. Elsewhere He spoke of "true riches" (Luke 16: 11) and "treasure in heaven" (Matt. 6: 20). All these phrases characterize the "exaltation" of the humble Christian.

The words of Jesus in Luke 14: 11 may well have been in James's mind: "Everyone who exalts himself will be humbled; and he who humbles himself will be exalted". The words used in Luke for "humble" and "exalt" are the same words used by James in these verses.

**1: 10** Next the RICH MAN is addressed, and he is exhorted to BOAST IN HIS HUMILIATION. It seems reasonably certain that this rich man also is a Christian "brother". This has, however, been disputed. Those who think that he is not a Christian use the following arguments:

(i). If the rich man were a Christian, this would mean that his new humiliation was a real, actual humiliation, whereas the "exaltation" which the poor Christian now enjoys is a spiritual state. It is argued that James would not confuse in a single sentence a spiritual and a literal use of words.

(ii). Elsewhere in this epistle the rich are always bad people, outside the Christian community (cf. 2: 6–8; 5: 1–6).

(iii). If the rich man were a Christian, the word "brother" would be explicitly used here as in the previous sentence.

These three arguments, however, can be countered, as follows:

(i). There seems to be no reason at all why in the same sentence a literal and metaphorical use of words, even the same words, should not occur. For instance, that key utterance in the teaching of Jesus, about losing life in order to save it, involves the use of the word "life" in these two different ways.

(ii). James undoubtedly regards wealth as a great danger to the Christian life, and we know that some of the fiercest opposition to the early church came from wealthy pagans who feared that the Church would interfere with the source of their money-making. But that does not mean that some rich people may not have been among those won for Christ and His Church. James, knowing the danger of wealth, would well feel it incumbent upon him to offer solemn warning to these wealthy Christians.

(iii). The word "brother" in the original Greek stands right at the beginning of the whole sentence, and it is most natural to understand it as referring to both parts of the sentence, and to translate: "Let the brother who is poor . . . and the brother who is rich . . ."

Moreover, if the rich man here is not a Christian it means that both the words "boast" and "humiliation" have to be loaded with sarcasm, and his "humiliation" would have to refer to his pagan wealth which, in spite of appearances to the contrary, is a disgrace in God's eyes. This variant interpretation appears to be very strained.

We take the rich man, therefore, to be a Christian and expound the passage from this point of view.

We have noted how Paul writes as though the Christian community at Corinth were drawn largely from the poorer classes, but this does not mean that rich people were not included also. Indeed even at Corinth it is clear that there were wealthy members, because at the communal meal, associated with the Lord's Supper, to which each person brought his own food, there were those who over-ate and over-drank, to the humiliation of their poorer Christian brothers, who could not even satisfy the pangs of hunger. In Acts we have even more explicit evidence of the presence of some rich people in the community. The venture in communal living, to which their new-found love for one another led the early Church in Jerusalem, required that those who had possessions and goods should sell them for the benefit of the whole community (Acts 2: 44-45). At Acts 4: 34 also we read that "as many as were possessors of lands or houses sold them" in order that the money could be made available for common use. These owners of property would probably include some richer people, and Barnabas in particular is named as one who disposed of his property for the good of all the society. Lydia, and Aquila and Priscilla probably fall into the same class, and perhaps also the less honourable Ananias and Sapphira.

In his mission churches Paul accepted among the members both rich and poor, and since it was only at Jerusalem that we read of the rich selling their property for the benefit of their poor brothers, rich and poor would remain within the Church, though undoubtedly in every church those who were better off in this world's goods were expected to share their good fortune with their less fortunate fellow-Christians. Indeed one of James's most scathing denunciations is reserved for the Christian who has the means of helping a destitute brother but does nothing more than speak fine, but empty words (2: 15-16). In 1 John 3: 17 such denial of the law of love for neighbour is declared to prove that the "love of God does not abide in him". All the New Testament writers equally insist on the practical application of the basic law of loving neighbour as self, especially when that neighbour is a fellow Christian. Paul, however, does not require the rich man to dispose of his riches. He treats of this problem of social inequalities within the Christian group in 1 Cor. 7: 20–24, and his advice is clear: "Each one, my friends, is to remain before God in the condition in which he received his call" (N.E.B.). At the same time a Christian must be "unattached" to his material circumstances, so that success in them will not elate him nor failure throw him into despondency. "Buyers must not count on keeping what they buy, nor those who use the world's wealth on using it to the full" (1 Cor. 7: 30–31, N.E.B.). If this seems timid advice, not wholly in tune with the radical ethics of Jesus, we note that Paul gives as his reason for avoiding large-scale upheavals: "For the whole frame of the world is passing away" (7: 31). It is clear that James also gives his counsel on the basis of this same assumption, as 5: 7–8 make clear.

Here in this preliminary warning to the rich we become aware of the concern that James feels about the danger of riches to the individual Christian and to the Christian community. In this as in so much else he is faithfully reflecting the teaching of his Lord, though this aspect of His teaching has not always been emphasised in the Church as it should have been. This emphasis gives offence, and we are always in danger of trying too zealously to avoid giving offence.

It is appropriate to remind ourselves of the words of Jesus on this subject, so that we may be in a position to determine how far James faithfully reproduces the mind of Jesus.

Some parts of the Old Testament regard wealth as the mark of God's favour. But Jesus did not adopt this point of view. It was all too obvious that many wealthy people were very wicked people and that it was their very wickedness which in some cases enabled them to become wealthy. Wealth to Him, so far from being the sign of God's favour, is treated as the arch-enemy of God and called "Mammon", the chief rival of God in man's affections. It is not the rich whom He proclaims to be "blessed", but the "poor" (Luke 6: 20), and rebuke and pity are mingled in the words: "Woe to you who are rich" (Luke 6: 24). It is noticeable that Luke in his version of the Beatitudes reports the plain words "poor" and "rich" without spiritualizing their meaning as Matthew does. Jesus also said: "It will be hard for a rich man to enter into the Kingdom of God" and even went further in saying: "It is easier for a camel to go through a needle's eye than for a rich man to enter the Kingdom of God"—that is, it is not only hard, but virtually impossible. Indeed nothing short of a miracle from God can make it possible (Matt. 19: 26). The severe words to the Rich Young Ruler: "Go, sell that thou hast, and give to the poor and thou shalt have treasure in heaven" may be explained away as an unusual injunction used only for one particular case, but in honesty we should recognize that words equally severe appear at Luke 12: 33 and there they are addressed to all disciples. The devices we use to explain away these stern words of Jesus are perhaps an illustration of what He called "the deceitfulness of riches" (Mark 4: 19). The Parable of the Rich Fool (Luke 12: 16–21) and the words that follow it are perhaps most of all akin in emphasis to this passage in James, where the rich man is warned of the transitoriness of his tenure of life and therefore of his hold on his wealth. When, therefore, James speaks of wealth and its dangers, he is faithfully presenting a truth which he received from his Lord. The sternness of this stricture on wealth is explained by Hort as due to the fact that wealth all too easily leads "to the substitution of another God for Jehovah and the denial of the brotherhood of man".

The rich man, now that he has become a Christian, is exhorted to "boast" (find his joy and satisfaction) not in the pleasures and privileges that wealth can secure for him but "IN HIS (NEW) HUMILIATION". This may mean that by becoming a Christian he has actually had to forfeit the sources of his income and lose business connections on which his profits depended; it may even mean that he has suffered, through persecution, the actual destruction of property. More likely, however, the words are used metaphorically, and imply that as a committed member of a small and despised minority group, regarded by the pagans as narrow-minded, bigoted and unsociable, he is now treated by his former associates as "queer", so that they cease to include him in their circle of friends. He finds himself shut out from the social activities which previously filled his life, partly on the grounds of conscience, and partly because he is now avoided by his former acquaintances. In this sense he is deprived of much that he once cherished. To be treated by the "best people" as a social outcast is indeed for such a man a "humiliation". John Wesley, as his evangelical enterprise led him into more and more unconventional methods, found that he alienated many influential friends, but the call of God was insistent. When he felt compelled by faithfulness to God to preach in the open air, and thus to defy all recognized standards of ecclesiastical conduct, he comments on his action, in his own private record, thus: "I consented to be yet more vile".

Paul, the great precursor of all evangelists, had to drink this same bitter cup to the dregs. By becoming a Christian he had to forego much that previously he had treasured. He writes: "What things were gain to me, these have I counted loss for Christ . . . for whom I suffered the loss of all things, and do count them but dung that I may gain Christ and be found in him" (Phil. 3: 7–8). In the eyes of the non-Christian it seems unspeakable folly to discard obvious advantages for what to him seem imaginary gains. Paul had to be content to be in their eyes "a fool for Christ's sake" (1 Cor. 4: 10). But what to the outsider appears as utter loss is for the Christian great gain—he has found Christ, and friends in Christ, and with Christ life has become new and full of meaning; the present is full of Christ, and yet in the future there is still more of Christ. It is not merely, as Mayor puts it (p. 41) that "The rich should cease to pride himself on wealth or rank, and rejoice that he has learned the emptiness of worldly distinctions", but, more positively, he has grasped enough of the "unsearchable riches of Christ" to be able to ignore the allurements of material wealth. Calvin's words do better justice to his real gains, as well as to his apparent losses: "Since it is incomparably the greatest dignity to be introduced into the company of angels, nay, to be made associates of Christ, he who estimates this favour of God aright will regard all other things as worthless" (p. 285).

The words of the Magnificat come to mind in this context: "He hath exalted them of low degree . . . and the rich he hath sent empty away" (Luke 1 : 52), and also Jeremiah 9: 23–24: "Let not the rich man glory in his riches . . . but in this, that he understands and knows me, saith the Lord".

THE FLOWER OF THE GRASS. This is to us a strange phrase, since we do not think of grass as bearing flowers. The N.E.B. more satisfactorily translates as "flowers of the field", what we should call "wild flowers". The original Greek does in fact mean "flowers of the grass", but James is here quoting from the Septuagint, the standard translation in his day of the Old Testament into Greek. In the original Hebrew of the Old Testament, however, the phrase means "flowers of the field". It seems justifiable, therefore, to use this phrase rather than to perpetuate the inaccurate translation of the Hebrew in the Septuagint.

The passage quoted by James is from Isaiah 40: 6–7. The same passage is quoted also at 1 Peter 1 : 24–25, and the same mistranslation of the Septuagint is reproduced there ("flowers of the grass").

Even in the most favourable circumstances the life of the green grass and the wild flowers in Palestine is very brief. The summer heat soon withers them up. As Jesus noted, the grass which is today in the field is tomorrow dried up and fit only to be used as fuel in the oven (Matt. 6: 30). In the Gospels green grass seems to be regarded as such a rarity as to deserve special mention when it comes into the story (Mark 6: 39; John 6: 10). When, however, the normal heat of the sun is heightened by the scorching South East wind, known as the Sirocco, its life is even shorter. We should remember that James writes of a climate very different from the temperate zones, where flowers and green grass flourish for many months each year.

HE WILL PASS AWAY. This is normally taken to refer to the rich man, though it is possible for the word to be translated: "*It* shall pass away", and some have suggested that it refers to the man's wealth. But in the quotation from Isaiah it refers to human life as a whole: "All flesh is grass", and the brevity of life generally is likened to that of the grass. Here too in James it may well be used of human life generally, of both poor and rich. Both alike share the shortness and uncertainty of life.

If wealth were the subject of "pass away", that would be in accord with its proverbial insecurity. Many besides Job have found themselves bereft of it by one sudden disaster.

If, however, the subject is the rich man, the difficulty is that his life (even apart from his wealth) is no more unstable than that of others, though it is true that money breeds a false sense of security, and the rich man more than the poor man needs to be reminded of life's insecurity. In so far as the rich man is identified with the evil man, the whole witness of the Bible is that God's judgement will indeed overtake him unfailingly (cf. Psalm 37: 9–10, 17).

If the reference is to the shortness of human life generally and the wisdom of putting one's faith in something more enduring (Wisdom 2: 4; 5: 9), for the Christian of that time this reminder would be sharpened by the expectation of the imminent end of the world. For the first generation of Christians believed this to be nearer than their own death. James shared this view as is evident from 5: 7–9. When he speaks of the brevity of human life, it may hold something of the same significance as Paul's words in 1 Cor. 7: 31: "For the fashion of this world is passing away".

**1: 11** The quotation from Isaiah 40 gave as the reason for the withering of the grass the fact that "the breath of the Lord bloweth upon it". This may mean that God sends His wind upon it. These words about "the breath of the Lord" are not, however, quoted by James. Instead he writes: "THE SUN RISES WITH ITS SCORCHING HEAT". In the cool of the night the fresh grass is green, but with the dawn comes the scorching heat of the sun. The word translated "heat" may mean the South East wind, the dreaded sirocco (as in Gen. 41: 6, Jonah 4: 8, Luke 12: 55). When it blows it is like the hot air from an oven and in the space of a few hours vegetation is dried and dead. It may, however, be used of any excessive heat (as in Matt. 20: 12) and this is probably its meaning here.

Students of Greek will notice that the four verbs of verse 11 are in the Greek aorist tense. This is usually translated by the past tense in English, but our translation rightly renders them here by the present tense, since in Greek this is a special aorist known as the Gnomic aorist, used, according to Hort, "of general statements founded on repeated experience". This use is discussed in Moulton's Prolegomena, p. 135. James uses this tense because it stood in the Septuagint from which he quotes.

WITHERS THE GRASS AND ITS FLOWER FALLS. N.E.B. translates "the flower withers, its petals fall".

ITS BEAUTY PERISHES: literally "the beauty of its appearance".
N.E.B. has "what was lovely to look at". These words are James's
own, not from the quotation. He reveals something of the same
appreciation of the loveliness of God's creation which we find in the
words of Jesus, who said that the simple beauty of the wild flowers
exceeded that of the splendour of Solomon's court (Matt. 6: 29).

SO WILL THE RICH MAN FADE IN THE MIDST OF HIS PURSUITS. In view of
this conclusion it may seem more natural to take the subject of "will
pass away" in verse 10 as also the rich man, but it need not necessarily
be so. The word "pursuits" does literally mean "journeyings", but
probably here it is used metaphorically, and should be translated here
as "pursuits" or "business". If, of course, his wealth depended on
widespread commerce, then his "business" would involve actual
journeys. Even in the midst of his success, this rich man, like the
"Rich Fool", finds that his soul is required of him.

> 1: 12–15. *Blessed is the man who endures trial, for when he has
> stood the test he will receive the crown of life which God has promised to
> those who love him.* 13. *Let no one say when he is tempted, "I am
> tempted by God"; for God cannot be tempted with evil and he himself
> tempts no one;* 14. *but each person is tempted when he is lured and
> enticed by his own desire.* 15. *Then desire when it has conceived gives
> birth to sin: and sin when it is full-grown brings forth death.*

In 1: 2–4 the theme was the correct bearing of the Christian man
in time of trial. Here James takes up this theme again, almost as
though verses 5–11 were a kind of parenthesis. It was noted at verse
2 that the Greek word for "TRIAL" carries a double meaning: (i) a heavy
ordeal of suffering or distress and strain; (ii) an enticement to do evil,
that is, what we normally mean by the word "temptation". Because
the same Greek word meant both these things, a Greek writer could use
it without having to determine precisely in which of these two meanings
he meant it to be understood. Sometimes it was one, sometimes the
other, and sometimes both were included.

1: 12 Here the first of these two meanings appears to predominate,
as in verse 2, and R.S.V. translates the word as "trial", an ordeal
which a Christian is urged to face with steadfast courage—such things
as illness, unpopularity, financial loss, sorrow, persecution. By the
time, however, that verse 13 is reached the other meaning has come to
the fore, and James is writing about "enticement" to evil, by which he
would mean such things as lust, dishonesty, untruthfulness, jealousy,
hate, self-seeking.

Those who endure trials (in the first sense of the word) are pronounced "BLESSED". This word is used to describe those who have found the secret springs of life's deepest happiness, the quality which John Wesley spoke of as being "happy in God". It is something quite other than freedom from outward trouble. It is an inner quality, capable of being sustained even when outward circumstances are most unfavourable. "Blessedness" is something a Christian may begin to taste here on earth, but its fulness lies beyond the sphere of this earthly life. "That, that is the fulness, But this is the taste." Even in our present experience, no matter how adverse our outward circumstances, we may know something of blessedness, but its full content is reserved for hereafter.

In verse 2 it is the onset of troubles which is to be greeted with joy. Here it is not so much the troubles themselves, as the power to face them with steadfast courage which is the source of the blessedness. There the trouble was welcomed as an opportunity to prove our ability to meet it worthily. Here the courageous "endurance" of the ordeal is commended as the secret of entry into spiritual treasure.

Our Lord often used the word "BLESSED" (e.g. Matt. 5: 1-12) to commend and encourage those who adopted the Christian attitude to life, and these are very often the people whom the world at large would have thought most to be pitied—the poor, the sorrowful and the persecuted. This beatitude is similar, and has much in common with the one spoken by Jesus in Luke 6: 22-23.

Ability to "ENDURE" takes an honourable place in the qualities expected in the Christian. It means to face troubles and distresses with steadfast courage, without discontent or self-pity, without thought of "giving up" or turning back. Calvin says it means confronting them in such a way "as to rise above them". Paul reminds us that love "*endures* all things" (1 Cor. 13: 7), and Jesus promises the fulness of salvation to him "that *endures* to the end" (Matt. 24: 13), and similarly in Luke 21: 19 He says: "By standing firm (*enduring*) you will win true life for yourselves" (N.E.B.; cf. also 1 Pet. 2: 19-20).

Some commentators claim that this word "endure" proves that the "temptation" here meant is an ordeal rather than an inducement to evil, since such "temptation" would have to be resisted (as at James 4: 7) or avoided (1 Tim. 6: 11), rather than endured. This is probably true, though it might be possible to speak of "enduring" even "enticement to evil", in the sense of standing up to it and not giving way to it.

Here, however, temptation is taken to mean some ordeal which "tests" the quality of a man, and proves what kind of Christian he is. If he proves to be a steadfast man whose faith and obedience no suffering or threat can weaken, he can be declared to be an "approved" (Greek *dokimos*) man, that is, one who has STOOD THE TEST in "the fires of affliction" (cf. verse 3 where the word "testing" is used in a similar sense). Jesus said that the man who put his hand to the plough and kept looking back was not "fit" for the Kingdom of God. The man who endures without looking back may be thought of as "fit", "approved". What is basically the same word is also used by Paul in Romans 5: 3-4, where he writes that persecution produces "endurance" (Greek *hypomenē*), and "endurance" produces "character" (*dokimē*), which the R.V. translates as "probation", but which the N.E.B., more accurately, renders as "proof that we have stood the test".

We have noted that the Christian may find inward compensations in "blessedness" even in the midst of outward woes. But in addition to the rewards that accrue to us on the journey, there are still more splendid rewards at the journey's end. It is of these primarily that James speaks when he says: HE WILL RECEIVE the crown of life.

Some high-minded Christians deplore the introduction of any appeal to the thought of reward into the Christian life, and certainly it is a poor kind of Christian faith which expects to be rewarded by material gains and worldly comforts and financial benefits. The New Testament does not speak of such rewards for the Christian. But that there are rewards assured to the Christian is without question the teaching of the New Testament—though it must be acknowledged that the rewards are of the kind that only a true Christian would be able to appreciate. Jesus certainly did not shrink from speaking of rewards. "Great is your reward in heaven", He said (Matt. 5: 12; cf. Matt. 5: 46; 6: 1, 2, 4, 6, 17, Luke 6: 35). Paul also makes reference to unimaginably good things which "God prepared for them that love him" (1 Cor. 2: 9, cf. also 1 Cor. 3: 8, Col. 3: 24). Even the word of Jesus about the need to be ready to "lose life", if we are to gain it, implies the promise of true "life" to those who seek it aright.

It is in accord with this word of Jesus that the reward which God waits to bestow on His faithful children is here described as the "CROWN OF LIFE". It would be a mistake to press for any special meaning in the word "CROWN". It had come to be used frequently, almost conventionally, for some great reward or special benefit. In the New Testament it refers generally to the reward at life's end. In 2 Tim. 4: 8 we read of a "*crown* of righteousness" laid up for the Christian "on that day", and in 1 Pet. 5: 4 of "the *crown* of glory" awarded at the Last Judgement. In Rev. 2: 10 not only is the general context of thought similar to this in James (there is reference to "persecution" and "testing" and "faithfulness unto death") but there the reward as here is "the *crown* of life".

In modern times a crown is usually made of very precious materials and is intrinsically valuable. In ancient times, however, it was usually of little value in itself, its value lying entirely in the honour it represented. Nor was its main use to denote royalty. In the Greek world its chief purpose was to reward prowess in athletic contests, and it was made out of leaves. In itself valueless, it denoted a high honour. The Jews cared little for athletic skill, and for them the crown was more often a symbol of joy on some festive occasion (Ezek. 16: 12, Wisdom 2: 8), or a sign of special dignity or honour (Prov. 16: 31, Job 19: 9, Wisdom 5: 16).

Here, quite clearly, the word is used metaphorically of some high honour to be received with joy. Paul can speak of a crown as indicating a *present* privilege. His converts at Thessalonica, for instance, are his *"crown* of boasting" (N.E.B. *"Crown* of pride"). But usually in the New Testament a "crown" seems to refer to some ultimate reward at life's end, and this is the meaning of the *"crown* of life" here.

We noted that when James thus speaks of this reward in terms of "life" he has taken his cue from the words of Jesus, and other writers of the New Testament also follow this lead. Our Lord Himself constantly spoke of the ultimate prize which God could bestow on human beings as "Life", that is a new quality of Life, Life with a capital L. This occurs not only in the passage already referred to (on p. 44) from Mark 8: 35–37, but also in Mark 9: 43, John 10: 10 and many others. Sometimes He adds the word "eternal" to indicate the special quality of the Life which is meant ("eternal" meaning the quality characteristic of the New Age dawning upon the world in the coming of Christ to earth) as at Mark 10: 30, John 12: 25, etc. The same phrases are found also in Paul who can speak of God's final gift to His children as "LIFE" (that which is mortal in us is to be "swallowed up in life", 2 Cor. 5: 14), or alternatively as "eternal life" (Gal. 6: 8, Rom. 2: 7; 6: 23).

As in so many other things, this Christian way of speaking springs out of Old Testament origins. In Deut. 30: 19–20 God sets before His people the solemn choice between LIFE and death, and commands: "Therefore choose life . . . to love the Lord thy God, to obey His voice and to cleave unto Him, for He is thy life". Jesus, when asked how "eternal life" could be gained, made reference to the keeping of the Ten Commandments, and added, quoting in part Lev. 18: 5: "Do this and you will live" (Luke 10: 28).

It is this Life, the supreme gift of God, which James says GOD HAS PROMISED. It is called a "CROWN" because it is a source of joy, a high privilege, a wonderful honour. It is the mark of God's approval, the symbol of His "Well done".

The actual text in the Greek does not include any word for God. It says simply "He promised", but quite clearly "God" is meant, and translators do in fact normally introduce the name of God as subject. The omission of it is probably due to James's reluctance as a Jew to use the divine name unnecessarily, lest he fall into the grievous sin of using it carelessly. The "promises" referred to may be those found in the Old Testament Scriptures, or else the word of our Lord who re-affirmed them. "For all the promises of God find their 'Yes' in him" (2 Cor. 1: 20).

The ones who are to receive this gift are "THOSE WHO LOVE GOD". This was a common way of describing true believers in God. In the Old Testament it is found, for instance, at Exod. 20: 6, Deut. 7: 9 and 30: 19–20, quoted above. It came especially easily to the lips of Christians because Jesus had selected and emphasized from the Old Testament commands the two which, He declared, comprehended all the others. The first of these was to "love God" (Matt. 22: 37). Those who love God are those who respond in obedience to the word of Christ. Paul too uses this phrase, as for instance in 1 Cor. 2: 9 and Rom. 8: 28. It appears, however, to be a phrase which he took over from the current use of the Church rather than one he himself specially cared for. It occurs again in James 2: 5, where it is closely associated with the second of the two great commands, to love our neighbour as ourselves (2: 8).

**1: 13** Here the second meaning of "trial" begins to predominate, and to "tempt" means to "induce to evil" rather than merely to "test". In fact R.S.V. now uses the word "tempt", though it is the same Greek word which in the preceding verse is translated as "test".

The main purpose of this section is to administer a sharp rebuke to those Christians who wish to find an excuse for their sinning, in order to free themselves from personal responsibility for it. They turn the blame on God, who, they say, is responsible for the evil things that overcome them. They say: "I am tempted by God". The modern equivalent of this excuse may be found among those who say: "God made me as I am; I am not responsible for these strong feelings and appetites which I am not able to control. What I am and what I do is God's fault". In this way they try to make it possible for themselves to go on sinning without suffering the twinges of an uneasy conscience.

The origin of evil and the power of evil to seduce and subdue us is a problem for which there is no easy answer. Even if we say that Satan is responsible, we are still left with the question: How did Satan come to have this power? Any course in systematic theology would have to face this problem and provide the best answer possible. But James is not a theoretical theologian. It is not intellectual problems with which he is here concerned. His interest is in what John Wesley would have called "practical divinity". Others may deal with speculative problems; he wants primarily to get Christians to behave as better Christians, and so he meets this issue at an entirely practical level.

He would recognize that God does allow men to be "tested" in order that they may be "proved". Job was "proved", and in a similar way Satan asked to have Peter to sift him (Luke 22: 31). Our life on earth would not serve God's purpose were there no occasions by which our moral and spiritual muscles could be exercised and thereby strengthened and proved. But though God permits "testing" He never seeks to induce man to do evil. Of that James is quite certain.

It is a sad characteristic of our depraved human nature not only that it does evil, but that it seeks to evade responsibility for its evil doing. This continuing truth about us all is vividly brought out in the story of Adam and Eve, where Eve blames the serpent for her sin, and Adam blames Eve for his. When we cannot blame other people, we turn the blame on God for creating us the kind of people we are. The writer of Ecclesiasticus faced this self-deceit, and firmly rebuked it: "Do not say, 'Because of the Lord I left the right way.' . . . Do not say, 'It was He who led me astray' " (15: 11–12, R.S.V.). This excuse, writes Hort, "is the vice of men whose religion has become corrupt, not of men who have none at all".

GOD CANNOT BE TEMPTED WITH EVIL. Literally this could be translated, "God is untemptable". There is nothing in God to which evil can make its appeal. And it is impossible to think of One so wholly free from evil as being in any way directly responsible for it in another. James affirms this without argument. To him it is an axiom too obvious to need any supporting reason to make it believable. In the same way Paul when confronted by the suggestion that God might be "unjust", unfair in his treatment of men and women, cannot even consider the possibility. He dismisses it, not pausing to give his reasons, with the words: "Quite impossible!" ("God forbid", Rom. 9: 14). The utter goodness of God, completely free from blemish or imperfection, is a basic assumption not only of James and Paul, but of all New Testament writers.

Therefore, GOD HIMSELF TEMPTS NO ONE. It is possible that one-time trusted agents of God may overstep their rights and become tempters. Our own human nature, already corrupted, devises evil uses for powers within itself which God meant only for good. But where evil attracts and seduces, that is something which cannot at all be ascribed directly to God.

Sometimes, it is true, the words of the Bible suggest that God does "tempt" (e.g. A.V. of Gen. 22: 1). But this is in the sense of "test" and R.S.V. does in fact use the translation "God tested Abraham" instead of "tempt" as A.V. It was probably with the intention of emphasizing this point that the translators of the N.E.B. altered the familiar petition of the Lord's Prayer from: "Lead us not into temptation" to "Do not bring us to the test". Paul has a wise word in 1 Cor. 10: 13 about this kind of "tempting" and God's part in it. Calvin points out that Scripture speaks of God as "hardening" or "blinding" men who set themselves against God, but he notes that this is a punishment for sin, not a "temptation" to it.

**1: 14** James uncompromisingly asserts man's inescapable responsibility for his own sinning. Certainly outward circumstances may make temptation almost unendurably strong, and sometimes perversions inflicted by others in childhood weight the scales very heavily against some men. When it is the sin of others we are dealing with, it is well to bear this in mind. But when it is our own sin which is in question, to try to shirk the responsibility for it is the mark of a poor type of Christian, just as to blame one's tools is the mark of a poor workman. If there are excuses for failure, we can trust in the understanding mercies of God, but it is not for us to invent excuses, but to accept responsibility. As James says, if we sin, we are to blame. John Wesley reminded people of his own day: "Even the injections of the devil cannot hurt, before we make them our own". It is only after we have permitted and encouraged "lust" that it breaks out into action.

This spring of evil in human life is described as our OWN DESIRE. Both A.V. and R.V. gave the translation "lust", but in English this word tends to be restricted to improper sexual desire. The Greek word, however, while including this, is used also for desires of many kinds. It is, for instance, the word used to translate the "covetousness" forbidden in the tenth commandment. It could equally well describe any other strong desire, such as greed for gain, craving for vengeance or power or prominence, or sadistic pleasure in inflicted cruelty. Man's heart is full of these evil desires, and when the thin restraints of civilized life are removed, they soon appear in all their crude ugliness. It was his knowledge of this that made Jeremiah say: "The heart of man is deceitful and desperately wicked" (17: 9).

It is by these various longings that man is LURED out of his normal restraints (and protections) and ENTICED by attractive inducements into evil. The words are taken from the craft of hunting. The animal, safe in its lair, must first be LURED out by some cunning device, and then ENTICED by some tempting bait into the trap carefully laid for it. So man's desires become the agents of evil to trick him to his downfall, drawing him away from standards of conduct he habitually follows, and within which he would be safe, and enticing him into evil by making it appear pleasing and harmless.

**1: 15** This verse reveals a deep understanding of human nature. James uses the word SIN in a sensible, practical way, though some might think a not very profound way. Different writers use the word differently. Some mean by "sin" a malignant power abroad in the universe, ever seeking to gain entrance into human life. Others use it of the deep sinfulness within the human heart, even when it finds no expression in word or act. Others insist that sin is far more than just conscious acts of disobedience to God's will, and that sin, like an ice-berg, is mainly below the surface, and that most of our sinning, perhaps the worst of it, is sin that we ourselves are unaware of. All these mean-ings of sin point to important truths. Perhaps we need several different words for these different things. James, however, as at other times, is severely practical, and he means by "sin" some act or thought in which a person is knowingly disobedient to the perfect will of God, something to which in a measure at least he gives his consent. This certainly is one kind of sin, and James would probably not wish to deny that there are other kinds. But it is this kind that here he is dealing with.

James distinguishes between DESIRE and "sin". We must be sure that we understand what James means by "desire". He does not mean the "desire" which is encouraged and welcomed and gloated over. That he would include under sin. It is rather the involuntary, instinc-tive, awakening of desire. If, for instance, a man feels that he has been grievously wronged by another, a feeling of resentment and hostility arises uninvited in his heart. This James would not call "sin"; he would call it wrong "desire". If the man does the Christian thing, recognizes the resentment for the evil thing it is, seeks to hand it over to God for Him to remove, and by every means in his power turns from it and seeks to exclude it from his thoughts and have love put in its place, then that is temptation or "desire" as James calls it, but it is not sin. But if the Christian, "lured and enticed" by the intensity of his feelings, and the anticipated pleasure of "getting his own back", perhaps even deceived into thinking this course of action permissible, allows himself to foster and dwell on bitter, angry thoughts, which inevitably lead on to words and actions of like kind, this is sin. It is offensive to God and we are accountable for it, because we have assented to it. When James speaks of sin (as Calvin reminds us) he does not speak of "the beginnings of sin" but of sin "when it breaks forth".

This inward act of consenting to the evil feeling or desire and allowing it to linger and swell within our hearts James speaks of as desire "CONCEIVING" sin. The metaphor is drawn from the process of child-birth. The first act that leads to the birth of a child is when the woman's womb receives the male sperm, that is, when she conceives. So the first act that leads to sin is when "desire" is allowed to linger and grow in the heart, "to be conceived" there. This warns us how foolish are those who say: "It does not matter what goes on in my thoughts, so long as it does not find expression in outward word or act". As surely as conception in the normal course leads to birth, so does the harboured ("conceived") desire lead to outward sin. Indeed the lustful thought itself, if it is fostered and encouraged, is itself a grievous sin, as our Lord made perfectly clear (Matt. 5: 28).

The emergence of inward desire, inflamed by long brooding over it, into outward acts or words of sin is not, however, the end of the matter. Such sin is itself the latest stage in a process of development; it also sets on foot a further process which will advance step by step to an inevitable goal—unless something is done to check and change it. That sure end is described as "death". SIN WHEN IT IS FULL GROWN BRINGS FORTH DEATH. The final consequences of sin, when they go on to the bitter end, consist of "DEATH".

In establishing this link between sin and death, James is repeating in his own way what Paul also has emphasized. "The wages of sin is death" (Rom. 6: 23) is his way of putting it. So too in Rom. 8: 6 he says "The work of the flesh is death" (cf. also Rom. 5: 12–21, and Wisdom 1: 12 and 16).

This thought of the final result of sin as death is characteristic of the Bible. In the early days of Hebrew thought, the place where it was thought the shades of the dead lingered on in some vague kind of existence was called Sheol. Those who dwelt there were regarded as cut off from God (cf. Ps. 115: 17), so that death at that time meant not only the end of physical life, but separation from God. Later it was believed that God would not leave in this comfortless place those who had lived honourably for Him, but He would raise them back to life in a great act of resurrection. This hope, somewhat tenuous before the time of Jesus, became the confident assurance of the early Christians because God had raised Christ from the dead, and they too were to be raised together with Christ. But this hope of victory over death was never thought of as something that was naturally man's right. If man remained a disobedient and unrepentant sinner, it was his doom to the last to be cut off from God, just as the dead in Sheol had been thought to be cut off. So it was natural that the end of the sinful man, unredeemed by Christ, should be called "death", the opposite of eternal life, and involving separation from God. The word "death", therefore, came to carry a double meaning. It might mean just physical death, the end of physical life; or it might mean spiritual death. Paul could speak of people, still living, who were "dead in trespasses and sins", but there was a tragic finality about the fate of those who were already spiritually dead when physical death overtook them.

When James uses "death", he may mean that spiritual deterioration during a man's lifetime which draws him far away from God in wickedness and spiritual hardening. He may also mean the final verdict of God at the Last Judgement upon his wretched way of life, when He says: "Depart from me". This is "death" in its most dreadful form. It is the extreme opposite of the crown of life bestowed on those who in God's sight stand "approved" (verse 12).

1: 16–18. *Do not be deceived, my beloved brethren.* 17. *Every good endowment and every perfect gift is from above, coming down from the Father of lights with whom there is no variation or shadow due to change.* 18. *Of his own will he brought us forth by the word of truth that we should be a kind of first fruits of his creatures.*

James constantly addresses those to whom he writes as "BRETHREN" (see note on 1: 2), and occasionally adds the adjective "BELOVED", as here and at 1: 19 and 2: 5. This characteristically Christian mode of address is found also in Paul's writings (1 Cor. 15: 58, Phil. 4: 1).

**1: 16** Paul also uses the solemn warning, "DO NOT BE DECEIVED", to call attention to an error in thought which has consequences in wrong conduct. There may even be a suggestion that the error is partly due to willing self-deception, which is thought to excuse the evil conduct which results from it. In Gal. 6: 7 he speaks sharply to those who claim that evil conduct does not result in retribution: "Be not deceived. God is not mocked". Similarly in 1 Cor. 15: 33 he uses this warning for those who argue that death ends everything, and that no judgement follows death; therefore the sensible thing to do is to indulge in all the material pleasures possible before death (cf. also 1 Cor. 6: 9).

Here James has been warning his readers against the demoralizing tendency to excuse their failures on the ground that God made them as they are, evil as well as good, and to overlook the great mercies which God has poured into our lives. Such self-pity, with its shirking of responsibility, is a ready cause of moral defeat. On the other hand, the attitude which "counts our blessings" and remembers gratefully our many privileges finds a constant stimulus towards that obedience which pleases God.

The powers of evil, if they cannot force their way into human life by a frontal attack, are subtle enough to be able to deceive the Christian by turning his thoughts from his rich store of blessings, and inducing him to brood on his real or imagined hardships. In this way discontent becomes the seed-bed of all kinds of evil.

**1: 17** EVERY GOOD ENDOWMENT AND EVERY PERFECT GIFT. In the original Greek these words read like a line of poetry (a hexameter). Some scholars, including Ropes and Dibelius, are inclined to regard it as a quotation from an unknown poem. Others, however, think that the rhythmic form of the words is accidental, though indicative of the writer's sense of rhythm in what he wrote.

The general meaning of the words may appear to be clear, but in fact the precise significance of some of the details is disputed. God is declared to be the author, not of the evil things which some are attributing to him (as in 1: 13), but of all that is good, and, by implication, of only that which is good. Our Lord Himself had insisted that His followers should think of God in this way, as One who gives "good things" to those who ask Him (Matt. 7: 11, cf. John 3: 27).

Moffatt translates these words as: "All we are given is good, and all our endowments are faultless". But this affirmation of the natural innocence of human nature does not represent the Greek, where the affirmation that they come "from above" seems to carry the main emphasis. The good things which are ours are "from above", that is, from God.

If we ask whether we should detect a difference in meaning between "good endowment" and "perfect gift", or treat them as parallel ways of saying substantially the same thing, no agreed answer can be given. Probably the second alternative is to be preferred, the second phrase being used not to indicate something different, but to emphasize the inclusive truth that everything that is good is God's gift to man. If, however, a distinction is to be made, the first phrase must apply to those good gifts which all men share, and the "perfect gift" to the special privileges accorded to Christians through their knowledge of Christ.

A further difficulty arises from uncertainty about the exact meaning here of the Greek word translated by the R.S.V. as "endowment" (Greek *dosis*). Most translators agree with R.S.V. and translate as "gift" or some equivalent, but the normal meaning is "giving". It is the same word which is used at Phil. 4: 15 where it is translated: "No church entered into partnership with me in *giving* and receiving except you only". Since this is the usual meaning of the word and its only other occurrence in the N.T. carries this meaning, it may seem reasonable to accept this as the meaning here, as N.E.B. does: "All good giving . . . comes from above". Hort strongly insists on the translation "giving", reminding readers that this was the rendering in both the Geneva and the Bishops' Bible. He comments that the two words used here for "endowment" (*dosis*) and "gift" (*dōrēma*) "are emphatically distinguished". In support of this, we note that Moulton and Milligan, in their lexicon of Greek words found in the papyri, include no instance of *dosis* meaning "gift".

In other literature, however, roughly contemporary with the N.T., *dosis* is found with the meaning of "gift" (see Arndt and Gingrich), and many translators agree with this translation in R.S.V. Ropes too writes of *dosis*: "Here parallelism makes the latter sense (i.e. "gift") probable", since "In James there is no special distinction intended, the repetition being only for rhetorical effect". Dibelius adopts the same point of view, and it is on the whole preferable.

IS FROM ABOVE, COMING DOWN. . . . Ropes supports R.S.V. in this translation of the Greek, but it may equally well be rendered: "comes down from above", as in N.E.B. (supported by Dibelius). But the difference in meaning is slight.

"From above" (Greek *anōthen*) means "from God" (as in 3: 17, John 3: 31; 19: 11), and this gives perfectly good sense, the phrase that follows ("from the Father of lights") being added for the sake of precision. It seems unnecessary and artificial to insist that to avoid this repetition some other meaning must be found for it. Hort, however, takes this point of view and argues that here it means "from its first beginning" (a meaning similar to that found in Luke 1: 3 and Acts 26: 5).

FROM THE FATHER OF LIGHTS. It is probable that the word "Father" does not here mean much more than "Creator", (as in Job 38: 28: "Has the rain a father?"). But it certainly serves most appropriately to anticipate the following metaphor about a new birth, with the implication of "sonship", which follows in the next verse.

The N.E.B. translates "lights" as "lights of heaven". This is an interpretation rather than a precise translation, but it gives the meaning well. The "lights" here are the heavenly bodies, sun, moon and stars, as in Gen. 1: 14 which speaks of "lights in the firmament of the heavens", and "the greater light to rule the day, and the lesser light to rule the night". Ps. 136: 7 also speaks of God as Him "who made the great lights". Ropes, and others, quote the Jewish benediction which precedes the Shema: "Blessed be the Lord our God, who hath formed the lights".

This description of God serves to emphasize that the greatest of man's blessings, even the sun itself, the source of light and heat, and the moon which relieves the frightening blackness of the night, are the gracious gifts of God to man. It serves, also, as an opportunity to emphasize that, no matter how great God's gifts may be, He is greater than His gifts. The sun and the moon give their light, but intermittently. The darkness of night constantly overwhelms the bright light of the sun's day-time shining; the moon's light is always growing, or dwindling, and then, for a time, utterly failing. Even when sun and moon are at their brightest, storm clouds may obliterate them. In contrast the goodness of God towards His children is unfailing and constant, not subject to phases or interruption: WITH WHOM THERE IS NO VARIATION (cf. John 1: 5 where God's true "light shines in the darkness" without being obscured, and 1 John 1: 5: "God is light and in him is no darkness at all". Cf. also Isa. 60: 19–20).

Moffatt sees here a reference to the stars (as distinct from sun and moon) and suspects an allusion to astrology, and its claim that human life is controlled by the stars. This, however, is not necessary, and James's meaning is clear if we understand the Lights to be sun and moon and stars.

OR SHADOW DUE TO CHANGE. Our best Greek manuscripts are not agreed about the precise form of words which James used here.

R.S.V. translates the reading most commonly accepted (*ē tropēs
aposkiasma*, literally meaning, "or a shadow of turning"). The A.V.
has "with whom is no shadow of turning", as though it meant: "with
whom there is not the slightest suggestion of any change". But though
the word "shadow" in English may bear this meaning, it is very
doubtful if the Greek word *aposkiasma* can. R.V. has "shadow
cast by turning", and N.E.B. "No play of passing shadows".
Arndt and Gingrich suggest: "no darkening which has its basis in
change".

The Greek word *tropē* may be used with the sense of "solstice",
but this does not give a good meaning here. If it could be applied to
an eclipse, that would be more suitable, but we have no evidence for
such a use. It is more probable that the word is used in a general
sense of "change". Greek words from the same root are used elsewhere
to affirm the unchangeableness of God. Philo speaks of Him as *atreptos*
(not subject to change)—see Arndt and Gingrich.

Shadows are caused by bright light, and change in the source of
light is reflected in the changing shadow. At midday when the sun is
overhead there is little shadow; at sunset the shadows are long. In
the morning they fall towards the west, and in the evening towards the
east. But with God all is light. His goodness is not occasional or fitful,
but unceasing and unfading, steady and persistent.

The obscurity of these Greek words has roused special interest in a
textual variant which is found in three early manuscripts. This is not
the only variant, but is the one with strongest support. The manuscripts which give this reading are ℵ B and P[23]. ℵ and B are the two
best Uncial manuscripts representing the Alexandrian tradition. Both
are dated about A.D. 400 or a little earlier. P[23] is one of the fragments
of papyri found at Oxyrhynchus in 1914, and may be a hundred years
or more earlier. The difference in the Greek is slight. It may be
represented thus: the commonly accepted text is *ē tropēs aposkiasma*,
and that in ℵ B P[23] *hē tropēs aposkiasmatos*; literally, no variation
"which consists in the turning of a shadow". Ropes appears to favour
it and claims that it "makes excellent sense" (p. 163). Curiously
enough Hort, who usually accepted the combined authority of ℵ and
B, in this instance treats their reading almost casually, and contents
himself largely with suggesting how it may have arisen. Dibelius,
against Ropes, finds himself unable to discover any "excellent sense"
in it. Indeed for him the more commonly accepted one also appears to
offer no satisfactory meaning either. As a result he allows himself the
luxury of a conjecture, and suggests a reading which, he argues, may
have been the original one. In the Greek his conjectured reading would
be: *ē tropēs ē aposkiasmatos*. This literally could be translated: with
whom is no variation "caused either by turning or by shadow".

Since, however, this has no manuscript authority, and since the text most widely supported does not appear to be unduly difficult, not many scholars are inclined to support Ropes's preference for the Alexandrian reading, and fewer still approve of Dibelius's conjecture.

*Note on* THE GIFT OF GOD.

Verse 17 lays great stress on the good things which are ours, as men and as Christian believers, as the free gift of God. In the relationship of God with man, it is always God who is the Giver, and man who receives. Of nothing is this more true than the rich privileges of the Christian life itself, of the "new birth" to which verse 18 refers. "This new life in Christ is at every stage the Gift of God".[1] In this emphasis James once again shows himself at one with the other writers in the New Testament.

Jesus Himself vividly represented this abundant, almost extravagant, giving on the part of God. In Luke 6: 38, for instance, using metaphors from the action of a generous shopkeeper, who gives far more than the exact measure which is asked for, He says that God gives us "good measure, pressed down, shaken together, running over". The same emphasis occurs also in Paul. He drew on every word in the Greek language he could think of which has the meaning of "gift", and when these did not suffice he appropriated a fairly ordinary word, *charis*, meaning "favour", and poured into it all that Christian theology now thinks of in association with the word "grace"—the free, unconditioned, spontaneous generosity of God to man in Christ. In Rom. 5: 15–17 the phrase "free gift" and the word "grace" tumble over each other as he seeks to underline how wonderful and unlimited is the generosity of God to man.

All the good things of the Christian life are described in the N.T. as the gift of God. The Kingdom of God is His gift. "Fear not, little flock, it is your Father's good pleasure to *give* you the kingdom" (Luke 12: 32). The coming of the Holy Spirit into human life is always God's gift, which men must be content to receive humbly and undeservingly —never earn or deserve or achieve (cf. Acts 2: 38, Luke 11: 13). The same is true of salvation. This is "by grace"; it is "not your own doing"; "it is the GIFT of God" (Eph. 2: 8). When salvation is described in terms of "eternal life", this also is affirmed to be "the *gift* of God" (Rom. 6: 23, John 17: 2, etc.). On this matter the New Testament speaks with one voice, and James is in harmony with the others.

1: 18 OF HIS OWN WILL. This phrase also emphasizes the generous goodness of God, and links it specifically with the new birth into the Christian life. This is not something which man can organize for

[1] *The Message and Mission of Methodism*, p. 19.

himself; it is not a psychological readjustment which a man can achieve for himself. It is a gift from God, offered to man by God's free choice. He was not subject to external pressures. It was not something that He owed to man. It was a generous decision prompted only by the inexplicable love of God for His creature man. N.E.B. translates "of set purpose". Perhaps here J. B. Phillips is to be preferred: "By his own wish". Some commentators who already have a predilection for doctrines of predestination have sensed something of the kind here, but this is to read into the text something which is not present in it.

HE BROUGHT US FORTH. This verse is aptly introduced by Calvin with the comment: "This is special proof of God's goodness that He has regenerated us unto eternal life". This is the "perfect gift" which God offers us in Christ, the gift of "regeneration" or "the new birth", an event by which our life makes a new start, in which God is recognized as our Father, and we know ourselves to be His sons.

Some scholars have disputed this interpretation, and denied that there is any reference here to the new birth. Those who understand the epistle as a whole as originally a Jewish writing, only slightly modified to give it the appearance of a Christian epistle, understandably must make this refer to mankind in general, brought into being at the creation to hold a special status among the rest of God's creatures. It is surprising, however, to find Hort taking this point of view, and arguing that "us" here means mankind generally. Among more recent writers Rendall[1] and L. E. Elliott-Binns[2] argue strongly in support of Hort.

The Greek word for "he brought forth" (*apokyeō*) does not, however, easily lend itself to Hort's explanation. It does not mean "create". It has already been used in 1:15 for sin "bringing forth" death. Its normal meaning is of a mother giving birth to her child, though more loosely it can sometimes be applied to either parent in their responsibility for the birth of their child. We may, therefore, confidently follow Ropes: "The figure of begetting was not used for creation, whereas it came easily into use with reference to the Christians who deemed themselves 'sons of God' ". The implication is very strong that by this new birth "we" have been brought into a relationship with God which is that of "child to Father". J. B. Phillips even translates this word as "He made us his own sons".

### Note on THE NEW BIRTH.

This reference in James to the life of the Christian as something equivalent to a "New Life" brings him once again into line with the general testimony of the New Testament.

[1] *The Epistle of St. James and Judaic Christianity*, pp. 63ff.
[2] *New Testament Studies*, Vol. III, No. 2, pp. 148ff.

Our Lord Himself frequently spoke of a new quality of life into which He sought to bring men (e.g. Mark 8: 35; 9: 45, Matt. 7: 14). Sometimes its newness is indicated by the addition of the epithet "eternal", especially so in the Fourth Gospel. He spoke of the need to "turn" and "become as little children", and this suggests being "born again", since we become children by birth. The Fourth Gospel speaks not only of believers receiving "power to become children of God" and being "born of God" (1: 12–13) but explicitly uses the phrase "born anew" (3: 3, 7, though the R.S.V. margin translates: "Born from above"). Paul does not use this precise metaphor, but shows that he knows the necessity of a similar radical change in human life: "If anyone is in Christ, he is a new creation . . . the new has come" (2 Cor. 5: 17). An even closer parallel to James, because the new birth is associated with the activity of the Word of God, is found in 1 Pet. 1: 23: "You have been born anew . . . through the living and abiding word of God".

This radical change is brought about by THE WORD OF TRUTH. This phrase, borrowed from the O.T. (e.g. Ps. 119: 43), was quickly taken over into the accepted vocabulary of the Christian Church. It occurs frequently in the N.T. (e.g. 2 Cor. 6: 7, Eph. 1: 13, Col. 1: 5, 2 Tim. 2: 15). In John 17: 17 also we read: "Thy word is truth".
It is probable that "the truth" was a synonym for the Gospel, and "the word" here means "the proclamation". N.E.B. translates here: "by declaring the truth". Jesus Christ is Himself the Truth in John 14: 6, and Eph. 4: 21 speaks of "the truth" as it is "in Jesus". Earlier we noted the correspondence between this verse in James and 1 Pet. 1: 23, where, we read, Christians are "born anew" . . . "through the living and abiding word of God". In verse 25 the explanation is offered: "That word is the good news which was preached to you". The "word of truth", therefore, is the proclamation of the truth of the Gospel. It may be tempting to wonder if "word" here may carry some of the special meaning it does in the opening verses of the Fourth Gospel. But this is improbable.
The verse, therefore, declares that the new life offered to us in Christ is God's intention for us, and God's free offer to our need. It reaches us and becomes effective in us through the proclamation by others of God's truth, as it has first of all become clear to them. It is as Paul wrote in Rom. 10: 17: "Faith comes from what is heard, and what is heard comes by the preaching of Christ".
God's purposes designed for mankind a renewal of their human nature through the offer of the Gospel, and the end which this was intended to achieve is THAT WE SHOULD BE A KIND OF FIRST FRUITS OF HIS CREATURES.

"FIRST FRUITS" is here used metaphorically. This is indicated by the Greek word (*tina*) here translated "a kind of". J. B. Phillips gives the effect by introducing the phrase "so to speak".

"First fruits" (Greek *aparchē*) is a common phrase in the Bible. Quite literally it meant the first part of a crop to be gathered in. According to Lev. 23: 10 this had to be brought to the priest as an offering to God. The offering of this first part was an acknowledgement that the whole crop, in a sense, belonged to God, since it came from God as God's gift to man. Further significance attaches to the word because this offering was required to be "without blemish" (Lev. 23: 12), that is, first not only in order but also in quality. Three ideas were, therefore, combined in the thought of the "first fruits". They symbolized something which in a special sense was the property of God, something which was representative of a larger whole still to be gathered in (Phillips here translates the word as "first specimens"), and something which was the best men could make it, since it was to be offered to God.

The word is used metaphorically in the N.T. in different contexts. Paul has a remarkable use of it to describe the present gift of the Holy Spirit in the life of the Christian. This, he says, is a foretaste (*aparchē*) of the full life with God in heaven (Rom. 8: 23). Jesus Himself also, in His triumph over death by His resurrection, is described as "the first fruits" from the dead (1 Cor. 15: 20). He, alive from the dead, is the first of a great company who like Him will conquer death (a similar thought occurs in Rom. 8: 29, where Christ is described as "the firstborn of many brethren").

A commoner use, and one nearer in meaning to this one in James, is found in Rom. 16: 5 where Epaenetus is described as the "first fruits" of Asia (R.V.). R.S.V. rightly does not retain this metaphor, which carries no clear meaning in English, and translates: "the first convert in Asia for Christ". Similarly in 1 Cor. 16: 15 the household of Stephanas is called the "first fruits of Achaia" R.V. (R.S.V. "the first converts in Achaia").

In Rev. 14: 4 faithful Christians are described as "redeemed from mankind as first fruits for God". This suggests a small group, specially dedicated to God and of fine Christian quality, perhaps with the suggestion that they are the first pioneers of a much larger company who will follow their lead.[1]

Similarly here in James the Christians addressed are reminded that God had not brought them into His Kingdom merely for their own sake. They are the privileged pioneers in a great movement which will add many, many more to their company. Those who have

---

[1] The text in 2 Thess. 2: 13 is uncertain, but the reading which includes this word (*aparchēn*) is translated in the R.S.V. margin: "God chose you as the *first converts* to be saved".

already entered the Christian life by this new birth represent what God intends for all His creatures. By implication, they have received their privilege in order that they may be God's agents in communicating that privilege to others. A true Christian is a witnessing Christian and a true Church is a missionary Church.

Some scholars have pressed the metaphor further and related it closely to Genesis 1, where the first human beings were created "in the image of God". They urge that God's purpose in recreating Christians is that in them the broken image of God may be recovered. So Moffatt comments here: "The very object of our being is to reproduce God's nature". This certainly reflects teaching to be found in Scripture (e.g. Col. 3: 10: "the new nature . . . being renewed . . . after the image of its creator"), and it may have been in James's mind as he wrote this.

OF HIS CREATURES: The Greek word (*ktisma*) here translated "creature" is used commonly of the material things in creation rather than human life. Those who believe that this passage refers to creation rather than to regeneration point this out, and argue that here James means that human life is the "first fruits" of the inanimate creation. Usually, however, scholars allow that here the word does mean "human beings"[1]. Christians to whom James writes are "new creatures in Christ", the first in a long line to follow. Certainly the idea of Christians as a "new creation" is found in Pauline writings (2 Cor. 5: 17, Gal. 6: 15, Eph. 2: 10; 4: 24).

> 1: 19-21. *Know this, my beloved brethren. Let every man be quick to hear, slow to speak, slow to anger, 20. for the anger of man does not work the righteousness of God. 21. Therefore put away all filthiness and rank growth of wickedness and receive with meekness the implanted word, which is able to save your souls.*

The R.S.V. treats these three verses as a unit. Others,[2] however, prefer to expound 1: 19-20 as a unit, and verse 21 as introducing the four verses which follow.

The K.J.V., instead of "KNOW THIS" (Greek *iste*) reads "wherefore" (Greek *hōste*). This is due to a variant reading in some late Greek manuscripts, which K.J.V. follows. The more reliable manuscripts, however, read *iste*, from the verb "to know". The form *iste* could be either indicative or imperative. If indicative, it would be translated "you know" (as in R.V.). This makes it a gentle reminder to the readers of their awareness that their Christian faith has made them new

---

[1] Arndt and Gingrich on *ktisma*: In Jas. 1: 18 it "is to be thought of as referring chiefly to men".

[2] e.g. Dibelius, *Der Brief des Jakobus*, p. 106.

creatures in Christ, as the preceding verse declares, and this implies
that conduct appropriate to their high privilege is expected of them.

Most commentators, however, prefer to take the word as an imperative, as R.S.V. does. This makes the reminder of their privilege rather
sharper, as though it were something they were in danger of forgetting.

Moffatt in his translation prints these words merely as a conclusion
to verse 18, and not as an introduction to verse 19, rendering the words:
"Be sure of that, my beloved brothers".

**1: 19** For "BELOVED BROTHERS", see notes at 1: 2 and 1: 16.

The words in verse 19 are explicitly addressed to EVERY MAN, that
is, to each Christian in the group. They are a warning against carelessness in what we say.

Warnings on this subject are very common in Jewish teaching, both
in the Old Testament itself, and in the later Rabbinic instruction. The
Book of Proverbs frequently returns to this theme, for example:

> "He who guards his mouth preserves his life;
> He who opens wide his lips comes to ruin" (Prov. 13: 3).

Similar warnings appear also at Prov. 10: 19; 29: 20, etc. In the
Apocrypha, Ecclesiasticus often repeats such warnings, as

> "Be quick to hear, and deliberate in answering (5: 11)."

Strack-Billerbeck[1] quote many similar sayings from Jewish Rabbis:
"Silence is a fence for Wisdom", "Silence is a hymn of praise to
Thee, O God", "Silence is the spice of Speech".

The recommendation to be QUICK TO HEAR and SLOW TO SPEAK, has
often been taken as addressed to those who speak specifically God's
message, either as preachers or as counsellors. In this case, they are
urged to wait patiently on God, so as to be able to receive from Him
the word they must speak, before presuming to speak in His name. If
this is the meaning, then the further advice that they be SLOW TO
ANGER must mean that when they are confronted with unfair criticism,
stubborn opposition, or sullen unconcern, they must keep their words
free from any note of irritation or denunciation, since such signs of
anger, so far from pre-disposing potential hearers to give heed to their
words, are much more likely to antagonize and estrange. Or it may be
that the warning against anger is there because an irritated and resent-
ful mind is not likely to be able to hear God's voice and submit to His
directions.

The introduction of the word ANGER does, however, raise the question
whether these words are in fact addressed particularly to preachers of
the Word. Probably rather they refer to our ordinary conversation, and

---

[1] *Kommentar zum Neuen Testament aus Talmud und Midrasch*, Vol. III, p. 758.

are a reminder that even our "idle words" (Matt. 12: 36), that is, our casual conversation, should be so watched as to make them pleasing to God and effective in bearing a Christian witness. In this case the words would apply to any situation in which there is discussion, leading to argument and dispute, when angry protests are made, and charges and accusations are bandied about. The Christian man is urged, in such circumstances, to be ready to listen to arguments and explanations put forward by others, and himself to speak only after he has considered all that others wish to say, and then to speak without annoyance or resentment, since a discussion conducted with hot feelings, even if we imagine they are in the service of God, are not likely to discern His will or further His purposes.

James has much to say elsewhere about this subject of unwise conversation and returns to it at 1: 26; 3: 2–5; 3: 6–12; 4: 11. On this matter he is a little more emphatic than other New Testament writers, but others also stress the obligation of guarded speech. Our Lord's words about it are very clear: Matt. 5: 37; 7: 1; 12: 36–7; 15:8, Luke 6: 45, etc, and also Paul's: Col. 3: 17; 4: 6 (cf. also Eph. 4: 29, Titus 2: 8).

ANGER (orgē) is listed as one of the Seven Deadly Sins, but few Christians in fact treat it with this seriousness. The New Testament, however, makes it clear that it is always to be regarded as an ally of Satan, not of God. No doubt there is the possibility of a righteous indignation, whose anger is directed solely against wrongdoing, but our sinful human nature is rarely capable of it. Too easily we represent what in fact springs from wounded self-esteem and thwarted pride as "righteous indignation". In Paul's writings when anger is named, it stands in company with obviously evil qualities, which a Christian must seek to discard (e.g. Col. 3: 8, Eph. 4: 31). It is true that in Eph. 4: 26 there appears to be a kind of permissive acceptance of anger (though a slightly different word, parorgismos, is used): "Be angry but do not sin: do not let the sun go down on your anger". These words, however, should not be understood as an approval of anger, but rather a clear insistence that if anger does occur, it must be clear from all that taint of self which makes almost all anger sin, and moreover, even if it be free from sin, it must not be allowed to continue overnight.

There is another Greek word sometimes translated as anger— thymos—which means a passionate outburst of anger. It is probable therefore that this word for ANGER (orgē) may refer not so much to a passing display of temper, but rather that which expresses persistent dislike of another person and hostility to him. Certainly where the verb from the same root is used in Matt. 5: 22 it is the persistent harbouring of resentment, rather than a quick and passing outburst, which is forbidden.

It is this same word (*orgē*) which is used elsewhere for the Wrath of God, and this clearly does not mean an outburst of temper, but a relentless opposition to evil, which leads to its punishment and ultimately to its destruction. Anything in man worthy to be called "righteous indignation" will share this same quality. But ANGER like vengeance (Rom. 12: 19) is really God's prerogative, and is not to be usurped by sinful man, who is too full of self to be able to exercise it disinterestedly in the service of what is right. Certainly as individuals we are forbidden the use of this weapon, though in representative positions of responsibility a Christian man may have to learn how to become an instrument of God's Wrath (Rom. 13: 4).

**1: 20** This verse is a brief, pointed sentence which exposes vividly the wrongness of human anger. However right it may appear to the angry man, it does not in fact WORK THE RIGHTEOUSNESS OF GOD. Scholars discuss whether in this context WORK means "produce" or "practise", but for all practical purposes the distinction is not important.

If we treat these words as addressed to those who speak publicly for God, they are a reminder that the scolding tone and whip of sarcasm do not produce the good results the Christian preacher hopes for. If, however, the advice applies more to ordinary conversation, then it means that if the Christian speaks words prompted by anger he will not be doing right in God's eyes; he will not be treating his fellows in a fair and right way; and if others are looking to him to gain some impression of the God he claims to worship, then his irritability, evident in his words, will provide something very far from a right picture of the God he serves.

RIGHTEOUSNESS in the Bible is a very big word, which combines in itself meanings which in English are felt to be distinct. In some contexts its main emphasis is on "*being right* with God", but elsewhere it primarily indicates "*doing right*", as God commands the right. In Paul's writings the former meaning tends to predominate, but in Matthew, for instance, it is usually the second (e.g. Matt. 6: 33; 5: 20). Whichever of the two meanings, however, is uppermost, we may be sure the other is not wholly absent, since the Biblical writers could not conceive of a man who was right with God, who did not from that right relationship begin to *do* what was right in relation to God and other people. In James the second meaning of the word is uppermost, as in Matthew, the moral rather than the spiritual emphasis predominating.

The gist of this verse is: What is right in God's eyes, what is fair and just to our fellowmen, is never likely to be achieved by anger. If, therefore, we feel deeply that some wrong ought to be exposed and corrected, the time for speech and action is not when a wave of anger is passing through us, but later when we can think and see clearly, and the thing concerned still stands out as an evil needing to be removed.

**1: 21** Some commentators attach this verse to those which follow, and not to verses 19–20. But R.S.V. and N.E.B. treat it as the conclusion of the verses which precede, and we follow their lead. In this case the evil things which we are bidden to discard must be related to the anger just reproached. The defilement mentioned must be in part at any rate that caused by ill-tempered speech.

The word used here for PUT AWAY may be used for the removal of dirt from the body, but in the N.T. commonly means the laying aside of clothing. Its metaphorical use with regard to evil qualities is a feature of several of the N.T. writers, and is found in Rom. 13: 12, Col. 3: 8, Eph. 4: 25, Heb. 12: 1, 1 Pet. 2: 1 (where it is also linked with "wickedness", as here), and 1 Pet. 3: 21. It expresses what elsewhere might be known as repentance, the turning from evil in order to turn to God.

FILTHINESS is translated by N.E.B. as "all that is sordid". It is the same word as is used in the Greek version of the O.T. for the "filthy rags" of Isa. 64: 6. It can be used to describe any defilement, and so in a moral sense comes to mean what makes a man unclean, and unacceptable to God. In English we may be inclined to restrict its use to sins of a physical nature, drunkenness and vice, but here it must include anger. Anger makes a man dirty and offensive to God, and yet we are inclined to whitewash it as if it were a trivial fault, a mere weakness of temperament. Here it is clearly branded as a serious sin, not inappropriately to be reckoned as one of the Seven Deadly Sins.

What we have to discard is not only all filthiness, but also THE RANK GROWTH OF WICKEDNESS (*perisseian kakias*), which is translated in K.J.V. as "superfluity of naughtiness". "Superfluity" or "excess" cannot, however, represent its real meaning here, since that would seem to imply that wickedness which is not excessive may be tolerated. Calvin suggested as the translation the "immense chaos of wickedness"—that is, *all* evil in the overwhelming abundance with which it confronts us. The N.E.B. represents the same general meaning by "the malice which hurries to excess".

"Abundance" is the normal meaning of *perisseia*, but some commentators argue that in this instance it means "that which survives", or "the remnant". Certainly a cognate Greek word *perisseuma* may bear this meaning, though it is unusual for *perisseia*. This meaning would, however, make good sense in this context, for it is appropriate to exhort Christians who have already discarded some of their former wickedness to discard also the remaining wickedness which still clings to them, like a bad "hang-over" from a pagan past, as one commentator has described it. Calvin, for instance, comments: "This doctrine is very useful, for spiritual generation is not a work of a moment. Still some remnants of the old man ever abide in us. We must necessarily be

through life renewed".[1] James here summons his readers to a decisive
act of discarding as it were the grave-clothes which still cling to the
resurrected Lazarus.

WICKEDNESS is the usual translation of the Greek word *kakia*, but it
may carry the more precise meaning "malice" or "ill-will", and in
this sense is found in close company with such words as anger, spite,
passion, ill-feeling, cursing and angry shouting (see especially Col.
3: 8 and Eph. 4: 31). This meaning clearly suits very well this context
in James, where in the previous verse anger is explicitly condemned for
the evil thing it is. It is, therefore, probably to be preferred.

Sometimes in Paul the exhortation to "put off" evil qualities is
followed by the plea to "put on" (as a new garment) good qualities
(as in Col. 3: 10). James, however, does not continue with this
metaphor of dressing and undressing. He does not wish here so much
to commend the outer virtues which should adorn the Christian, but
rather to plead for an inner change which may lead on to outward
change later. So he alters the metaphor to one suited to the planting
of a seed. He urges: "RECEIVE the implanted word", just as in the
Parable of the Sower (Mark 4: 20) certain soil is described as "*receiving
the word*".

The tense of the Greek imperative here (for both "put away" and
"receive") implies a decisive action. It is not, therefore, favourable
to an exposition which seeks to insist that this exhortation applies to
something which has to be *continually* received.

What we are to receive is THE IMPLANTED WORD. The Greek word
(*emphytos*) translated "implanted" does, in fact, in secular Greek,
usually mean "inborn", and some commentators have retained this
(as in R.V. margin). Hort, for instance, defines the phrase as meaning:
"the original capacity involved in the creation in God's image which
makes it possible for man to apprehend a revelation at all".[2] Some
identify it with the moral sense implanted by God in every man
(Rom. 2: 14-15) or "the true light which enlightens every man" as
he comes into the world (as some translators render John 1: 9, but
R.S.V. and others do not agree with this understanding of the verse).

It would, however, be hardly appropriate to urge people to "receive"
what was already within them as an inborn characteristic. There can
be little doubt therefore that here, as in other Christian writings,
*emphytos* can be used to describe not natural, inborn gifts but later gifts
of grace which are received and allowed to take deep root within our
human nature. In this sense, in Barnabas 9: 9, the "gift of Christ's
teaching" can become "implanted". "IMPLANTED" therefore, or just
"planted", as in N.E.B., makes a good translation. It means taking
the adjective proleptically, as Calvin recommended: "Receive the

---

[1] *Commentary on the Catholic Epistles*, p. 293.    [2] *The Epistle of St. James*, p. 38.

word, so that it may be securely planted", or "deeply rooted", as
Ropes suggests.

It is significant to notice this metaphor of "sowing" this "word"
and then looking for salvation as its fruit, in connection with the same
metaphor which is implicit in Gal. 5: 22, where the Holy Spirit is
thought of as a seed, deeply planted, and bearing rich fruit in Christ-
like qualities.

The WORD is probably to be understood as the same as the "word of
truth" in 1: 18, meaning the "message of the Gospel". In Eph. 1: 13
this "word of truth" is equated with the "gospel of your salvation".
At 1 Pet. 1: 23 are those who have been "born again through the
living word of God", which is "the good news which was preached to
you" (1 Pet. 1: 25). It is interesting to notice that 1 Pet. 1: 23-25 has
further links with Jas. 1: 21 by being associated with "salvation"
and also with "putting off" malice (kakia).

Some have asked whether the "WORD" here may carry some of the
profound meaning that it bears in John 1, but this is probably to read
too much into the term as it is used in James.

This "word of God", the message of the Gospel, is to be received
WITH MEEKNESS (praytēs). "Meekness" is not a satisfactory translation,
but the measure of difficulty in finding a better one is indicated by the
great variety of translations used in modern versions. "Gentleness"
is often preferred, but N.E.B. here has "quietly", Moffatt "modestly",
Phillips "humbly", Weymouth "with a humble spirit", Basic English
"without pride". Meekness in modern English has come to suggest
timidity and colourless neutrality. In the Bible it did not mean this
or we should not read: "The man Moses was very meek" (Num. 12: 3).
If it can be used of Moses it describes a quality to be found in combination with heroic courage and indomitable purpose. In general it may
be said to mean a full consecration to an unselfish purpose to the complete exclusion of self-seeking and self-assertion, and of any spirit of
resentment and retaliation. It is a spirit which enables a man to learn
from others and to accept with glad contentment whatever the pursuit
of God's will brings to him. Here it means primarily a readiness to
learn, to accept correction, to submit one's life uncomplainingly to the
total control of God. It stands in contrast to "anger" and "malice"
both of which come into existence only when the human will is exerted
in defiance of God's.

This word of God, when deeply planted in our lives and allowed
to flourish without hindrance to its growth from self-seeking or illwill,
IS ABLE TO SAVE YOUR SOULS.

It is instructive to collect the affirmations in the N.T. of what God
IS ABLE to do. Outstanding among them are Eph. 3: 20, Heb. 2: 18,
Heb. 7: 25, 2 Tim. 1: 12 and Jude 24. (Others worth referring to are

c

Acts 20: 32, Rom. 4: 21; 11: 23; 14: 4, 2 Cor. 9: 8, Phil. 3: 21, Heb. 5: 7, Heb. 11: 19. Cf. also Mark 9: 23 and 10: 27).

SALVATION is referred to elsewhere in this epistle at 2: 14; 4: 12; 5: 20. Some have argued that here it means "full salvation" in the sense of the final deliverance from all sin into Christian perfection. If so, it is the offer of the means for removing every evil thing, and enabling us to fulfil the command to be perfect (Matt. 5: 48; cf. also 1 Thess. 5: 23, 2 Pet. 3: 14). This would be in line with Heb. 7: 25 and Jude 24, quoted above under *God is able*.

It may be doubted, however, whether this can be taken as the primary significance of "salvation" in James. Certainly the context of the word in 4: 12 and 5: 20 suggests that for James "salvation" was an "eschatological" word, and meant ultimate salvation from the power of death and from the verdict of rejection at the Last Judgement, as also in Rom. 13: 11.

Undoubtedly in the N.T. "salvation" can be spoken of as a privilege already appropriated and made our own (e.g. Eph. 2: 8); it is also a continuing experience of the Christian (1 Cor. 1: 18); but there is a third sense in which its completion lies beyond the sphere of this earthly life (Rom. 13: 11). It is the third sense which is predominant here.

"SOULS" here means the real self, that part of us which may survive the destruction of the flesh in death and be saved into eternal fellowship with God, into the privilege of "being with Christ" (Phil. 1: 23), and "at home with the Lord" (2 Cor. 5: 8). "Soul" has the same meaning in 5: 20 (cf. also 1 Pet. 1: 9).

1: 22–25. *But be doers of the word, and not hearers only, deceiving yourselves. 23. For if anyone is a hearer of the word and not a doer, he is like a man who observes his natural face in a mirror; 24. For he observes himself and goes away and at once forgets what he was like. 25. But he who looks into the perfect law, the law of liberty, and perseveres, being no hearer that forgets but a doer that acts, he shall be blessed in his doing.*

This section is an emphatic warning against sentimental and unpractical religion. There is a kind of religious man who can enjoy listening to a preacher, and being present at a public act of prayer, but fails to translate his faith into effective action in daily life, fails to make obedience to Christ in the common acts of life the essential feature of his religion which it ought to be.

1: 22 The readers are called upon to BE DOERS OF THE WORD AND NOT HEARERS ONLY. The command "be" is perhaps hardly adequate to represent the strength of the Greek word, which literally means "become". Tasker suggests it be translated: "Make sure that you are".

The "WORD" which must be put into practice as well as listened to is the "word" already referred to in 1: 18 and 1: 21, which can make men into "new creatures in Christ", and, by becoming deeply rooted within them, can lead on to salvation. But for this goal to be reached, the "word" must be treated, not just as something we are expected to listen to and approve, but also something we must obey, something we must "do".

"Hearing" is a necessary part of the Christian life. "Faith comes by hearing", says Paul (in Rom. 10: 17, Gal. 3: 2, 5), but "faith" which stays at the stage of hearing, instead of moving forward to the next stage of practical obedience, is a case of "arrested development". It is a childish, immature kind of religion, something less than adult faith. To listen to a sermon on humility or forgiveness may seem a commendable religious act, but the truly religious act really starts when the listener turns what he has heard into deeds, and, in obedience to Christ, acts self-effacingly and forgivingly.

This emphasis in James establishes another close link with the teaching of Jesus. The Sermon on the Mount (Matt. 5–7), which includes some of the most practical of the teaching of Jesus, ends with the parable of the Two Houses, one built on an insecure foundation of sand and doomed to collapse under stress, the other founded on rock and destined to stand firm. The two builders represent types of Christian. The "jerry-builder" is one "who hears the words but does not do them", whose relationship to Christ is devotional and sentimental, but not obedient and practical. The good builder, on the other hand, is one "who hears the words and *does* them" (cf. also Luke 11: 28).

Paul, speaking of his fellow-Jews in Rom. 2: 13, makes a similar point: "It is not the hearers of the law who are righteous before God, but the *doers* of the law will be justified".

Worship, Bible Reading, Sacraments (which represent the "hearing" element in religion) are all important, very important, but important not for themselves but for what they lead to. They are Means of Grace, the channels by which God's Grace normally reaches us. They are not, however, to be valued as if they were ends in themselves. They are not the goal of true religion. If true religion is obedience to God in the common ways of life, they are effective to the extent in which they lead people into such obedience, if they help to create in men a disposition to obey God, and to provide the spiritual power which can make obedience possible. W. Barclay writes: "It is still possible to identify Church attendance and Bible reading with Christianity, and to believe that the man who faithfully attends Church, and who diligently studies his Bible, is a good Christian. Those who act like

that have come less than half the way, because they have failed to
see that the really important thing is to turn that to which they have
listened into actions and deeds".[1]

John Knox in *The Ethics of Jesus in the Teaching of the Church*[2]
speaks of the danger "of supposing that contemplating the good is
the same as being good; that we are less selfish because we admire
unselfishness; that we are less proud because we admire humility. . . .
In the same way one may feel that to confess one is selfish is as good as
being unselfish, and that to admit one is proud or lustful is as good as
being poor in spirit or chaste; that one achieves virtue by paying tribute
and acknowledging one's lack of it". The danger of being content to
"hear" without "doing" is somewhat similar to this.

Those who are disposed to find satisfaction in "hearing", without
moving forward to "doing", are described as "DECEIVING THEMSELVES".
The Greek word used (*paralogizomai*, as also at Col. 2: 4) suggests
behaviour which is inconsistent and irrational. (It is not the same Greek
word as that translated "deceive" in 1: 16.) One is tempted to translate
it by the word so commonly used in popular psychology today—"ration-
alization". This is "a trick the mind has of allowing us to evade the
pain of facing our real motive by supplying a 'reason' for our behaviour
which has all the appearance of being entirely satisfactory".[3] No doubt
the priest and Levite could have provided good reasons why they
should hurry on to their religious duties, and not stay to care for a
man who was lying unconscious at the roadside. So we too find
specious reasons for pious inaction, when practical acts of obedience
would be costly and inconvenient. We may sometimes even deceive
ourselves into thinking they are the real reasons.

**1: 23** One who remains only a hearer, is one in whose heart the
word has been planted (1: 21), but has not gone on to bear the fruit
of obedience.

Such a person is compared to a man who looks at his reflection in a
mirror and does nothing about it. If he noticed anything calling for
action—that he needed a shave, a wash, a hair-cut, or a tidy-up—it is
forgotten at once as other things claim his attention. Perhaps the point
of the simile is no more subtle than this. It likens the man who hears
and forgets to the man who looks and forgets. W. Barclay takes it in
this simple way: "He is like a man who looks in a mirror and who sees
the smuts which disfigure his face, the dishevelment of his hair, and who
goes away and forgets what he looks like, and so omits to do anything
about it".[4] Blackman also pleads for a similar simplicity of interpretation: "The emphasis falls on the forgetfulness"; and of the deeper

---

[1] *The Letter of James*, p. 29.          [2] p. 32.
[3] Leslie D. Weatherhead, *Psychology and Life*, p. 63.
[4] *The Letter of James*, p. 29.

significance that some commentators read into the details he writes: "It is reading too much in". Dibelius too favours this simple approach and complains that those who read profound allegorical meanings into the passage are forcing Western ideas of logical consistency on to what is an oriental use of picture language, in which the details are not to be pressed.[1]

We must, however, note some of the subtleties of meaning which other commentators have felt to be significant.

The English words "HIS NATURAL FACE" translate five Greek words: *to prosōpon tēs geneseōs autou*. They could be translated quite literally as "the face of his birth", i.e. the face he was born with, or "the face of his (present) existence", i.e. his face as it now is. These two possibilities lead to two variant interpretations.

Hort represents the *first* when he insists that the Greek word *geneseōs* must mean "birth", and so his "face", as it is here referred to, means the face he had at birth, before it was spoiled by sin, "the reflection of God's image in humanity" (p. 39). That is, the man sees in the mirror what God meant him to be, something which should rebuke him and summon him to penitence, but he is quickly able to forget it as other interests claim his attention; and so he carries on as though nothing disturbing had taken place. So is the man who hears the Word of God: he may be at first disconcerted by it, as it recalls to him the innocence of his former life, now lost, but he quickly forgets the impression it made.

The difficulty of this interpretation is that it relies on the doubtful claim that the Greek word *geneseōs* must mean "birth" and not "existence". A greater difficulty, however, is that if a man looks in a mirror, he does in fact see the man he now is, not the earlier innocence, which was once there, but which has now been lost.

The *second* interpretation is, therefore, the more probable of the two, and is nearer to the simple exposition with which we started this section, and which we believe is the best way of understanding this passage. Mayor may be taken as representative of this approach. He sees here a sharp contrast between the reflection of himself which a man sees in a mirror, a reflection of himself as he now is, and the image of what he was meant to be, as it stands revealed in the "perfect law of liberty". In the mirror a man sees just what he is, not some reminder of what he might have been by which to compare what he is. Moreover he is so familiar with the face he sees that he does not notice the marks in it that denote moral deterioration. The "perfect law", however, can provide that startling contrast which is able to penetrate the protective cover of familiarity.

This interpretation depends on the validity of translating the Greek

[1] *Der Brief des Jakobus*, p. 110.

word "geneseōs" as "existence" rather than "birth", so that the phrase means "the man's face as it now is", and not "the innocent face of the new-born baby". Dibelius insists that this is a perfectly possible meaning, and provides evidence in other Greek writers for his claim.[1] Certainly this is what one does in fact see in a mirror.

The word "glass" is used for "mirror" in K.J.V., but in ancient times a mirror was made of polished metal rather than glass

**1: 24** Some commentators have tried to make the Greek word for "observes" mean just a quick, unheeding glance. The word itself does not, however, carry this precise significance, nor does the tense of the Greek verb, as it is used in verse 23 (where it is a present tense). In verse 24, however, though it is the same word which is used again, the tense of the verb is different (aorist), and this change of tense does lend support to Mayor's suggested translation of the opening words of verse 24: "Just a glance and he is off", rather than to R.S.V.'s: "HE OBSERVES HIMSELF AND GOES AWAY". "Off he goes" would well represent the feeling of the Greek, as though the mirror and what he has seen in it have been dismissed from his mind, as soon as he turns from it. The Greek tense also behind the words "AND AT ONCE FORGETS" is an aorist and could be represented by: "Immediately he has forgotten all about it".

WHAT HE WAS LIKE: Hort refers this phrase to the image of God in man, before it becomes unrecognizable through disobedience to God. It can, however, mean simply: "What he looked liked" (at the time of looking in the mirror).

**1: 25** This man, quick to forget what he has seen, is contrasted with the man WHO LOOKS INTO THE PERFECT LAW. The word for "look into" literally means "to stoop down" in order to have a close look. It is used in John 20: 5 and 11 of the disciples who looked into the open tomb on Easter Day, to ascertain that it was in fact empty. It is used also in 1 Pet. 1: 12 to describe angels who long to be able to penetrate more deeply into the wonder of what Christ did for men on Calvary. It is a word which suggests that very close attention is being given to what is being examined. It is what he sees in the "the perfect law", as the result of this close scrutiny, which stabs his spirit wide awake, and leaves him deeply dissatisfied with what he now is. This law proves a tutor to bring him to Christ (see Gal. 3: 24).

He not only examines this law with great care, but also "PERSEVERES". This probably means that he perseveres in the study of it, "lives in its

---

[1] For instance, he quotes Homer's *Odyssey* 19: 178 where this same phrase is used to indicate the ordinary face of a person, in contrast to the face when it is "loaded with cosmetics". Also in Wisdom 7: 5, after describing the humility of human birth, the writer comments: "No king has had a different beginning of existence" (*archēn geneseōs*), where "*archēn*" refers to birth, and "*geneseōs*" must carry the more general meaning of "existence".

company", as N.E.B. translates. Some, however, think it means that he does not forget the truth of what he has seen, but rather lets it continue to rule his life, as he puts into practice what he has learned in theory. At any rate, he is no longer a HEARER THAT FORGETS BUT A DOER THAT ACTS.

The two striking phrases: "THE PERFECT LAW" and "THE LAW OF LIBERTY" deserve careful consideration.

THE PERFECT LAW: James no doubt inherited from his Jewish past a deep regard for the Law of the Jewish people. He would have repeated frequently, "The Law of the Lord is perfect" (Ps. 19: 7), and many similar words which express the deep veneration of the Jews for their sacred Law. But no Christian would be able to refer to the Law of the Old Testament as the perfect law, even if he did retain some deep respect for it. For the Christian the perfect law could refer only to the understanding of the will of God for man, as it had been brought to its highest point in the life and teaching of Jesus. It might well include such collections of the teaching of Jesus as we find in the Sermon on the Mount (Matt. 5 to 7), where the words: "You must be *perfect*" (Matt. 5: 48) occur. It was also in that context that Jesus spoke when He said that He had come to "fulfil the Law" (Matt. 5:17), that is to make it "perfect". All the teaching of Jesus about the conduct which God approves would be part of this "perfect law", and certainly his summary of the Law and the Prophets in the two great commands to "love God" and to "love one's neighbour" (Matt. 22: 34–40). It is the second of these which James later refers to as the "royal law" (Jas. 2: 8), and Paul acclaims as "the fulfilling of the Law" (Rom. 13: 10). Parry writes: "The perfect law here referred to is, then, the law of conduct laid down by the Lord Jesus, complete in contrast with that law in which scribes and Pharisees saw their embodiment of righteousness, but, still more, complete as exhibiting to human eyes the perfection of God the Father Himself. . . . The character and action of God is the standard embodied in this law".[1]

Any reference, however, to a "perfect law" must take account of the memorable words of Jeremiah in 31: 31–34. In this passage the prophet deplores the inadequacy of God's law, however good, if it is imposed on a man only from outside and remains external to his own nature. In that case the Law merely represents a stern duty, which a sincere man feels he must obey from a strong sense of obligation, but does so with a heavy heart, against his own inclination, and with a sense of being made to carry an unbearable load. In this case it is more than human nature can endure, and is doomed to failure. If the law of God, he declared, is really to rule men's life, it must be inwardly accepted by them, it must be "written on their hearts". This was the

[1] *St. James*, p. 27.

penetrating insight of Jeremiah. He saw man's need of it, and heard God's promise that in time this "new covenant" would indeed be ratified and inaugurated. But for him it remained an unfulfilled dream about the future. It was Jesus who at last made it a reality.

What it means for the "law to be written on the heart" becomes clear from Ps. 40: 8, where, by the parallelism of Jewish poetry, it stands as an equivalent to finding "delight in doing God's law". God's law is perfect only when the human heart has been so changed (this is the New Covenant) that a man not only knows what he ought to do, but *wants* to do it. By conversion he has been enabled to "love what God commands". The achievement of this change in human life, this *New* Covenant, Jesus associated with His death on the Cross. It was to inaugurate it that He shed His blood, the blood which was to be the blood of the New Covenant (1 Cor. 11: 25). One purpose of His death is to make us hate the sin that crucifies the Son of God afresh, and come to live not for selfish ends but for Him, "who for our sake died and rose again" (2 Cor. 5: 15) and "make it our aim to please Him" (2 Cor. 5: 9). This is to be a "new creation in Christ" (2 Cor. 5: 17).

There is clearly a close link between this thought of God's perfect law "written in our hearts" and James's thought of God's word "implanted" in our hearts (Jas. 1: 21), deeply rooted and effective there, since it controls the springs of human action and energy.

This link with Jer. 31: 31-4 also enables us to understand what at first may seem the paradoxical description of the perfect law as "THE LAW OF LIBERTY" (a phrase which recurs at Jas. 2: 12). Law often appears to be something that curbs freedom. But this is only when the Law represents a requirement which we do not want to fulfil. If the Law prescribed exactly what we *wanted* to do and forbade what we did not want to do, then freedom to do what we liked, and obedience to the Law, would become identical. This is what has happened to the real Christian. He has been enabled to "delight in the will of God", to enjoy doing what God asks him to do. This obedience to God is a wonderful freedom ("His service is perfect freedom"), and this freedom of the child of God is freedom to do what most we love doing—pleasing God.

Before this can happen there is needed a wonderful work of God's grace in the human heart. And if it is to continue, that work of grace must be daily renewed.

Freedom, or liberty, is one of the great privileges of the Christian life. It is offered in the preached words of Jesus (Luke 4: 18, and also John 8: 32 and 36). It is a recurring theme of the Apostle Paul, who writes of "the glorious liberty of the children of God" (Rom. 8: 21). He also declares that "For freedom Christ has set us free" (Gal. 5: 1) and "where the Spirit of the Lord is, there is freedom" (2 Cor. 3:17). It means freedom from the dominating power of evil in our lives, freedom from religion viewed as a burdensome duty (i.e. the Law), and freedom from the sickening dread of death and the fear that life itself is empty meaninglessness, and, above all, in this context, freedom from the attitude which regards moral goodness as an external set of rules we feel we have to obey, but do so with reluctance and resentment.

James, however, does not merely speak of liberty, but also of "THE LAW OF LIBERTY". Along with this new freedom, there is also a continuing law. This is implied in the saying of Jesus where the promise of release is accompanied by the offer of a yoke. The will of God continues to be the rule by which the Christian must order his life. Even Paul clearly recognized this. He could speak most vehemently against the Law, when it was regarded as a moral code or a scheme of religious observances, by obedience to which a man thought he could establish himself before God, so that in God's presence he could feel himself proud and self-sufficient because of his achievements. The Law, viewed as a means of salvation, was to Paul anathema, a delusion, a device of Satan, leading men away from God, instead of to Him, and building them up in a wholly false delusion of self-achieved safety. But he was well aware that for the redeemed man there was still the obligation to please God, not as a device for extracting from God salvation as a reward for human merit, but for the sheer delight of pleasing God, to whom we owe all that we are, and who has done for us more than we can ever begin to estimate. To guide such a man in his longing to please God there is still a law, which serves in his life as a useful signpost when he is uncertain what is pleasing to God and what is not. This continuing law in the life of the Christian is what is here described as "the perfect law", and "the law of liberty".

James, of course, is not the only New Testament writer to make this paradoxical association of law and freedom. Paul in Gal. 5:13 writes: "You were called to *freedom*", but "through love be servants of one another. For the whole *law* is fulfilled in one word, 'You shall love your neighbour as yourself'". This law of love is both a fulfilment of the law and an expression of Christian freedom. Further, in Rom. 8:2 Paul writes: "The *law* of the Spirit of life in Christ Jesus has set me *free* from the law of sin and death". This freedom, however, made possible for man by the abundant grace of God in Christ, has been bestowed, not to enable man to be careless and casual about moral conduct, but "in order that the just requirement of the law might be fulfilled in us, who walk not according to the flesh but according to the Spirit" (Rom. 8:4).

This continuing law in the life of the Christian may sometimes be called "the law of Christ" (Gal. 6:2, 1 Cor. 9:21), or else the "law of faith" (Rom. 3: 27). These are Paul's equivalents for what James calls "the perfect law" or "the law of liberty".

The Christian man who has been redeemed and regenerated (Jas. 1: 18), who has received into his life that power from God which can save his soul (1: 21), who now sets himself, in his new-found freedom from the power of evil, to please God by fulfilling the perfect law of God made known through Christ, is now pronounced "blessed": HE SHALL BE BLESSED IN HIS DOING.

This is the second "beatitude" in James, the earlier one occurring at 1: 12. The word "blessed" is the same Greek word as the one used in the Beatitudes of Jesus (Matt. 5: 3-10).

We note the concluding emphasis "IN HIS DOING", so characteristic of James, and especially of this paragraph. But in this also he faithfully reflects the emphasis of his Master, who said: "Blessed are those who hear the word of God and *keep* it!" (Luke 11: 28) and "Not everyone who says to me, 'Lord, Lord', shall enter the kingdom of heaven, but he *who does the will* of my Father" (Matt 7: 21, 24-27), and also: "If you know these things, blessed are you *if you do them*" (John 13: 17).

1: 26-27. *If any one thinks he is religious, and does not bridle his tongue but deceives his heart, this man's religion is vain. 27. Religion that is pure and undefiled before God and the Father is this: to visit orphans and widows in their affliction, and to keep oneself unstained from the world.*

Scrupulous observance of religious practices cannot be regarded as a substitute for personal purity of life or for an attitude of personal goodwill towards all, especially those in need. This practical goodwill is shown, negatively, by the avoidance of any words which may bring hurt to another (verse 26), and, positively, by offering personal help to people who are in need (verse 27).

The link with the preceding verse, if one need be sought, can be found in the similarity of emphasis. In verses 23-25 "hearing" is rebuked if it does not lead on to "doing". So here all outward forms of religion are rebuked, if they do not lead on to the practice of that personal purity of life and charitableness of conduct which, in a healthy Christian life, inevitably spring from it.

1: 26 IF ANY ONE THINKS he is religious: Most modern commentators (in company with R.V., R.S.V. and N.E.B.) prefer this translation, but that of K.J.V. "If any man *seem* to be religious . . ." is a possible rendering of the Greek. If K.J.V. is accepted, the warning in the words is addressed to those who see this "religious" man's life and, in spite of its obvious failings, are inclined to be so impressed by it, as to make it the model of their own life. The other translation (as in R.S.V.) is preferable, because it makes better sense for the warning to be addressed to the man himself, who fondly imagines that his regularity at worship and sacraments, his observance of saints' days and holy days is of the very essence of religion, and is, therefore, careless of other elements of true religion, which in fact are even more important.

The words "religious" and "religion" translate the Greek words *thrēskos* and *thrēskeia*. They are not very accurate translations but it is difficult to find a better. The Greek words refer primarily to the outward aspects of religion—public acts of worship, sacraments, religious disciplines such as fasting, systematic praying, and almsgiving (as commented on by Jesus in Matt. 6: 1–18). We do not seem to possess in English a word which describes only these outward acts of religion, as distinguished from inward religion, which consists of true faith in God, a sincere obedience to God's will in our daily lives, and true charity towards others, as part of our obedience to the known will of God. So most modern translators have to be content with the word "religion", though in English the word normally includes inward as well as outward religion. Phillips tries to indicate the difficulty by putting the word "religious" in inverted commas, to suggest that its usage here is rather different from the normal one.

This protest of James against the ritual element in religion when valued and stressed apart from the moral element is fully in line with the message of the great prophets of Israel. They denounced "sacrifice" (representing the outward form of religion) if it was practised apart from justice and mercy. They insisted that what God required of His people was not elaborate sacrifices, but "to do justly, to love mercy and to walk humbly with thy God" (Mic. 6: 6–8; see also Isa. 1: 10–17; 58: 6; Zech. 7: 4–10). The word of God in Hos. 6: 6, "I desire mercy and not sacrifice", was one of these prophetic words which our Lord Himself referred to more than once (Matt. 9: 13; 12: 7). He Himself took up this emphasis into His own teaching, and James is faithfully reflecting it (cf. Mark 12: 33).

In this passage, therefore, "religion" means the outward forms of religion. If they are used as God meant them to be used, as means of grace to enable us to submit our lives in obedience to the whole will of God, they are a valuable, even necessary part of the religious life. One of the commonest faults, however, into which religious people are prone to fall, is to come to regard these outward forms as of value in themselves. Observance of them is felt to be of the very essence of religion, in comparison with which purity of life and compassion for the distresses of others are of smaller importance. It is this attitude which earns for religious people the reputation of hypocrisy. It was this that Jesus deplored so deeply in the Pharisees, and led Him to rebuke them as "hypocrites". The real outward marks of a religious man are honesty and personal integrity in all his dealings, and fairness and kindliness in all his treatment of others, and it is very sad when religious people themselves forget it.

James isolates, for special rebuke, a sin which even very religious people are apt to make light of, perhaps even sometimes to be rather proud of. It is the sin of an "unbridled tongue". He DOES NOT BRIDLE HIS TONGUE (N.E.B. "has no control over his tongue"). James has already made one reference to this danger (in 1: 19) and will return to it again at greater length (3: 1–12). The kind of restraint he here asks for in the Christian is perhaps the twofold restraint of truth and love, which Paul also requires (Eph. 4: 15). Anything we say, whether *to* another or *about* him, should be able to pass the two tests: Is it true? Is it kind? A third test, which springs from concern for the good of the community, is: Am I doing any good by repeating it? The bridle, which James recommends, would hold the tongue back from speaking words that fall below this threefold standard. Sharp, hurtful words, sarcastic and sneering, are ruled out, and also words, however gently spoken, which hint at evil or bad motives in another.

Very often the habit of criticizing others springs from a root of bitterness and jealousy within ourselves, which we have not allowed Christ to remove. Or it may come from unacknowledged pride, since criticism of another is thought to reflect credit on ourselves, either for our cleverness in making the criticism or for our supposed freedom from the fault we impute to others. Calvin speaks frankly of this unpleasant fault. He calls it "a vice under which hypocrites commonly labour, that is the wantonness of the tongue in detraction. . . . They who have put off the grosser vices are specially subject to this disease. He who is neither an adulterer nor a thief nor a drunkard, but, on the contrary, seems brilliant in some outward show of sanctity, will set himself off by defaming others, and this under a pretence of zeal, but really through the lust of slandering. . . . They seek praise from the defects of others".[1] Concern for truth and moral standards can too easily be accepted as an excuse for unbridled words. But to make such excuses is for a man to DECEIVE HIS HEART.

James has already referred to the subtle power of human minds to deceive themselves (1: 16, 22; cf. also Gal. 6: 7) into thinking an evil thing is for them permissible. He knows, as Jeremiah did, that "the heart is deceitful above all things" (Jer. 17: 9). The Devil can avail himself of this deceitfulness, by persuading us that harsh and bitter words are justified by the high purpose with which they are spoken—to expose evil, to warn others, to protect public morality. But the Devil is adept at inducing us to do evil by representing it to us

[1] *Commentary*, pp. 298–299.

as good. He disguises himself as an angel of light (2 Cor. 11: 14), and seeks to persuade us that un-Christian methods are justified if the ends we seek are Christian.

In English the word "heart" is often used to describe the emotional or even sentimental part of us. In the Bible, however, it is used more widely to include reason and will, as well as feeling. Here it is little more than a variant for "himself". Indeed N.E.B. renders: "He is deceiving himself".

Such RELIGION IS VAIN: No amount of outward piety can compensate for a biting, sarcastic, fault-finding tongue. It is VAIN in the sense that it utterly fails to fulfil the purpose of true religion, which is to do honour to God and to offer Him the obedience He longs to receive.

**1: 27** Having rebuked one grave fault which sometimes disfigures the conduct of Christian men, often without their realizing it, James proceeds to underline two positive qualities which should mark the life of a truly religious man.

True religion is here called RELIGION WHICH IS PURE AND UNDEFILED BEFORE GOD. The Pharisees insisted on purity of religion, but theirs was an external purity—freedom from physical contact with the heathen Gentile or prohibited types of food, neither of which was regarded as impure by our Lord (Mark 7: 15ff.). Here pure and undefiled does not mean "pure" as the Mosaic Law prescribed it, but rather as God had made it known in Christ. It means a perfect love for God, and a perfect love for one's neighbour.

The purity required is not according to some human rules, or man-made traditions (Mark 7: 3, 5, 9) but BEFORE GOD, that is, in God's sight.

GOD AND THE FATHER: This is not a very happy translation of the Greek. It sounds almost as though "the Father" is someone different from "God", which, of course, is not the case. The words mean: "God, who is the One we know as Father". "Father" became the characteristically Christian word for "God". Others had used this word about God, but the Christians appropriated it as specially their own. In this they followed the usage of their Lord, who always spoke of God in this way, and taught His disciples to do the same. He is even recorded as using (in the Aramaic) an intimate and affectionate form of the word, "Abba" (e.g. in Gethsemane, Mark 14: 36). This word left so deep an impression on His disciples that soon Gentile Christians were using it as well, even though they had no knowledge of the Aramaic language (e.g. in Gal. 4: 6, Rom. 8: 15). The Christians dared to think of the transcendent Creator of All Things as "Father", a word which carried authority, but also expressed trust and affection. Because of this, they found it easy to think of fellow-Christians as "brothers" (1: 2, 16, 19, etc.).

It may be that James introduces the word "Father" here because he is going on to insist on the family loyalty that should characterize all Christians, making them specially concerned for the less fortunate members of the Christian family. These less fortunate ones are here described as "ORPHANS AND WIDOWS". It is not, of course, that loving care is to be limited to them. Rather they are named to represent all those who suffer distress. In ancient times they more than others were liable to the miseries of want and insecurity—children too young to fend for themselves and left fatherless, and women, perhaps with the responsibility of a young family, left alone without the breadwinner of the family, the one to whom they looked for provision and protection. They often faced want, and they were always in danger of exploitation and ill-treatment. In the Bible their pitiable plight is often referred to. The man who tries to defraud them is pronounced "cursed" (Deut. 27: 19). The good man is urged to act as father to the fatherless and husband to the widow (Ecclus. 4: 10). God Himself is described as "Father of the fatherless and protector of widows" (Ps. 68: 5). In the early church widows were the special object of compassionate care (Acts 6: 1). One of the callous acts with which our Lord charges the very religious Pharisees is that, in spite of their pretensions to piety, they take advantage of the helplessness of widows (Mark 12: 40). In contrast our Lord Himself is shown to have a special concern for widows. He is aware that the dead boy at Nain is the only son of his mother, and she is a widow (Luke 7: 12). He points out the sacrificial giving of one widow who is desperately poor (Mark 12: 42).

"IN THEIR AFFLICTION" probably refers to their continuing unhappy plight as orphans and widows, though it may mean "in any particular distress that overtakes them", in which they would feel especially the lack of the man of the house. Unless the husband had been a very rich man, his dependants would be in real need, since in those days there would be no relief from public funds, and for ordinary people at any rate no possibility of personal insurance.

The Christian is urged to "VISIT" such people in their trouble. This implies not only bringing to them means to relieve their need, so far as that is within our power, but it also indicates that the personal care is also there. It is not sufficient to make some off-hand allocation of available funds, and then feel that our responsibility is done. The offer of loving interest and personal concern is needed as well as financial help, sometimes needed even more.

This emphasis on practical, loving care for needy people recalls to us our Lord's parable of the Sheep and the Goats, where the test which the Judge applies to determine true religion is whether human need, in whatever form it confronts us, has awakened our practical sympathy and help, since, if only we realised it, it is Christ Himself who comes to us, *"incognito"*, in the sufferings of any human being. It is interesting, therefore, to notice that this very word "VISIT" (*episkeptomai*) is used twice in that parable (Matt. 25: 36, 43).

Rev. Dr. W. E. Sangster, for sixteen years minister at Westminster Central Hall, London, was supreme as an evangelical preacher. When, however, the bombing made normal life in London impossible from 1940–45 he made the deep cellars of the Hall into shelters for frightened and homeless people, and himself slept in them for five years, supervising the welfare of thousands and bringing them love and cheer. His son in the biography of his father writes: " 'Service before services' was his motto".[1]

The Apostle Paul does not fall behind even in this emphasis. He writes: "Neither circumcision nor uncircumcision is of any avail" (i.e. outward forms of religion are vain) "but faith working through *love*" (Gal. 5: 6).

The second positive characteristic of true religion is TO KEEP ONESELF UNSTAINED FROM THE WORLD, i.e. personal integrity, shown in complete honesty, moral purity, and absence of self-seeking.

"THE WORLD" is here used as John uses it. In his writings it means the world of men as it is in its alienation from God and rebellion against Him. It is almost synonymous with "evil", because the "world" is now in the power of evil. This "world" is also the environment in which the Christian must live. Its customs and habits are tainted with evil. Therefore the pressures which come to the Christian from the social life about him are in the direction of evil. He has constantly to be on the alert against this pressure, sometimes direct and threatening, more often insidious and unnoticed. That is why Paul pleads: "Do not be conformed to this world, but be transformed by the renewing of your mind" (Rom. 12: 2). The stain of the world is evident in us when we allow its pressures to lead us into dishonesty, untruthfulness, impurity, and indifference to human need. This makes us unclean in the sight of God.

[1] *Dr. Sangster* by Paul Sangster, p. 192.

# CHAPTER TWO

2: 1–7. *My brethren, show no partiality as you hold the faith of our Lord Jesus Christ, the Lord of glory. 2. For if a man with gold rings and in fine clothing comes into your assembly, and a poor man in shabby clothing also comes in, 3. and you pay attention to the one who wears the fine clothing and say, "Have a seat here, please", while you say to the poor man, "Stand there", or, "Sit at my feet", 4. have you not made distinctions among yourselves, and become judges with evil thoughts? 5. Listen, my beloved brethren. Has not God chosen those who are poor in the world to be rich in faith and heirs of the kingdom which he has promised to those who love him? 6. But you have dishonoured the poor man. Is it not the rich who oppress you, is it not they who drag you into court? 7. Is it not they who blaspheme that honourable name by which you are called?*

**2: 1** On the opening words of address, MY BRETHREN, see the note at 1: 2.

Christian people are instructed to SHOW NO PARTIALITY. The word here translated partiality (*prosōpolēmpsia*) was usually rendered in the older versions, "respect for persons", and appears in some modern translations as "favouritism". It means showing a greater degree of consideration for one who stands high in the social scale than for one who socially is unimportant. It is a fault specially to be deplored in a judge, who is expected to be scrupulously fair in his judgements, and to be unaffected by any private sympathies he may feel for some litigants, whether on account of their social class, political allegiance, national loyalty, or his own personal acquaintance with them.

Condemnation of this fault is found often in the Old Testament. Moses instructs those whom he appoints to help in the administration of justice: "You shall not be *partial* in judgement; you shall hear the small and the great alike; you shall not be afraid of the face of man, for the judgement is God's" (Deut. 1: 17). And not only judges, but all the people, are commanded by God, through him: "You shall do no injustice in judgement; you shall not be *partial* to the poor or defer to the rich" (Lev. 19: 15).

The importance of this impartiality is emphasized also in the New Testament. Here it is primarily proclaimed as an essential quality in God's nature. This is found not in just one or two writers, but in many.

Clearly it came to be regarded among all Christians as a truth about God which was of supreme importance for them. In Acts 10: 34 Peter declares: "I perceive that God shows no partiality". This means that people of all races are equally precious to Him. Gentiles no less than Jews are seen to be the object of His loving care. Paul writes: "God shows no partiality" (Rom. 2: 11). The same truth appears in 1 Pet. 1: 17 where God is described as One who "judges each one impartially according to his deeds". Similar affirmations are found in Col. 3: 25 and Eph. 6: 9 (cf. also 1 Clem. 1: 3, and Barn 4: 12).

It is characteristic of the faith of the New Testament writers that the truths they believed about God they found exemplified in the life of Jesus. In the gospels we read that observers noticed in Him this quality of transparent integrity. Even His enemies are reported as saying: "Teacher, we know that you are true and care for no man; for you do not regard the position (*prosōpon*) of men" (Mark 12: 14; cf. Matt. 22: 16; Luke 20: 21).

It is left to James, however, to use this particular word to insist precisely that this quality of the character of God and of Jesus Himself should find its place also in the Christian believer. He emphasizes it here in 2: 1 and also in 2: 9. There can be little doubt, however, that the kind of conduct here required by James was a standard which came to be commonly accepted among the early Christians. Indeed the acceptance of it was one of the driving forces in the Gentile Mission of the Church. Christians rejoiced to believe in God as One who loved Gentiles equally with Jews, and felt that a similar impartiality of concern for people of all races could rightly be expected of them. This idea is present even when this particular word is not used, e.g. in Gal. 3: 28: "There is neither Jew nor Greek, there is neither slave nor free, there is neither male nor female: for you are all one in Christ Jesus", and in the reports in Acts of Peter's visit to the house of Cornelius.

It was one of the great truths about God, which Jesus brought into the world, that God loved equally people of all races. He had no favourites. This applies also to a man's status in society, which counts for nothing with God. Slaves and the very poor are at no disadvantage with Him. It is this aspect of the word which is uppermost in the mind of James in this passage, and which leads to the N.E.B.'s translation: "Never show snobbery". What we believe about God affects profoundly our own way of life, since what may be called the moral qualities of God are qualities a Christian must seek to reproduce in his own life, as he aims to be an "imitator of God" (Eph. 5: 1, cf. Matt. 5: 45).

Then as now in the secular world a rich and prosperous man could count on receiving much greater consideration than a poor and unsuccessful man; a man from the dominant race counted for more than one from a subject people. This, however, is not as God meant it to be. It is rather a mark of the sinfulness of the world. The Christian in his attitude towards his fellowmen is called on to reflect the nature of God, by showing no partiality, and not to conform to the sinful world, in which such partiality is a normal characteristic.

Behind the fighting lines in the first world war a Christian group of men opened rest houses for Christian fellowship, in which all soldiers, irrespective of rank, were welcome. It came to be known as Toc H. Over the entrance was printed a parody of a famous quotation: "Abandon all rank, ye who enter here". Whatever differences of rank had to be observed in the military world outside, within the Christian fellowship all were equal. So it should be within the Church.

Partiality in our treatment of others is, James declares, quite inconsistent with our profession, if we HOLD THE FAITH OF OUR LORD JESUS CHRIST. In this matter, as in many others, a Christian should not be "conformed to this world", but "transformed by the renewal of our mind to prove what is the will of God" (Rom. 12: 2).

FAITH is a most important word for the Christian. It has already been commented on at 1: 3, and will need further treatment at 2: 14ff. Here it means much more than just an intellectual assent to the statement that Jesus is Lord and Christ. It implies an attitude to Him which allows Him to rule our lives. It means total commitment of our lives to Him in obedience. Partiality in our treatment of others is clearly wrong because it is sharply at variance with all Christ stands for.

The R.S.V. translates the Greek words quite literally as "the faith of our Lord Jesus Christ". In modern idiom the meaning is better represented by the phrase "faith *in* our Lord Jesus Christ".

For a note on LORD JESUS CHRIST see 1: 1.

The words "THE LORD OF GLORY" are also ascribed to Christ by Paul in 1 Cor. 2: 8. They may mean either that Christ now reigns "in glory" (cf. Luke 24: 26), or that we think of Him as our "glorious Lord". It is a common Hebrew idiom to use the genitive of a noun for what in English we should express by an adjective, and Biblical Greek sometimes followed this Hebrew idiom. In Rom. 8: 21, for instance, a literal translation of the Greek words, as reproduced in the R.V., is: "the liberty of the glory of the children of God". Modern versions, however, revert to the rendering of the K.J.V. and translate them as "the glorious liberty". So here they may be rendered as "glorious Lord".

These Greek words, however, do lend themselves to an entirely different translation, which is attractive, if not wholly convincing. The words could, in fact, be translated: "Our Lord Jesus Christ, who is the Glory". "Glory" in the New Testament can be used of the splendour of God's presence as men are sometimes permitted to glimpse it. Certainly it is true that this splendour of God has been shown to us in Jesus Christ, and elsewhere the New Testament writers proclaim this truth with confidence. "He is the *glory* of my people Israel" (Luke 2: 32); "He reflects the *glory* of God" (Heb. 1: 3); "We have beheld his *glory, glory* as of the only Son of the Father" (John 1: 14). If James did mean this here, he would be in line with other writers of the New Testament; but probably the other meaning is the one James intended.

**2: 2–3** Since God, as we have come to know Him through Christ, "shows no partiality", His people should do the same. Unhappily, writes James, this does not always happen. Rich visitors to Christian services are given attentive, even obsequious, consideration, whereas poor people coming in receive the most casual, even contemptuous treatment. This is wholly inappropriate in those who profess faith in Christ and claim to live in obedience to His will.

The GOLD RINGS and FINE CLOTHING are the outward signs of a man who is rich.

The word used here for "ASSEMBLY" is the Greek word *synagōgē*, which could be translated "synagogue" and mean a place for Jewish worship. But some of the early Christians called their own meeting places by this name, and there is no doubt that a Christian assembly is here meant.

In contrast to the well-dressed rich man, one who attends in SHABBY CLOTHING can be recognized at once as a POOR MAN. The casual treatment he receives is very different from the flattering courtesies offered to the rich man. They PAY ATTENTION (see the same word in Luke 1: 48 and 9: 38) TO THE ONE WHO WEARS THE FINE CLOTHING, secure a comfortable seat for him, and courteously invite him: "HAVE A SEAT HERE, PLEASE". Apparently there was a shortage of seats, and some of the congregation had to stand or sit on the floor, so that to have a seat at all was a privilege.

The word translated "PLEASE" (*kalōs*) may carry a rather different meaning. It literally means "well" or "pleasantly", and some modern translators agree with the K.J.V. in making this refer to the comfort of the chair. K.J.V. has: "Sit thou here in a good place", and Phillips has "Please sit here—it's an excellent seat". It may, therefore, be a specially comfortable seat which is offered to the rich man. N.E.B., however, agrees with R.S.V. in translating *kalōs* simply as "please", which is an idiomatic meaning which the word came to bear.

In contrast, the poor man receives very off-hand treatment. It seems that anything will do for him, because he is poor. He is told he can stand, if he likes, or, if he must sit, he must make do on the floor. The very sad thing about this is that the Christian steward says:

"Sit at *my* feet". This is a good translation of what the K.J.V. translated literally as "Sit here under my footstool". The unhappy implication of the word *"my"* is that not only is the poor man treated worse than the rich man, but worse even than the Christian who receives him. This Christian official has a seat, but does not offer it to the poor newcomer, who is not important enough for that. If the church member had given up his own seat to the rich man, and himself been content to sit on the floor with the poor man, the situation would not have been so deplorable as it is; but he too has a seat as well as the rich man.

This word of rebuke to a first century church still comes as a rebuke to some modern churches. In some areas it has been customary for rich people to pay "pew-rents" and therefore to expect to occupy their pews on all occasions. It would have been felt by them as an intrusion if a rich man had taken their seat. It would have been intolerable if the intruder had been a poor man. The words of James here are, unhappily, not wholly out of date.

**2: 4** HAVE YOU NOT MADE DISTINCTIONS AMONG YOURSELVES? The word here translated as "made distinctions" (*diakrithēte*) has two possible meanings:

(a) It may mean to "judge between" two people, and it is this meaning which R.S.V. represents. Similarly Phillips: "You make class distinctions in your mind". Such distinctions are wrong among Christians, since for those "in Christ" there is "neither slave nor freeman", which in modern terminology means: "neither poor nor rich, neither lower class nor upper class".

(b) The Greek word may, however, indicate "wavering", or "inconsistency", as it does in 1: 6, where R.S.V. translates as "he who doubts", and where it is equated with the "double-minded man, unstable in all his ways". This alternative rendering is preferred by N.E.B.: "Do you not see that you are inconsistent?" They are confessing a complete obedience to Jesus Christ, and yet in their conduct are defying and affronting Him.

Since the Greek word carried both meanings, it is not impossible that James had both in mind when he used it here.

By acting as though the poor man is not entitled to the same courtesies as the rich man, they have BECOME JUDGES. There is a play on words here in the Greek. We noted one meaning of *diakrithēte* is to *"judge* between", so now they can be rebuked for acting as *"judges"*. Passing critical judgements on others was clearly forbidden by Jesus: "Judge not, that you be not judged" (Matt. 7: 1), and it is doubly wrong if the judgement is based on merely outward factors. God reads the heart (1 Sam. 16: 7), and Christians, if they are to judge, should assess a man on his character, not on his appearance.

The use of the word "judge" also reminds us that "partiality" was a particularly abhorrent offence in one who was trusted to act as judge (see note on verse 2). If we assume the responsibility of a judge, we ought to be bound by his standards of conduct. We should not be JUDGES WITH EVIL THOUGHTS (N.E.B. "by false standards"), accepting the superficial standards of the world, instead of God's.

**2: 5** James uses various devices for commanding his readers' attention. Now he writes: LISTEN. It makes one wonder whether these words of his were originally spoken to hearers, rather than written for readers.

BELOVED BROTHERS: see 1: 2 and 1: 16.

James now adds a further reason why his readers should not despise the poor and flatter the rich. The basic reason is that it is wrong and in defiance of God's will. In addition to this, however, it is an observable fact that it is from the poor that people are much more readily won into the Christian faith, and it is the rich who are usually found ranged in bitter hostility against the Christians. Moreover, it appears that this was not just a matter of chance, but the result of the deliberate strategy of God. God had chosen what was "foolish in the world to shame the wise, and what was weak in the world to shame the strong" (1 Cor. 1: 27).

It is basic to the teaching of the New Testament that a man becomes a Christian, not so much by his own deliberate decision to take sides with Christ, but rather as a result of God's choosing of him. "You did not choose me", said Christ, "but I chose you" (John 15: 16; 6: 70). So here GOD HAS CHOSEN THE POOR.

In this sense of being God's chosen people the Christian community believed themselves to be taking over the destiny of Israel. They were the New Israel. The people of Israel had been profoundly aware that they were "God's chosen people"—not because they were better or cleverer or more reliable than others, but simply because God had chosen them, in spite of their obvious faults and frailties. God had "elected" them, chosen them to be His own people, as an act of His own free grace, not at all as a reward of merit. Deut. 7: 6-7 states this movingly: "It was not because you were more in number than any other people that the Lord set his love upon you and chose you, for you were the fewest of all peoples; but it is because the Lord loves you".

The Christian community accepted such words as equally true of themselves, the new people of God, claimed by God to do the work the Old Israel had refused to do. They were within the Christian Church not because they had been more deserving than others of this high privilege, but simply because God in the grace of Christ had reached down to their need, offering His forgiveness, and claiming them as His own. They are not self-chosen, but chosen by God. This emphasis is everywhere in the epistles (Rom. 8: 33; Eph. 1: 4;

Col. 3: 12; 2 Thess. 2: 13, etc.). It is a constant wonder to the early Christians why they should have been selected, and so many others, certainly no worse than they had been, had apparently been passed by.

Already the poor have been mentioned at 1: 9–10, and we noted in that connection the severe words spoken by Jesus about the dangers of wealth. It was the poor who in the main welcomed His teaching (Mark 12: 37). It is from their number that God chose His servants (Luke 1: 52). It is to them that the Kingdom of God belongs (Matt. 5: 3; Luke 12: 32). At Corinth, and perhaps in many other areas, it was from the poorer classes that the Christians were chiefly drawn (1 Cor. 1: 26–29). They are called "THE POOR IN THE WORLD" to indicate that it is by "the standards of the world" that they are poor, or "poor in the sight of the world", as N.E.B. renders it. By other standards, however, they are rich.

Commentators note that for the Hebrews the word "poor" had come to be almost identified with the "devout", the kind of people to whom worldly prosperity meant little because obedience to God meant everything. It may be that this rather specialized meaning of the word is partly in James's mind here. Certainly the rich appear to be identified with those who care little for God and God's people.

When God chooses a "poor man" it is to make him rich, but not rich as the world counts riches. He is to become RICH IN FAITH. This recalls phrases used by Jesus. He spoke of those who were "rich toward God" (Luke 12: 21), and also about "true riches" (Luke 16: 11) and "treasure in heaven" (Matt. 6: 20). In the epistles the word "rich" can also be used with a spiritual significance (see 1 Cor. 1: 5; 2 Cor. 8: 9; Heb. 11: 26). Here their riches are described as consisting of "FAITH", that is, that attitude of heart and mind which is ready and able to appropriate and make its own all the gifts of God's grace.

God's freedom from "partiality" is clearly shown in His choice of the poor and unimportant in the world to be not only "rich in faith", but also "HEIRS OF THE KINGDOM". Although this is the only use of the phrase "the kingdom (of God)" in this epistle, it is another instance of the faithfulness of James to the teaching of Jesus. Though it occurs only rarely outside the Synoptic Gospels, there it represents the central theme of the preaching of our Lord. The substance of the proclamation with which His ministry begins is: "The Kingdom of God is at hand" (Mark 1: 15). It was the subject of many of His parables (see, e.g., Matt. 13). It was the gift of God to those who turned to Jesus in faith, not at all the achievement of human endeavour ("It is my Father's good pleasure to give you the Kingdom"—Luke 12: 32). It is specifically related to the poor. They are pronounced "blessed" and the Kingdom is promised to them (Luke 6: 20). In contrast He says: "How hard it is for those who have riches to enter the Kingdom of God" (Luke 18: 24).

In English the word "kingdom" tends to suggest an area with boundaries. In the Greek, however, its meaning is better represented as "The Rule of God". It is this which is the supreme blessing life can bring, when we are controlled not by Satan, or our own divided will, but entirely by the Rule of God. Jesus sometimes used it as a variant for "life" or "eternal life" (see Mark 9: 45 and 47). Here, Ropes suggests, it is practically equivalent to "salvation" (and this is borne out by a comparison between Luke 18: 25 and 26).

This "Kingdom" is part of the blessing which Jesus made available during his earthly ministry to those who were willing to receive it (Luke 11: 20; 17: 21), but its fulfilment lay in the future. We still need to pray: "Thy Kingdom come". Of this Kingdom, James assures us, the poor whom God has chosen are destined to be HEIRS.

Here again we meet the language of Jesus Himself. He too spoke of "inheriting" the Kingdom (Matt. 25: 34) and also of "inheriting" eternal life (Matt. 19: 29; Mark 10: 17; Luke 10: 25; 18: 18). Paul also writes of "inheriting the Kingdom" (1 Cor. 6: 9–10; 15: 50; Gal. 5: 21; Eph. 5: 5) and other writers use the metaphor "inherit" in connection with "a blessing" (1 Pet. 3: 9) and with "the promises" (Heb. 6: 12; cf. also 1 Pet. 1: 4).

The word originally meant to receive a legacy bestowed simply by the goodwill of the testator, probably as the result of some family relationship, and not usually based on the merit of the recipient. It may be that this original sense had been partly lost, and that the word had come to mean little more than just "acquire", but the original meaning has a special significance for Christian usage. We receive God's blessings, not because we have deserved them but because, as adopted sons in God's family, it is His gracious will that we should have our share in His treasures, that we should be "heirs of God", "fellow heirs with Christ" (Rom. 8: 17).

This inheritance is one which God HAS PROMISED TO THOSE WHO LOVE HIM. For the latter phrase, see 1: 12.

**2: 6** The fact that God has chosen the poor to be heirs of His Kingdom, makes it more than ever shameful that some of His own people HAVE DISHONOURED THE POOR MAN, humiliating him by discourtesy and lack of consideration. Similarly Paul rebukes the well-to-do Christians at Corinth, because at the "love-feast" they bring plenty of good food for themselves and ignore their poorer brethren who actually go hungry: "You despise the Church of God and humiliate those who have nothing" (1 Cor. 11: 22). Paul and James alike grieve at this breach of the true spirit of Christian brotherhood.

Their preferential treatment of the rich over against the poor is not only a disgrace to their profession as Christians. It is also a mark of something less than good sense, because it is the rich, whom they treat with such elaborate attention, who, so far from being the ones who deserve well of the Christians, are the very ones who stir up trouble for them, both by private agitation and persecution, and also by setting in motion legal proceedings against them.[1] We note this fact in the story of Acts, where persecution of the Christians is often set on foot by rich people, when they begin to feel that their sources of income are being jeopardized by the success of the Christian mission. At Philippi, for instance, Paul found himself in real danger after he had cured a fortune-teller of the evil spirit which possessed her, because her owners realised that "their hope of gain was gone" (Acts 16: 19). Similarly at Ephesus the makers of small silver replicas of the shrine of the goddess Diana created serious trouble for him when they realised that their trade was losing customers (Acts 19: 27). So in many missions, both overseas and at home, the source of much serious opposition has been the apprehension of the rich that the sources of their income are being threatened by the spread of the Christian faith. Sometimes their influential social position and their acquaintance with legal procedure made it possible for them to DRAG YOU INTO COURT, though often they had to operate in less legitimate ways, and use whatever unofficial means were in their power to OPPRESS YOU.

**2: 7** The hostility of the rich is not confined to hurtful actions against the Christians. That perhaps they could bear with patience. But these enemies also speak with sneering contempt of the honoured name of Christ Himself, that HONOURABLE NAME BY WHICH YOU ARE CALLED. This is more difficult for the Christian to bear without protest. In 1 Peter also we read of disciples being "reproached for the name of Christ", and suffering "as a Christian" (4: 14, 16).

The Greek words "the name by which you are called" could equally well mean: "the name which was invoked over you". The first meaning is in accord with the O.T. references to the people of Israel as, for example: "you that are called by the name of the Lord" (Deut. 28: 10; cf. Jer. 14: 9; Isa. 63: 19). If the second meaning is preferred it would presumably refer to the moment of their baptism, when the name of Jesus would be invoked over them. Perhaps it is this meaning which lies behind the translation of N.E.B.: "the honoured name by which God claimed you", because baptism into the name of Christ was the acceptance of God's claim upon one's life.

---

[1] As soon as it was clearly recognised that Christians were not Jews (who had special privileges of meeting for worship), any Christians who met together were technically liable to prosecution.

2: 8–13. *If you really fufill the royal law, according to the scripture,* *"You shall love your neighbour as yourself," you do well.* 9. *But if* *you show partiality, you commit sin, and are convicted by the law as* *transgressors.* 10. *For whoever keeps the whole law but fails in one* *point has become guilty of all of it.* 11. *For he who said, "Do not* *commit adultery," said also, "Do not kill." If you do not commit* *adultery but do kill, you have become a transgressor of the law.* 12. *So speak and so act as those who are to be judged under the law of* *liberty.* 13. *For judgement is without mercy to one who has shown* *no mercy; yet mercy triumphs over judgement.*

This paragraph, like the preceding one, is concerned with the sin of "showing partiality"; that is, treating people differently according to their social status. The word occurs in 2: 1 as well as 2: 9. This indeed is the link between the two sections.

It is as though the one who is being rebuked for showing "favouritism" to a rich man, as against a poor man, protests that his concern to be attentive to the rich man arose from an eagerness to practise the command to "love his neighbour". Such a protest would spring either from dishonesty or self-deception (a danger which James warns against in 1: 22 and 26). If in fact "love for neighbour" had been the motive, the poor man would have been as well treated as the rich, since both are equally "neighbours". Calvin's comment (p. 305) is bluntly true: "They were officiously attentive to the rich, not from love, but from a vain desire of attaining their favour". Friendliness to others is indeed a fulfilment of God's law as expressed in Lev. 19: 18: "You shall love your neighbour as yourself", but friendliness to the rich at the expense of the poor is a defiance of that Law as stated in Lev. 19: 15: "You shall not be partial to the poor or defer to the great".

**2: 8** The R.S.V. reads: "IF YOU REALLY FULFIL THE ROYAL LAW . . ." The Greek word (*mentoi*) translated "really" can sometimes bear this meaning. In this case its purpose is to draw the readers' attention to a sharp contrast with the following verse (2: 9). It may equally well be translated as "however", and both R.V. and N.E.B. understand it in this adversative sense. The meaning of the passage is not seriously affected either way.

THE ROYAL LAW probably refers to the whole of God's Law, rather than to the single precise commandment, now quoted. This commandment, however, of love for one's neighbour is thought of as summarizing the moral aspect of God's total Law.

Why is it called "ROYAL"? John Wesley says concisely that it is because it is "The Law of the Great King". Others associate it with the "Kingdom of God", which is central in the teaching of Jesus (see on 2: 5). In this case the "royal law" is that which describes the mode of life expected of those who have entered into the Kingdom of God (Matt. 5: 20; 7: 21, Mark 9: 47, etc.) and are living by its laws. Dibelius (p. 133) doubts this: "Probably this is not James's meaning. Rather" (by the adjective "royal") "he intends to represent the law as one which is supremely important, admitting of no exceptions, and completely binding". Moffatt too, in his commentary, is inclined to take "royal" in this sense, and suggests "supreme" as an equivalent. Hort takes its meaning to be "the law which governs other laws" (cf. "royal priesthood" in 1 Pet. 2: 9).

The word "FULFIL" (*teleō*) means to "carry out", "put into practice", and is a different word from the one Jesus used to describe His own purpose and intention to "fulfil the law" (*plēroō*) in Matt. 5: 17. It is noteworthy, however, that in this passage which outlines what He means by the fulfilment of the Law Jesus also introduces the command to "love one's neighbour" (Lev. 19: 18) and draws out its full significance (Matt. 5: 43-48). In Mark. 12: 29-31 also we read how Jesus named the two great commands of the Law which comprehend all the others: to love God, and to "LOVE YOUR NEIGHBOUR AS YOURSELF" (from Lev. 19: 18). Paul, therefore, is only interpreting the mind of Christ when he too writes: "The whole law" (that is, on its moral side) "is fulfilled in one word: 'You shall love your neighbour as yourself,'" (Gal. 5:14). Again at Rom. 13: 8-10 he writes: "He who loves his neighbour has fulfilled the law. The commandments are summed up in this sentence, 'You shall love your neighbour as yourself. . . .' Love is the fulfilling of the law". So James here reiterates what his Lord had taught, and what Paul also had learned from Him.

If God's supreme law is followed obediently, especially in the sense in which it is most briefly, yet comprehensively, summarized ACCORDING TO THE SCRIPTURE (Lev. 19: 18) and also accepted by our Lord Himself as the perfect summary of the Law, YOU DO WELL. The authority of Scripture meant a great deal to the early Church (cf. 1 Cor. 15: 3). Only a known word of Jesus took precedence over it. When a word of Jesus was supported also by words from the Scripture, it appeared to be doubly sure.

When Jesus, however, accepted the words of Lev. 19: 18 as the perfect summary of God's moral law for man, He enlarged their meaning and widened their application. The people of Israel normally understood "neighbour" to apply only to their fellow-countrymen (and perhaps not even to all these). They could claim some justification for this in the actual text of Lev. 19: 18, for the whole verse reads: "You shall not take vengeance or bear any grudge against the sons of your own people, but you shall love your neighbour as yourself". Both the parallelism of the two parts of the verse (familiar to students of the O.T.) and also the sense of the passage suggests that "neighbour" was understood to mean the same as "a son of your own people". Jesus, however, lifted it far above such narrow limitations and gave it the meaning of "one's fellow man". In His answer to the question, "Who is my neighbour?" He told the parable of the Good Samaritan (Luke 10: 29–37) where the word "neighbour" clearly is meant to include even such hated foreigners as Samaritans, and indeed to mean any fellow creature whom we meet on life's way. The apostle Paul also understood it in this new way, and used as an equivalent of the word "neighbour" a phrase which means "the other man" (*heteros*), whoever he may be (Rom. 13: 8).

This summary of the Royal Law in the words of Lev. 19: 18 is basically the same as the word of Jesus, known as the Golden Rule: "Whatever you wish that men would do to you, do so to them: for this is the law and the prophets" (Matt. 7: 12). This is a positive instruction, which is more far-reaching than the less demanding negative one attributed to Hillel: "Whatever is hateful to thyself, do not to thy fellow", though Hillel is reputed to have claimed that this represented the whole Law so effectively that all else was to be regarded as commentary.

Jesus accepts Lev. 19: 18 as representing the best summary of God's will to be found in the O.T. He, however, Himself carried it to an even higher level, when He said: "This is my commandment, that ye love one another *as I have loved you*" (John 15: 12). The unselfish love of Christ for us, not just our own selfish love for ourselves, is to be the standard to which our love for others must aspire. Paul glimpsed this vision also: "As the Lord has forgiven you, so you also must forgive" (Col. 3: 13).

**2: 9** But in practising "love for neighbour" some SHOW PARTIALITY, that is, they choose whom they shall regard as neighbours and reject others. One's own countrymen may be included, and foreigners excluded. People of our own social class and those higher in the scale may be regarded as neighbours, but not those felt to be below us. But this is to "show partiality". We are not entitled to pick and choose those we will count as neighbour. To do so is to COMMIT SIN.

SIN is a word which occurs several times in James. It occurred at 1: 15, where its meaning was discussed. There it was distinguished from the "desire" which prompted it. "Desire" was the temptation which could conceive and give birth to sin. Sin was, therefore, the act of the will in disobedience to the known will of God. Later references to sin occur in 4: 17; 5: 15, 16, 20. Here its meaning is straightforward. It is an act of disobedience to God which incurs God's displeasure, an act which the doer consents to, even though he knows—or might have known, had he been willing to learn—that it is evil and wrong.

PARTIALITY in his treatment of others is the sin here condemned, because, as we have seen, it is plainly contrary to the command in Lev. 19: 15, and contrary also to the quoted command of Lev. 19: 18, at any rate in the sense in which it was understood and interpreted by our Lord.

Many Christians, while feeling that such "favouritism" is less than ideal, would regard it as "unfortunate", rather than grossly evil. James, however, will not allow this prevarication. If a thing is evil, he will call it evil (cf. Isa. 5: 20). And this partiality is an evil thing, a defiance of God's will. Therefore he who does it, COMMITS SIN. It is an affront to God, not an amiable weakness.

The word COMMIT stresses the deliberate nature of the action. It is not an error into which a man has fallen inadvertently, in a moment of carelessness. It is a purposed action which betrays an inner wrongness in our attitude to our fellowmen, and therefore reveals some wrongness in our thought and relationship to God.

YOU ARE CONVICTED BY THE LAW: the Law is here spoken of as if it were a living witness whose testimony exposes the guilt of the accused. Not only Lev. 19: 15, but also Deut. 1: 17 and 16: 19 prohibit discrimination against the poor in favour of the rich. The defendant could not plead ignorance of the Law, since it is declared in Scripture plainly and repeatedly. Therefore, they are exposed AS TRANSGRESSORS, which is a strong word, emphasizing the deliberate and defiant attitude of the wrongdoers (also used in Gal. 2: 18). They have not slipped unknowingly into error, but have knowingly overstepped the forbidden boundary (that is what the word literally means). So they stand condemned by their wilful disregard of the known will of God.

James seems to be aware of a somewhat flippant attitude on the part of the wrongdoers in this matter. They are inclined to dismiss their offence as at most a trivial fault, of very little importance. "In any case," they argue, "we keep God's law in all other and more important respects; so what does one little irregularity matter?" They feel that the large area over which they are obedient completely compensates for the small action, over which they are charged with disobedience.

**2: 10** To this plea for special indulgence towards their wrong-doing, James is severely firm: "WHOEVER KEEPS THE WHOLE LAW, BUT FAILS IN ONE POINT HAS BEEN GUILTY OF ALL OF IT". And in this he has firm support from other Jewish teachers. There were, however, some who took a more lenient line. They allowed acts of obedience to be set over against acts of disobedience, and provided that a man could claim a larger number of creditable acts than discreditable ones, the margin of merit was counted in his favour, so that failure at one point could be cancelled out by success at others. Moreover some Rabbis so magnified the importance of some laws, for instance the Sabbath laws, that provided these were scrupulously observed, a failure or two at other points could be overlooked.[1]

There is an echo of some such attitude as this in one of the clashes between Jesus and the Pharisees, when He rebukes them not only for emphasizing some points of the Law to the neglect of others, but also of emphasizing those which in fact were of slighter significance to the disregard of some matters of fundamental importance: "You tithe mint and cummin, and have neglected the weightier matters of the law, justice, mercy and faith; these you ought to have done, without neglecting the others" (Matt. 23: 23).

James, like Jesus, will have nothing to do with these expedients. God's Law represents the whole will of God for man, and it is not for us to pick and choose, selecting at our own discretion the items we will observe and those we can ignore. In this he represents the point of view reflected in the word of Jesus: "Not an iota, not a dot, will pass from the law until all is accomplished" (Matt. 5: 18–19).

It is true that there were some points in the Mosaic Law where it did not perfectly represent the final will of God and Jesus needed to correct them—for instance, those rules proscribing certain food as "unclean", so that to eat it meant defilement in God's eyes. Jesus declared all food clean (Mark 7: 1–23, especially 19). Moses also permitted a discontented husband to divorce his wife on comparatively slight grounds, and this Jesus corrected, to bring it in line with God's perfect will for man (Mark 10: 4–9). By making such adjustments, Jesus was "fulfilling" the Law (Matt. 5: 17), bringing it fully into line with the will of God as He alone perfectly understood it. But in that "perfect law", which truly represented the will of God, nothing could, for our own convenience, be set aside as optional. God's will for man was God's will. He had no right to exempt himself from the obligation to accept the whole of it.

Paul, also, knew that a loyal Jew was under obligation to keep *the whole law* (see Gal. 5: 3). And though his understanding of the Law changed as Christ interpreted it to him, there is no doubt he would have been horrified had any Christian claimed the right to disobey God at one point on the ground that he was obeying Him at many others.

So James is perfectly clear. To fail before one command of the law is to BECOME GUILTY OF ALL OF IT. This does not mean that to break one command is as blameworthy as to break them all, but to defy God at any point is to be guilty before God of breaking His Law. Whether

[1] Mayor (p. 86) quotes Shemoth Rabb. xxv: "The Sabbath weighs against all the precepts: if they kept it, they were reckoned as having done all."

it be at one point or many, God's Law has been violated. The extent of the guilt may vary, but the reality of it is the same. Before the Law of God the law-breaker stands condemned.

It is nowhere precisely stated in the O.T. that to be guilty of one disobedience is to be guilty before the whole Law. The nearest statement to this effect is in Deut. 27: 26: "Cursed be he who does not confirm the words of this law by doing them". In the LXX this is strengthened by the insertion of "all" before "the words of this law".

There are, however, a number of Rabbinic judgments which insist on this very point.[1]

**2:11** James takes an extreme instance to show the absurdity of claiming that to break only one command is different from breaking the law as a whole. HE WHO SAID, "DO NOT COMMIT ADULTERY", SAID ALSO, "DO NOT KILL". THEREFORE, IF YOU DO NOT COMMIT ADULTERY BUT DO KILL, YOU HAVE BECOME A TRANSGRESSOR OF THE LAW. Both adultery and murder are plainly forbidden by God. It is ridiculous to argue that one need not be regarded as a serious fault just because the other has not also been committed.

Not only are they both explicitly forbidden by God. They are also clearly in defiance of the law of love for one's neighbour. "Love," says Paul, "works no ill to a neighbour", but adultery does work ill to both partners in the marriage whose sanctity is violated. Murder also is the extreme consequence of lack of love for a fellow man. To hate him so intensely as to rob him of life itself is the complete antithesis of loving him.

If we could assume that James uses "adultery" and "murder" with some of the inner significance that our Lord gave to these words in Matt. 5: 21–22, 27–28 (where lustful desire is branded as evil, as well as lustful act, and where anger, resentment and contempt are shown to be under God's displeasure, as well as the act of murder) it would add even greater significance to the meaning of verse 11.

It may seem strange to find a man trying to excuse himself for committing murder on the ground that he has not also committed adultery. Yet there are cases where a man may be scrupulously upright in his faithfulness to his marriage, and even most severe in his condemnation of those who fall below these standards, who can nevertheless show himself cruelly hard and unforgiving to those he thinks have wronged him. Yet this attitude is condemned by our Lord in the same breath as murder itself is condemned (Matt. 5: 27–28). Such a man, though he may not actually kill, may very well refuse merciful help which alone could save life, or rescue a man from despairing death. His utter

---

[1] Hort quotes Shabbath (R. Jochanan) 70: 2: "If a man do all, but omit one, he is guilty of all and each". Mayor quotes R. Jose Galilaeus: "Qui reus est unius, reus est omnium".

integrity within his marriage seems to him to compensate for any wrong there may be in his cold heartlessness to those he regards as his enemies. It is a common frailty of human beings, as Samuel Butler satirically noted, to

> "Compound for sins they are inclined to
> By damning those they have no mind to".[1]

**2: 12** James has been pleading for total obedience to the whole of the known will of God. This will of God he has called in verse 8 the "Royal Law", and found its essence in the rule to love one's neighbour. Now, with a note of sharp severity, his pleading is reinforced by warning. He reminds his readers that, whether or not their conduct now is shaped by this Law, it will certainly be judged by that Law hereafter. No specious arguments and excuses and self-justification will avail on that solemn Day, but how we have acted, and how we have spoken to other people. So he insists: "SO SPEAK AND SO ACT AS THOSE WHO ARE TO BE JUDGED UNDER THE LAW OF LIBERTY".

This "royal law" has already been called the "LAW OF LIBERTY" at 1: 25, and comment on the significance of this name will be found there. This is the law which operates, not by outward enforcement, but when the love of Christ inwardly constrains. It is part of the freedom of the children of God, which issues in glad and spontaneous obedience to Him, for the sake of pleasing Him who has done so much for them, and in the glad assurance that what He commands is life's surest guide to deep and lasting happiness.

Our Lord in the Sermon on the Mount emphasized the importance of thought and desire, since they are the seed bed from which speech and action spring, whether for good or ill. James here, however, is concerned primarily with these outward consequences of our inner life—our actions and our words. In the treatment of the poor man callous words had accompanied contemptuous act. We are, therefore, reminded SO TO SPEAK as people who know that they must render an account of what they say at the Last Judgement. Here again James is true to the teaching of Jesus, who said: "On the day of judgement men will render account for every careless word they utter" (Matt. 12: 36). (See comment at 1: 26.)

The same thought of judgement must control also how we ACT. Our acts, as well as words, will confront us then.

Though this concentration upon conduct, and the absence of reference to faith, may at first appear at variance with other teaching in the N.T., actually in relation to the Last Judgement the emphasis on "works" is true to the general teaching of the N.T. as a whole. Present Justification, as Paul taught it, meaning the restoration of right

---

[1] *Hudibras* I, i, 215.

relationships between man and God, here and now, is the work of God's forgiving mercy alone, as it is offered to our faith through Christ. But at the Last Judgement enquiry is to be made into how this renewed relationship with God has been allowed to shape our conduct, whether our faith is or is not the "faith which works through love" (Gal. 5: 6). The parable of the Sheep and the Goats emphasizes that at the last it will not be our protestations of faith which will count, but the "little unremembered acts of kindness and of love" (Matt. 25: 31–45), the fruit of true faith. Paul too insists on this, when he speaks of judgement: "We must all appear before the judgement seat of Christ, so that each may receive good or evil, according to *what he has done* in the body" (2 Cor. 5: 10). And again: "When God's righteous judgement will be revealed . . . he will render to every man *according to his works*" (Rom. 2: 6; 1 Cor. 3: 8).

Some Christians claim to find such a reminder of coming Judgement, and the fact that our every word and act will there be brought forward to confront us, distasteful and even discouraging. But in fact it invests every moment of life with significance. If death comes to all, and beyond that nothing matters, then life is in danger of seeming an empty, pointless thing. But a belief that at the Last Judgement everything counts means that every moment of life is filled with the richest significance.

**2: 13** It is utter folly to excuse our sins cheerfully by insisting that God is bound to forgive, that it is His nature to be indulgent. There is forgiveness for true penitence, but God's JUDGEMENT IS WITHOUT MERCY TO ONE WHO HAS SHOWN NO MERCY.

James's thought here seems to move beyond the particular instance (of "partiality"), with which he began this section, to the affirmation of a truth of more general application. He insists on the fundamental importance of "MERCY" in any life which seeks to please God, and the strong displeasure of God against any failure in mercy. It is all too easy for one who sets himself to be morally upright, diligent, honest, and pure to become impatient of the gentler quality of mercy, perhaps even to regard it as a weakness. But mercy is something very near to the heart of God—happily for all of us, for we need God's mercy constantly.

Mercy is also one component of love for neighbour. If we do to others as we would like them to do to us, it means showing mercy to them in their times of need. It is similar to "compassion", and this was characteristic of Jesus, who was often "moved with compassion", and who commended the Good Samaritan because he too was "moved with compassion". The priest and Levite who hardened their heart without mercy against the needs of an injured man incurred His outspoken condemnation. In the parable of the Sheep and Goats, just referred to, that which commends a man to God is compassionate, merciful action towards all who are in trouble.

"Judgement" (or justice) aims to give to each man what is his due. It seeks to measure reward to merit. Mercy, however, looks not at deserving, but at man's need, and responds in generous kindness far beyond anything that is his due. God Himself is merciful, and it was to this quality in God that the publican in his broken-hearted contrition appealed: "God be merciful to me, a sinner." It was mercy, reaching far beyond mere justice, which prompted the owner of the vineyard to give a full day's wage to those who had worked only a small part of the day. It was mercy which moved the heart of the father when he saw his feckless son coming home in disgrace and near despair.

God, who Himself is merciful to penitent need, looks for mercy in His people. "I desire mercy" (Hos. 6: 6) is God's word, and one which Jesus often cited. If our lives have been filled with this quality, the Day of Judgement need not terrify us; but if our dealings with our fellows have been marked by harshness, and lack of generosity and of the readiness to forgive, then we shall find the same harshness reflected in the face of Him who is our Judge. JUDGEMENT IS WITHOUT MERCY TO ONE WHO HAS SHOWN NO MERCY. It was callousness which our Lord so strongly rebuked in the Pharisees, who could "devour widows' houses" and at the same time try to cover it up by lengthy prayers (Matt. 23: 14), and who brought a woman, taken in adultery, before him for his public condemnation (John 7: 53–8: 11).

Mercy, however, will receive mercy. This is in harmony with the clear assurance of Jesus: "Blessed are the merciful, for they shall receive mercy" (Matt. 5: 7). Since forgiveness of injuries is one aspect of mercy, we hear the same assurance again in the words which follow the Lord's Prayer in Matthew: "If you forgive men their trespasses, your heavenly Father also will forgive you; but if you forgive not men their trespasses, neither will your heavenly Father forgive your trespasses" (Matt. 6: 14–15). Similarly the unmerciful servant in the parable is condemned and punished severely because his Master's forgiveness towards him did not produce in him a corresponding forgiveness to his fellow man. A clear warning follows: "So also my heavenly Father will do to every one of you, if you forgive not your brother from your heart" (Matt. 18: 35).

This truth had been in part anticipated in the O.T. In Ps. 18: 25–26 we read: "With the merciful thou wilt show thyself merciful . . . and with the froward thou wilt show thyself froward" (R.V.). The Rabbis also sometimes emphasize this. Ropes, for instance, quotes Jer. Baba q. 8: 10: "Every time thou art merciful, God will be merciful to thee"; and also Rosh hash 17 a: "To whom is sin pardoned? to him who forgives injury".

But threat and warning do not have the last word, for MERCY TRIUMPHS OVER JUDGEMENT. Most commentators here seem to understand "mercy" as that which a man has shown during his earthly life, and which before God's Judgement Throne can call out God's mercy in response. The affirmation here would therefore mean that though every man comes to judgement deserving condemnation for his sins, yet his acts of mercy will reverse an unfavourable verdict into a favourable one. In this sense "mercy" wins the day as against judgement. Barclay (p. 43) states this interpretation quite explicitly: "The man who has shown mercy will find that mercy has even blotted out his own sin".

Others shrink from this emphasis, as seeming to allow human merit, here in the guise of mercy, to usurp the prerogative which belongs to God alone. Calvin voices this misgiving (pp. 308–9): "God's mercy alone is that which delivers us from the dread and terror of judgement. . . . Hard and forced is the explanation of those who regard mercy as put here for the person, for men cannot properly be said to rejoice against the judgement of God".

This may be so. Yet it would not be improper for James here, in his own way, to enforce what he understands to be the meaning of the Lord's beatitude: "Blessed are the merciful, for they shall receive mercy".

It may, however, well be that though James has felt it necessary to stress the reality of God's judgement, yet he feels compelled to conclude with a glad acknowledgement that in the end it is God's mercy which has the last word: It triumphs over judgement.

2: 14–17. *What does it profit, my brethren, if a man says he has faith but has not works? Can his faith save him? 15. If a brother or a sister is ill-clad and in lack of daily food, 16. and one of you says to them, "Go in peace, be warmed and filled," without giving them the things needed for the body, what does it profit? 17. So faith by itself, if it has no works, is dead.*

Already in 1: 22ff. James has spoken strongly against "hearing" which is not accompanied by "doing". Here he turns to believing (or, at any rate, professing belief) which does not produce actions to prove its reality. Christian conduct is the deep concern of James, and to him Christian confession of faith in God and Christ, or the claim to an experience of faith, is proved empty and unreal unless it leads on to Christian conduct in our treatment of others. A profession of sympathy which is no more than polite talk, and which does not lead to helpful action, when such action is in our power, is mere sentimentalism. So, says James, is a profession of faith which does not issue in the loving actions which spring from true faith.

James has just condemned lack of mercy in a Christian (2: 13). At the Last Judgement he has affirmed that mercy more than anything else will be the quality God will look for. Others, however, are claiming that "faith" is the one great essential; faith and faith alone matters in the Judgement, since "works" do not achieve our salvation; salvation by faith, not by works, is the essence of the Gospel.

James would not dissent from this if those who claim to have this faith do indeed have it, and are not just claiming it, and if their faith is the full, true faith. He knows, however, the test of true faith (by which it can be distinguished from spurious kinds of faith). It is that it inspires Christlike conduct, which includes compassion to all in distress. If such conduct is missing, it means that the faith is not genuine and the claim to have it is untrue.

Some claim to find in these verses and in the following paragraph evidence that James and Paul do not see eye to eye in this matter. Superficially indeed there are differences, but not fundamentally. It is rather, as Calvin comments here (p. 309): "The sum of what is said here is that faith without love avails nothing, and that it is therefore wholly dead." So Paul's words in Gal. 5: 6 could almost be taken as the text which James is here expounding.

2: 14 For "MY BRETHREN" see 1: 2.

WHAT DOES IT PROFIT? N.E.B. has "what use is it?"

IF A MAN SAYS he has faith: the discussion here is not really about the true nature of faith, though that is partly involved. Emphasis falls rather on the word "SAYS". It is about the claim a man makes to have faith, and the test by which the truth of his claim can be gauged. If, however, what this sentimental Christian professes is allowed the name of faith at all, then it is faith merely in the impoverished sense of an intellectual assent to certain ideas about God and Christ, which receives further criticism at 2: 19. Primarily, however, it is what Calvin calls "a false pretence of faith" which is being tested (cf. Matt. 7: 21, and 25: 45).

The word "FAITH" occurs in James at 1: 3, 6; 2: 1, 5, 14-27; 5: 15. Later we must discuss what it means for him, and his dislike of inadequate attitudes which masquerade as the true faith. Here, however, as in 2: 1, it is introduced without definition as an attitude of mind which can be assumed as the essential characteristic of any Christian. Christians, in the N.T., are commonly called "believers", and their religion is "the faith". It certainly includes belief in God, though its distinctive feature is faith in Christ. Nothing, however, of the precise content of this faith is here specified. Blackman understands it to mean "a general acknowledgement of Christ as Lord and a profession of loyalty to Him". Every Christian, therefore, claims to HAVE FAITH; but if such a person HAS NOT WORKS he is betraying the emptiness of his claim. If his faith is not virile enough to produce works, it is not true faith, or saving faith. It will certainly not be effective enough to SAVE HIM.[1]

BUT HAS NOT WORKS: James here uses the word "works" in a less technical sense than Paul. For Paul it is primarily the observance of the requirements of the Law, viewed as a means by which men may make themselves acceptable to God. For James its main emphasis is on "effectiveness"—as we say colloquially about something, "it works". If faith produces love, it is effective; it "works". If not, it "does not work", it is ineffective. Clearly compassionate love in action (as well as in feeling) is an essential part of what James means by "works"— this is clear from the following verse. If faith is so feeble that it cannot produce love, then it is also too feeble to "SAVE" a man. To such faith our Lord himself would say: "Why do you call me Lord, Lord, and do not what I tell you?" (Luke 6: 46).

Such stunted faith is not acceptable to Christ, nor can this FAITH SAVE a man. It is not the same kind of faith as that referred to in the firm promise: "*Believe* on the Lord Jesus Christ and you will be saved" (Acts 16: 31) nor in the affirmation: "By grace you have been saved through *faith*" (Eph. 2: 8). Faith which does not create in the believer a readiness to obey is not true faith or saving faith.

K.J.V. translates: "Can faith save him?" Certainly the Greek may be so translated, but it does not represent James's meaning here. James is not arguing that "faith" is not the means by which salvation is appropriated; rather he insists that this kind of ineffective faith, or an empty claim to faith, does not lead to salvation. So R.S.V. suits the context better: "Can *his* faith save him?"

The word "SAVE" is here used in a general sense. It is what Blackman calls "an unreflective use of the word". True salvation when its contents are specified includes our being put right with God, the realization of His forgiveness of our past sins, the claiming of His offer of victorious life here in the present, and an assured hope of the good things laid up for us by God beyond this earthly sphere. Probably in this context James is thinking mainly of the Last Judgement, and that which will enable us to hear the Lord's "Well done" (Matt. 25: 23), and to be spared the desolating verdict: "Depart from me" (Matt. 25: 41).

---

[1] Calvin comments (p. 310): "This is the same as though he had said, that we do not attain salvation by a frigid and bare knowledge of God, which all confess to be most true". The faith which saves is at the same time the faith which works.

**2: 15** James forces home his point with an apt illustration, with which all readers must agree. If a man is in real need and wanting help, sentimental good wishes without any attempt to assist him (when assistance could in fact be given) are obviously little better than empty mockery. It means the good wishes are not really genuine.

It is a BROTHER OR SISTER who comes in urgent need. These words could be used loosely of any fellow man or woman, any "neighbour", but usually they apply to fellow Christians, for whom we should feel a specially loving care. "As we have opportunity, let us do good to all men, and *especially to those who are of the household of the faith*" (Gal. 6: 10).

One wonders if James still has in mind the poor man who was slighted (at 2: 6). Certainly his constant care for the poor is evident here. This poor man IS ILL-CLAD AND IN LACK OF DAILY FOOD. For "ill-clad" K.J.V. has "naked". The Greek word (*gymnos*) could mean this, but usually it means "lightly clad", as those are who exercise in the gymnasium (an English word which comes from this very Greek word). But to be "lightly clad", by necessity and not by choice, in the harsh cold of winter is to be "ill-clad" and in distress. N.E.B. brings this out by translating as "in rags". He is also IN LACK OF DAILY FOOD, that is, he does not know from day to day where his next meal is to come from. The two phrases together mean "cold and hungry". In the parable of the Sheep and the Goats, which affords so many parallels to this section in James, our Lord comes to us unrecognized in those whom we meet who are hungry and ill-clad (Matt. 25: 35–36), and it is our merciful response to their need which is decisive in our favour at the Last Judgement.

**2: 16** To these unhappy people, short of adequate food and clothes, the only consolation offered is a cheerful greeting, with cordial good wishes for their future comfort, but no practical help at all. ONE OF YOU SAYS TO THEM, GO IN PEACE. This is a conventional Jewish greeting, used as acquaintances part from each other. We find it on the lips of our Lord (e.g. at Mark 5: 34, Luke 7: 50), though as used by Him it carried a much fuller meaning. The Hebrew word for peace was a rich word embracing all that goes to make for true welfare. Paul took this greeting over and combined it with the specifically Christian greeting. We find his wish of "grace and peace" to his readers at the beginning of many of his letters (Rom. 1: 7, 1 Cor. 1: 3, 2 Cor. 1: 2, etc. Also 1 Pet. 1: 2). In such a context these words would be used with care and fully meant. Often, however, the words "Go in peace" would be used simply as a convenient formula of departure, just as we say "farewell" or "goodbye", without realizing the good wishes originally intended in the words. N.E.B. seeks to represent this casual use of the words here by translating: "Good luck to you", and this slang phrase does perhaps suggest the spirit of indifference in which the words were spoken. It is just as we might say to a departing but delaying guest whom we wish to hurry on his way: "Have a good time", "Enjoy yourself", without really meaning it at all.

BE WARMED AND FILLED: his friend wishes for him the very things he so greatly needs, but does nothing to implement the wish. Mayor comments: "The sight of distress is unpleasant to these dainty Christians. They bustle out the wretched-looking brother or sister with seeming kindness and what sounds like an order to others to provide for their immediate relief, but without taking any step to carry out the order".

The Greek word here for "be warmed" is the one used of Peter "warming himself" at the fire on the night of his denial of Jesus (Mark 14: 67), but it may equally be used of wearing warmer clothing in order to keep out the cold.

The kind words are used to disguise the harshness of the actual treatment. To the speaker they may seem to exempt him from the need of any more practical kindness. So nothing is done to provide warm clothes or an assured supply of food. This is cheap generosity. Kind words and generous feelings cost us little. Generosity with time or money is costly, and this is avoided. Good wishes in words to those in need are regarded as the fulfilment of Christian obligation, WITHOUT GIVING THEM THE THINGS NEEDED FOR THE BODY (that is, for their bodily needs).

The apostle John similarly sharply rebukes such a sentimental and unpractical kind of faith, which does not issue in practical deeds: "If anyone has the world's goods and sees his brother in need, yet closes his heart against him, how does God's love abide in him? Little children, let us not love in word or speech, but in deed and truth" (1 John 3: 17–18). James, just as John, is saying that love is not love if it stops short of action.

WHAT DOES IT PROFIT? The opening words of the paragraph are repeated: What good is it? James asks.

**2: 17** Love which consists only of nice words and feelings, but does not go on to actions is a poor ineffective thing. So too, says James, is faith. If it is a matter only of nice feelings and easy words, and does not lead on to costly action for the service of others, it is not really faith at all; at best it is a lifeless, ineffective thing. It is as it were only the corpse of faith. FAITH BY ITSELF, IF IT HAS NO WORKS, IS DEAD.

The phrase "by itself" goes most easily with "faith". K.J.V. took it so and translated: "Faith, being alone", that is, unaccompanied by works. Calvin and Wesley so understood it. The R.V., however, took the words with "dead" and translated: "dead in itself". It is better with R.S.V. to follow the interpetation of K.J.V. and translate: "faith by itself". *If it has no works* is therefore an amplification of the phrase: BY ITSELF.

Faith, therefore, which does not work by love is described as dead, inactive, unproductive, sterile, barren. The same word is similarly used in Rom. 6: 11 and 7: 8.

Paul, had he wished to express such thoughts as these, may well have done so rather differently. He would probably have included more precise reference to the grace of God, and the fact that salvation is His gift; but he too would have felt it necessary to say that this changed life, which comes into being when God's grace and man's faith are united in man, must not stop at nice talk and nice feelings, but proceed to be productive of "good works". The words of Eph. 2: 8–10 express his thoughts on the relationship of faith and works: "By grace you have been saved by faith; and this is not man's doing, it is the gift of God, lest any man should boast. For we are his workmanship, *created in Christ Jesus for good works*, which God prepared beforehand, that we should walk in them". With James, Paul regarded faith as something meant to reach fruition in "good works".

2: 18–26. *But someone will say, "You have faith and I have works." Show me your faith apart from your works, and I by my works will show you my faith. 19. You believe that God is one: you do well. Even the demons believe—and shudder. 20. Do you want to be shown, you foolish fellow, that faith apart from works is barren? 21. Was not Abraham our father justified by works when he offered up his son Isaac upon the altar? 22. You see that faith was active along with his works, and faith was completed by works, 23. and the scripture was fulfilled which says, "Abraham believed God, and it was reckoned to him as righteousness"; and he was called the friend of God. 24. You see that a man is justified by works and not by faith alone. 25. And in the same way was not Rahab the harlot justified by works when she received the messengers and sent them out another way? 26. For as the body apart from the spirit is dead, so faith apart from works is dead.*

*Preamble.*

This passage, perhaps more than any other in James, has been the centre of special interest and lively controversy. In it James uses in close association the three important words: justification, faith and works. It is impossible to avoid the sharp comparison with similar passages in Paul where the same three words are the central theme. When these Pauline passages are examined side by side with this paragraph in James, it is impossible to ignore what appear to be striking differences. Some commentators have even claimed that they are contradictory, and that James is deliberately seeking to correct misleading statements found in Paul's letters. Certainly to a casual reader it must seem like that. Paul, for instance, in Rom. 3: 28 wrote: "We hold that a man is justified by faith apart from works of law"; whereas James in 2: 24 writes: "You see a man is justified by works and not by faith alone".

Since this issue is of such vital importance, especially to those who represent the evangelical tradition within the Church, we must begin by trying to clarify the meaning of these three words in the New Testament, and enquiring how far James and Paul use them in precisely the same sense or with some variation of meaning. What superficially appears to be a blatant contradiction between Paul and James, may arise from a difference in the meaning they assign to these words.

A further consideration must be borne in mind, which will at any-rate partly explain the discrepancy. The kind of error Paul is seeking to correct in Romans and Galatians is very different from the error which James is resisting, and our statement of a truth varies according to the error we are opposing. If we ourselves were arguing against antinomians, who believed that moral conduct in a Christian was of little importance, our arguments would be very different from those we should use if our opponents were "legalists" who believed that good conduct alone secured all the benefits of religion. So we must remember that in general Paul is urging his case against Judaizers, who believed salvation depended, in part at any rate, on doing the works of the Law, whereas James was ranged against antinomians who believed that inward faith was all that mattered.

It is unlikely that James actually knew Paul's letters and was attempting to correct passages in them, but he may very well have had to deal with Christians who knew something of Paul's teaching and distorted it to their own ruin. Paul himself knew of these people, who could even say: "Why not do evil that good may come?" (Rom. 3: 8), and, even worse, could claim that this was Paul's own point of view—"as some people slanderously charge us with saying".

Apart, however, from a difference of emphasis arising from a difference of opponent, there is also a difference in the meaning attached to "justification", "faith" and works", though the main difference lies with "faith" and "works".

To "JUSTIFY" is to declare someone innocent or righteous, or to treat him as such. In the O.T. it is the duty of the judge to "justify" the innocent and condemn the guilty, and so God in His capacity of Judge will never "justify the wicked" (Exod. 23: 7). While this gave confidence in God's scrupulous fairness, it also gave rise to a feeling of hopelessness among those who were deeply aware of wrongness in their lives: "How can a man be justified before God", asked Job (Job 25: 4, K.J.V.). "In thy sight shall no man be justified" (Ps.

143: 2, R.V.). Out of this dilemma arose the belief that there is forgiveness with God; He will cancel out the sin of the man who repents and comes humbly to God to be put right.

Usually in the O.T. this "JUSTIFICATION" from God is associated with His verdict on our lives at the Last Judgement, though His forgiveness is something which even in Old Testament days could be received and enjoyed during life on earth. The Gospels reflect in the main this twofold Old Testament usage. Jesus, reproving the casual attitude which makes light of words we utter in unguarded moments, says: "By your words you will be justified" (Matt. 12: 37), and the previous verse shows that this is linked with the Last Judgement when "men will render account for every careless word they utter". On the other hand in the parable of the Pharisee and the Publican our Lord says that it is not the scrupulous and spiritually proud Pharisee, but the sinful taxgatherer, with nothing to rely on but his own penitence and God's mercy, who goes home "justified" (Luke 18: 14). This cannot be wholly referred to the Last Judgement, but includes something at any rate of present experience.

James appears to follow this usage of the Old Testament and the Gospels. Justification means man's acceptance by God as "righteous". Predominantly it is associated with the Last Judgement, but can also have reference to God's acceptance of a man in this life. What Jeremias would call "present" and "eschatological justification" are not clearly distinguished.

Paul, however, makes a sharp distinction between them. When he uses the word "justify" he refers to the immediate privilege of our being accepted by God, here and now. Our ultimate encounter with God, when the final verdict will be pronounced, is spoken of by Paul in terms of "judgement" rather than "justification". This is a significant difference then: for James justification includes the final judgement, whereas for Paul it is only the here-and-now adjustment of our lives to God, with the final judgement treated as a separate issue.

It is of the very essence of Paul's Gospel that when a man awakens spiritually to find his life guilty before God, he cannot by his own efforts at keeping the moral law succeed in making himself innocent before God. Try as he may, he cannot wholly fulfil the will of God for him, and certainly nothing he can do in the present can cancel out the guilt of the past. He is utterly dependent on the forgiving mercy of God. This mercy has been offered to man pre-eminently in Jesus Christ and especially in His death on the cross. So he affirms: "We are justified by grace" (Rom. 3: 24).

So clearly is this a present privilege available here and now that he can sometimes speak of it in the past tense, as something already claimed and proved. Rom. 5: 1, for instance, is rightly translated by

N.E.B. with a past tense: "Now that we have been justified . . . " This present justification, according to Paul, is ours only by the sheer, unmerited grace of God in Christ.

Even Paul, however, when he writes of "judgement" or "eschatological justification", introduces the issue of conduct as well as the grace of God. "God will render to every man according to his works" (Rom. 2: 6), he writes. Also, "each one shall receive the things done in the body, according to what he hath done, whether it be good or bad" (2 Cor. 5: 10).

We must remember, therefore, that when Paul speaks of "justification" he excludes *final* judgement, whereas James appears to treat justification and judgement as a single unit. For Paul present justification is entirely of God's grace, but final judgement takes into account the "works" which should spring from a life made right with God. Since, for James, justification is not differentiated from judgement, his thought of justification takes account of works as well as faith.[1]

FAITH is the next word for consideration, and here there appears a more obvious difference in the usage of Paul and of James. When Paul speaks of present justification it is always as something which only God in His mercy can bestow on man, out of His free grace, and apart from this man cannot find it. It is beyond his power to achieve. But this gift is not bestowed high-handedly, without seeking the consent of the recipient. His willing response is sought, and that response is called "faith".

This faith, in the full sense in which Paul uses it, is complete openness to God. It is not anything we do, but only our readiness to let God have His way with us. He sees our need, and we are ready to let Him deal with it in His own way—whether by rebuke or correction, by healing or cleansing, by empowering or sanctifying. He decides what we need, and He supplies the need. We only withdraw our resistance to His will. That, for Paul, is faith, and that is all man needs to do in order to receive justification at the hands of God. If faith is used in this full sense, then Luther was right to interpret Paul (in Rom. 3: 28, etc.) as saying that we are justified by faith *alone*.

Faith of this quality, however, has the most far-reaching consequences, since it implies submitting our lives wholly to God in Christ for Him to cleanse, heal, rule and shape. When God rules our lives, one consequence is "love". True faith, says Paul, expresses itself in love (Gal. 5: 6) to our fellows, and if this result does not follow upon faith, Paul would feel there was some serious fault in the faith. Faith must bear fruit, just as the Holy Spirit in a human life must bear fruit.

When James criticises "faith", it is by no means the "faith which

[1] For a careful treatment of this subject, see J. Jeremias on "Paul and James", *Expository Times*, Vol. LXVI, pp. 368–71.

works by love" whose inadequacy he seeks to expose. Provided "love" had proceeded from the faith, he would have been well content. The faith he scourges angrily is not really faith at all. It is rather an unjustified claim to faith. It is the holding of accurate opinions about God and Christ, as though those opinions in themselves (apart from any consequences in life) made a man right with God. James looks for fruits to grow from true faith. They alone prove that faith is real. When there is coldness to another's need, and selfish indifference to the misery of others, he can only say that this proves that true faith is missing, and what is claimed as faith is not faith at all, but only a set of correct opinions.

There is also a difference between Paul and James in the meaning they give to "WORKS". When Paul speaks of "works" he usually means "works of the law". Indeed this is the phrase he uses consistently in Galatians, and sometimes in Romans, e.g. Rom. 3: 28. In the other references in Romans when he uses "works" alone, it is not unfair to assume that he means "works of the law". He insists that a man is not justified before God by such works. These "works of the law" mean a scrupulous observance of the rules of conduct prescribed in the Mosaic Law (and, perhaps, as amplified in the Rabbinic tradition). They include strict rules of diet, ritual cleanliness (cf. Mark 7), observance of statutory fasts, and the many regulations about the Sabbath, in addition to what we normally think of as the moral requirements, as outlined in the Ten Commandments. It was perfectly clear to Paul that such observances ("works") did not put a man right with God, and James would not have disagreed with him.

There is, however, another sense in which "works" occur, even in the Pauline literature. In this sense they are usually called "good works". Most noticeable is the occurrence in Eph. 2: 10, and this is most illuminating for helping us to understand James as well as Paul. In Eph. 2: 8 we have the great evangelical truth affirmed: "By grace you have been saved through faith; and this is not your own doing, it is the gift of God. For we are His workmanship, created in Christ Jesus *for good works*". Here "good works" do not mean "works of the law" but obedience to the will of God as made known in Christ, and above all they include "love". A Christian is justified by grace through faith in order that a further purpose may be fulfilled—that he may become a "new creature" in Christ, and as such may live his new life in "good works", that is, in obedience to the will of God (not, however, as interpreted in the Mosaic law, but in the life and teaching of Jesus, cf. also 1 Tim. 6: 18; Titus 2: 7; Acts 9: 36; Heb. 10: 24).

Now when James uses "works", he does so in this Christian sense. He does not mean by the word, obedience to ritual requirements of the Old Testament dispensation, but acts of love and mercy. In Heb.

10: 24 "good works" are precisely associated with "love", and it is this use of the word we find in James.

In this sense Paul would agree that "good works" are the outward sign of a recreated life. If they do not appear, doubt is cast on the reality of the faith, from which the new life springs. When James insists on "works" as the proof of faith, it is just this that he means.

The apparent difference between Paul and James, therefore, can be explained largely as a difference in the use of terms.

For Paul justification is God's present act in Christ of setting right the relationship with Him that man has broken. The faith he commends through which this takes place is the total committal of life, in trust and obedience, to God in Christ. The works, whose futility for putting us right with God he criticizes, are the detailed observance of rules governing ritual actions as well as moral behaviour.

For James the "works" he commends are acts of love and charity to our fellows in obedience to the Spirit of Christ. The faith whose inadequacy he exposes is just an intellectual assent to an article of belief, though it calls itself faith. Justification is not just God's immediate act of restoring man to right relationships with Him, but involves also the final verdict on a man's life.

Paul's emphasis is this: A man is justified by faith in Christ, and this cannot but produce in him good works, that is loving actions to others. James's emphasis is: True faith by which a man is justified proves itself in Christ-like conduct towards others, and if such conduct fails to appear, what claims to be faith is shown to be not faith at all.

The emphasis varies because the two apostles are addressing themselves to different kinds of errors.

**2: 18** There are a number of technical difficulties connected with this verse. Critical commentaries such as that by Ropes deal with them in full (pp. 211–214). Since, however, they do not greatly affect our understanding of the main teaching of the passage, we shall not here consider them in any great detail. Problems, however, are raised by the questions: Who is the "someone" who interposes a comment? The "but" which introduces the verse suggests that an objection is being raised to an earlier point, yet what is said agrees substantially with what James has just affirmed. Moreover, where does this comment end? In the middle of the verse, at "works"? or at the end (at "my faith")? Who are the "you" and the "I"?

Without pretending that there are not other possible solutions or arguing fully for the one we choose, we recommend one solution, which seems probable. We take the interpolated comment to consist only of the first half of the verse. For this we can claim the support of the translators both of the R.S.V. and the N.E.B., and also of such scholars as Ropes and Dibelius. The second half of the verse, beginning with "Show me your faith . . ." is the beginning of James's reply.

The pronouns "you" and "I", in the comment, are best taken not as personal references to James and the man who makes the comment, but just as a manner of saying: "One person . . . and another person . . ." It is a way of representing two types of Christian, one who emphasizes what we may call the root of the matter, that is faith, and the other the "fruit" ("works") which must grow from any good root.

It seems best also to take the opening comment, not as an objection to what James has been saying, but rather a friendly comment by a fellow Christian who is trying to do justice to both sides involved in the argument. He puts forward what he thinks may be acceptable as a formula of compromise, a solution tolerant enough to include both parties to the dispute. James has declared: "Faith without works is dead". This kindly person, who does not wish to be too harsh on anyone, suggests that there is room both for the man who emphasizes faith and the one who insists on works. Each may represent a different gift of the Spirit. Paul taught that "There are varieties of gifts" coming from "the same Spirit" (1 Cor. 12: 4). Indeed among such varying gifts, alongside "healing" and "prophecy", is included "faith". Perhaps, it is suggested, some Christians have "faith" and others have "works"; and not all are expected to have both. "YOU HAVE FAITH AND I HAVE WORKS" is his peace-making formula.

For James, however, this is merely evading the difficulty, not solving it. Faith and works are not to be regarded as alternative gifts of the Spirit, so that one or the other may be expected in a Christian, but not both. The only solution which James will accept is that if a man has true faith, it will be the kind of faith which produces "works". The works are not optional extras but an inevitable outworking of faith, which by their presence provide the only proof there is of the reality of the faith. He would underline Paul's affirmation in 1 Cor. 13: 2: "If I have all faith . . . but not love, I am nothing".

So James's reply is that we have no means of knowing whether or not true faith is present apart from what it does. He issues the challenge: "SHOW ME YOUR FAITH APART FROM YOUR WORKS". There is in fact no proof of the reality of faith other than the fruit it produces. If a Christian claims to have faith, but is, for instance, dishonest, or harsh and callous to others in their need, it shows that his so-called faith is not true faith. His claim to faith is only a claim, not a reality (as at 2: 14). But when in the life of a Christian love, patience, kindness, self-control appear, they prove the reality of the source from which they spring.

James is not objecting to those who urge the centrality of faith for the Christian, but only to those who describe as "faith" something which has no outward result in conduct. The kind of faith he values is what Paul calls the "faith which works through love" (Gal. 5: 6). So he continues: I BY MY WORKS WILL SHOW YOU MY FAITH. As Hort comments (p. 61): "The whole verse is little more than a paraphrase of (the word of Jesus) 'By their fruits ye shall know them' "(Matt. 7: 20).

A discussion of the meaning of the words "faith" and "works" in Paul and James respectively is contained in the preamble to this section.

**2: 19** James now describes more fully the so-called "faith" which he criticizes on the ground that it does not produce good works. Though it is so futile, some Christians are very proud of it, since they feel that because of it they have become intellectually superior to ignorant, polytheistic pagans. They have come to believe that there is only one God, and though they are still very selfish and lazy and ineffective as Christians, because this article of faith represents a higher truth than much of the contemporary religion round about them, they feel well satisfied with themselves, since they BELIEVE THAT GOD IS ONE.

This affirmation was the basic creed of the Jewish people, "Hear, O Israel, the Lord our God is one Lord" (Deut. 6: 4). The Christians took it over from their Jewish antecedents without question. Our Lord Himself cited it as part of His answer to the question: "Which commandment is the first of all" (Mark 12: 29), and Paul also, more than once, appeals to it as an elementary truth (1 Cor. 8: 4, 6; Eph. 4: 6). James does not find fault with his opponents for holding this belief. His complaint is that for them it is merely an assent of their intellect, which exercises no influence on their conduct. They do not accept and apply the corollary to it which our Lord equally emphasized: Thou shalt love thy neighbour as thyself. It is a good thing to possess an accurate theology, but it is unsatisfactory unless that good theology also possesses us.

A correct belief, held with the mind, but without influence on conduct is a poor thing. James illustrates this with devastating effect. Concerning the belief itself, he says: YOU DO WELL, but adds: EVEN THE DEMONS BELIEVE this. The very enemies of God Himself know this basic truth about God, but for all that they are still His enemies. The correctness of their belief does not make them other than demons, the declared enemies of God. The inadequacy of a merely intellectual belief in God could hardly be more plainly exposed.

The twentieth century does not find it easy to think in terms of "demons", but the reality of them is assumed in the New Testament, where we find it taken for granted that there is a vast world of evil powers ranged against God. Their ruler is variously spoken of as Satan, the Devil or Beelzebub (Mark 3: 22), and his individual agents are demons or unclean spirits. It was believed that these were seeking opportunity to invade human life in order to cause physical injury or moral ruin there. In the Gospels these evil beings are represented as recognizing Jesus as "the Holy One of God" (Mark 1 : 24). They, therefore, held correct beliefs about Jesus even earlier than His own disciples, but that did not make them other than demons, because their belief did not rule their lives. So here the demons know the truth about God, and its effect in their lives is to make them SHUDDER.

As they remember the nature of the One to whom they are opposed, they tremble with fear. Though they gain passing successes over God's people, and sometimes seem to gain great victories, nevertheless their final defeat and destruction is certain, because of the nature and the power of the One against whom they have rebelled. The time, they know, will come when "God will arise and scatter His enemies" (Ps. 68: 1). The power of Jesus to cast out demons was an anticipation of that final triumph of God over all forces of evil. The thought of their final fate makes the demons shudder in dread.

"The faith of a devil" has become a famous phrase among those who have studied the teaching of John Wesley. He used the phrase in the first of his published sermons to differentiate false kinds of faith from the true faith. The faith of a devil, borrowed from this context in James, means a mere assent of the mind to some truth about God and Christ, without that faith being allowed any power to shape and order the conduct.

**2: 20** James proceeds to give a conclusive illustration from the O.T. to demonstrate that in Scripture FAITH APART FROM WORKS IS BARREN.

The one addressed, who needs to be persuaded of this obvious truth, is called "YOU FOOLISH FELLOW". The word here translated "foolish" (Greek *kenos*) literally means empty, and so may mean one lacking in normal good sense. Epictetus, however, uses the word of a guest at dinner, who is actually somewhat ignorant, but makes great efforts to impress his fellow guests with his supposed knowledge. So it may be that James is suggesting that the opponent addressed here is not so much a genuine seeker after truth as one who is seeking to impress others with his subtle cleverness. The N.E.B. translates the phrase as "you quibbler", one who argues for the mere sake of arguing, even when others regard the matter as clear and settled. Perhaps the translators were representing the meaning of the word as used by Epictetus.

Faith which does not lead on to "works" is declared to be "barren" (Greek *argos*), that is, ineffective in that it fails to produce what it was created to produce, unproductive like a field, tilled and planted, which yet yields no crop.

**2: 21** The Biblical illustration which is quoted to prove that faith apart from works is barren, or, as in 2: 14, dead, is that of ABRAHAM.

Clearly he has become for New Testament writers the standard example of "faith". His life is used to illustrate "faith" in different ways.

Firstly, Paul appeals to Abraham (Rom. 4, Gal. 3: 6) as the embodiment of that faith which believes God's promises, however improbable their fulfilment may seem to human calculations. He quotes Gen. 15: 6, where Abraham believed God's promise that to him and his aged wife would be born a son. After long years of disappointment, it seemed incredible that it could happen. But "Abraham believed the Lord; and he reckoned it to him for righteousness".

The second kind of faith of which Abraham is the example is that cited in Heb. 11: 8. This is the moment in his life when God called him to leave a home with which he was familiar and where he felt secure and go out into an unknown land to face an unpredictable future. "By faith Abraham obeyed when he was called . . . he went out not knowing where he was to go." Faith here is obedience to a known command of God, when the outcome of that obedience is wrapped in uncertainty, and obedience seems fraught with danger and insecurity.

The third kind of faith, to which James here appeals, is that displayed by Abraham when he showed himself ready to obey God's strange but clear command to sacrifice his only son Isaac, a son specially dear because of the remarkable circumstances of his birth, and doubly dear because God's promises of a wonderful future for Abraham's offspring were all bound up with this boy. This kind of faith like the second includes obedience. This time, however, it was not obedience that involved possible and unknown dangers, but led him open-eyed straight into a most painful and costly act. This is faith *par excellence*, which is ready to obey God even when the cost of obedience is what to us seems utter ruin. It seems to anticipate something of Gethsemane and the prayer: "Not my will, but thine be done". Hebrews also refers to this costly act of faith at 11: 17, and perhaps it is this which is mostly in mind when in 1 Macc. 2: 52 Mattathias encourages his sons to be faithful: "Was not Abraham found faithful when tested, and it was reckoned to him as righteousness".

Abraham is therefore regarded as the supreme instance of faith, in all its different aspects.

He is called "OUR FATHER". He was regarded in a special sense as the Father of the people of Israel. Our Lord, in the parable of the Rich Man and Lazarus, uses the phrase: "Father Abraham" (Luke 16: 24). Matthew in his genealogy of Jesus is content to trace His parentage back to Abraham, since it was with him that the story of the people of Israel really began. The Christian Church, believing itself to be the New Israel, the True Israel, also claimed Abraham as their Father, and claimed that they were his sons in a truer sense than his merely physical descendants could claim, because it was his *faith* they shared. John the Baptist had denounced those who dishonestly put their trust in the fact that they were Abraham's children by physical descent, using this as a refuge from an accusing conscience (Matt. 3: 9, cf. John 8: 39). Paul, on the other hand, proclaims that Christians are the true children of Abraham, since it is they who have come to "share the faith of Abraham, for he is the *father* of us all" (Rom. 4: 16).

Abraham, the very epitome of true faith, WAS JUSTIFIED NOT BY FAITH ALONE, or by a mere show of words claiming to be faith, but BY WORKS, which sprang from the reality of his faith. This phrase sounds to be bluntly in opposition to Paul's words in Rom. 3: 28, mainly because Paul and James in their varying context are attaching different meanings to "faith" and "works". The seeming contradiction is discussed in the preamble to this section.

JUSTIFIED means "accepted by God", set free from the guilt which once separated man from God. Its use here springs from the sentence in Gen. 15: 6, which James quotes in verse 23: Faith "was reckoned to him as righteousness". If, in English, the connection is not immediately clear, it is because in English the close relationship between "justify" (Greek *dikaio*) and "righteousness" (Greek *dikaiosyne*) does not appear. The two words are actually from the same root. The similarity of the words would be represented if we used "justice" and "justify" instead of "righteousness" and "justify", though the word "justice" has come to have too restricted a meaning in English. In Genesis this phrase is used in connection with Abraham's faith in believing the promise of God about the birth of a son, and when Paul discusses it he refers it precisely to this one incident (Rom. 5: 3) and bases his argument on the fact that it happened both before the giving of the Law or the sign of circumcision. For James, however, it is regarded as a motto which stands, as it were, over the whole life of Abraham, and so James refers it here to his act of obedience in being ready to sacrifice Isaac. If Abraham had refused to obey what he understood to be a precise command of God, it would have proved in him the absence of true faith. His willingness to obey, in spite of such dreadful cost to himself, proved his faith in God. It was this faith, says James, which was reckoned as righteousness, which made him "just" before God, which therefore could be said to "justify" him. It is the act of obedience which "justifies" him, since that alone proves that Abraham's faith was real faith, and not the kind of empty assent to a theoretical truth which some people are claiming as faith.

Abraham was justified by the kind of faith which involves obedience, even costly obedience. James does not, in fact, mean that a man is justified by works apart from faith, but by that obedience which proves the presence of true faith. Calvin puts it this way: "James is speaking

of the proof Abraham gave of his justification". Ropes: "James insists
not so much on the necessity of works as on the inseparability of vital
faith and works". John Wesley: "James's justification by works is the
fruit of St. Paul's justification by faith". Hort: "Not for faith plus
works does St. James plead, but for *faith at work*".

Paul's emphasis is that Abraham's faith was a simple trust in the
truth of God's promise and a calm acceptance of its utter reliability
(Gal. 3: 6ff., Rom., 4: 1ff.). He appeals to it to show that when we
first come to God in our deep need of Him, all we need to bring to
Him is a simple trust in what He has promised, and nothing more.
That is the heart of the Gospel. *At that stage* we do not need to bring a
life of perfect obedience to all His commands.

James's emphasis, however, is on another aspect of faith. He insists
that true faith issues in costly obedience to God, as illustrated in
Abraham's readiness to sacrifice Isaac. True faith receives both the
promise of God and also the grace of God to cleanse and heal and
equip. Once healed and equipped it rejoices to offer complete obedience
to all the known will of God.

**2: 22** So Abraham was justified, WHEN HE OFFERED HIS SON ISAAC
UPON THE ALTAR. YOU SEE THAT FAITH WAS ACTIVE ALONG WITH HIS
WORKS. The story of this is told in Gen. 22. Abraham came to believe
that God demanded this terrible sacrifice of him. Perhaps he knew
of heathen fathers who sacrificed their children to the gods, and
wondered if his own faith in God could stand that test. God, however,
was not asking him to slay his son. What God wanted in Abraham
was the readiness to obey God even to that extent, though God did
not in fact want that particular kind of obedience. So Abraham is
spared the awful misery of the deed he was prepared to do, and God
said: "Now I know that thou fearest God, seeing that thou hast not
withheld thy son, thy only son from me" (Gen. 22: 12).

When obedience can go to that length, we know some mighty power
is active in it. That mighty power is "faith". N.E.B. translates: "faith
was at work in his actions". Literally the Greek words could be
translated: "Faith was at work in his works". Phillips paraphrases:
"Can't you see that his faith and his actions were, so to speak,
partners?" Moffatt has: "Faith co-operated with deeds". In this way
FAITH WAS COMPLETED BY WORKS. The obedience of Gen. 22 was the
fulness of the faith which first appeared in Gen. 15: 6. N.E.B. translates:
"By these actions the integrity of his faith was fully proved". The Greek
word (*teleio*) here translated "completed" contains the idea of a goal
(*telos*) being reached. "In these actions faith reached its appointed
goal", we might translate. Ignatius uses the same word (*telos*) in a
similar context: "Faith is the beginning, and love the end" (*telos*)
(Eph. 14: 1).

**2: 23** It was in this act of obedience, recorded in Gen. 22, that James claims "the Scripture (Gen. 15: 6) was fulfilled, which says, 'ABRAHAM BELIEVED GOD AND IT WAS RECKONED TO HIM AS RIGHTEOUS-NESS'". We noted in the previous verse that James removes this O.T. quotation from its precise context and treats it as a kind of motto over the whole of Abraham's life.[1]

HE WAS CALLED THE FRIEND OF GOD. This became an accepted title for Abraham. It is not found in the original story of Abraham in Genesis, but in Isa. 41: 8 words ascribed to God speak of "Abraham, my friend", and in 2 Chron. 20: 7 a prayer to God refers to "Abraham, thy friend". It is said that among the Arabs today Abraham is still commonly referred to in this way.

The phrase means one who is especially beloved by God (rather than one who befriends God). His unfaltering trust in God, proved by his unwavering obedience to God's will, partly, at any rate, explains this close relationship to God. We are reminded of the words of our Lord, where obedience and friendship are joined: "You are my friends, if you do what I command you" (John 15: 14).

**2: 24** The word "friend" also fits the relationship of one who is "justified", since for such a man the barriers of guilt and misunder-standing have been removed by the grace of God. So James summarizes his argument with the words: YOU SEE THAT A MAN IS JUSTIFIED BY WORKS AND NOT BY FAITH ALONE (verse 24). Sufficient has already been said about the apparent contradiction with Rom. 3: 28. Suffice it to say here that Paul no less than James would have felt it inconceivable that deliberate sin and selfishness and disobedience should continue in the life of a Christian who has been justified by faith (see Rom. 3: 8 and 6: 1–2). John Wesley used to say: "We know of no salvation but salvation *from* sin" (*not* of salvation *in* sin). Faith which does not bring victory over sin and progress in righteousness is not true faith.

**2: 25** One who is unconvinced by James's argument from Abraham might well reply that the instance of Abraham can hardly be regarded as typical, since he was a man so outstanding in goodness and spiritual insight. So James takes a further instance of a very different type of person, one indeed whose character was as bad as Abraham's was good, Rahab the harlot. In Joshua 2 the story is told how Hebrew spies secretly entered Jericho in order to discover its strength and weak-ness, to prepare the way for an attack. Their presence in the town was reported and they were in great danger. Rahab, however, gave them shelter in her house, and hid them away when the king's servants came

---

[1] In reference to this quotation of Gen. 15: 6 Dibelius writes: ". . . nicht als eine Ausfage über die religiose Stellung Abraham zu einer bestimmten Zeit, eben zu der Zeit, von der Gen. 15 handelt, sondern als einen Gottespruch, der über dem ganzen Leben Abrahams steht" (p. 153).

to arrest them. Later she allowed them to escape through a window which opened on the outside of the city wall. She is reported as doing this because she had heard of the great power of the God of Israel, and wished to be counted as one of His servants. She said: "The Lord your God is He who is God in heaven above and on earth beneath" (Joshua 2: 11). As with Abraham, her faith was not merely a theoretical opinion; it caused her to act daringly and effectively in the service of God and God's people. In this it was like Abraham's, though outwardly the two appear very different.

The fact that James calls her a "harlot" makes it clear that her disreputable character is an item in his argument. Some suggest that the sentence could well be translated: "Rahab, even though she was a harlot . . ." Calvin comments on this curious association of Abraham and Rahab: James "designedly put together two persons so different in character in order more clearly to show that no one . . . has ever been counted righteous without good works" (p. 316). Then, to make sure that his words are not misunderstood Calvin adds later: "We allow that good works are required for righteousness; but we take from them the power of conferring righteousness" (p. 317).

Many legends, extolling the later greatness of Rahab, developed in post-Biblical times, and even in the New Testament she is accorded a place of honour. Apart from James's reference to her, she is listed at Heb. 11: 31 among the heroines of the Faith, and her name stands in Matt. 1: 5 among the ancestors of our Lord.

**2: 26** Still another illustration or analogy is called upon to press home still further this point, that faith which is inactive is not true faith. He writes: AS THE BODY APART FROM THE SPIRIT IS DEAD, SO FAITH APART FROM WORKS IS DEAD.

It seems strange to us that in this analogy the body should be faith and the spirit works. We might have been inclined to approach it from the opposite angle, and say that as the spirit without the body is ineffective, so is faith without works. But to James faith which does not produce good works is very much like a corpse, "from which the breath of life has vanished" (Tasker). For James it is works which alone prove that faith is still alive. Perhaps he would even have said that it is doing good works which keeps faith alive, and unless it is so active in deeds of practical obedience, it soon dies. The words of the hymn-writer, Washington Gladden, interpret James's thought here, when he speaks of "Work that keeps faith sweet and strong".

In this context "spirit" means "the vital principle by which the body is animated" (Ropes). It does not carry the subtler meanings which Paul sometimes gives it in distinction from "soul" and "flesh".

In this controversial passage, therefore, James's emphasis on works does not arise from any desire to make light of faith, but only to distinguish clearly true, effective, practical faith from a "mere lifeless profession of orthodoxy". It is not works apart from faith which is praised but faith which is active in works. It is by these that faith can be demonstrated and proved. Apart from these practical outworkings of its inner vitality, faith remains unrecognizable for what it is or else betrays itself as a mere profession of belief which is in fact nothing more than empty words.

# CHAPTER THREE

*3: 1–5. Let not many of you become teachers, my brethren, for you know that we who teach shall be judged with greater strictness. 2. For we all make mistakes, and if any one makes no mistakes in what he says he is a perfect man, able to bridle the whole body also. 3. If we put bits into the mouths of horses that they may obey us, we guide their whole bodies. 4. Look at the ships also; though they are so great and are driven by strong winds, they are guided by a very small rudder wherever the will of the pilot directs. 5. So the tongue is a little member and boasts of great things. How great a forest is set ablaze by a small fire!*

This section is predominantly concerned with the evil that can be caused by an ill-controlled tongue. It begins, however, with a warning to Christians against over-eagerness to enter the ranks of "teachers". After that there follows a more general warning against the serious consequences that may follow unguarded utterance. It is true that teachers, more than most people, have to use speech in the course of their duties, and so are more than others under obligation to guard against the special dangers to which speech is prone. Verses 2–5, however, appear to be applicable to all conversation, and not just to the spoken words of teachers.

It would probably be better represented if a new paragraph were indicated as starting at verse 2. William Barclay in his Bible Reading Notes on James does, in fact, treat verse 1 as a separate unit, and expounds verse 2–5 as addressed to Christians generally rather than to teachers in particular—rightly, we believe.

**3: 1** One of the most notable developments in New Testament scholarship during this generation has been the recognition of the distinction in the New Testament between "kerygma" (proclamation) and "didache" (teaching). This development owes a great debt to C. H. Dodd's book on "The Apostolic Preaching", the main thesis of which has become accepted almost as a commonplace of New Testament studies. Alan Richardson summarizes the difference: "When preachers (originally the Apostles, later the accredited evangelists) had attracted 'hearers' by their proclamation in the market place of the cross and resurrection, they handed them over to the accredited 'teachers' for further instruction in the faith and for preparation for baptism".[1] The teaching would probably cover events in the life of Jesus, what Christians believed about Him, and the moral standards expected of them.

The status of the teacher may have been somewhat less official than Professor Richardson's words suggest, but in James we receive the impression that the teacher does hold a recognized and honoured place in the community.

The actual word "TEACHER" (of a church official) is, however, not a common one in the N.T. Though there are many references to "teaching", the noun teacher occurs only five times apart from this context in James.

In Acts 13: 1 there are named five men, who are recognized in the church at Antioch as "prophets and teachers", and included among them are Barnabas and Saul. No attempt is made, however, to distinguish between "prophet and teacher", or to indicate which of the men named may be regarded as one rather than the other. Clearly, however, they represent people of special responsibility in the church, since it is they who set apart Barnabas and Saul for a new missionary venture in the service of the church.

Paul in 1 Cor. 12 describes in some detail the various functions which need to be fulfilled by members within the Church. The whole Church is like a Body with varying limbs and organs, all necessary to the welfare of the whole. He specifies them as follows in 1 Cor. 12: 28: "God has appointed in the Church first apostles, second prophets, third teachers, then healers, helpers, administrators, speakers in various kinds of tongues". Here as in Acts 13: 1 "prophets and teachers" stand together as "officials" of great importance in the Church, second in prestige only to the apostles.

Somewhat similarly Eph. 4: 11 lists together "apostles, prophets, evangelists, teachers" (cf. also 2 Tim. 1: 11, and Heb. 5: 12). Teaching, though not teachers, is mentioned also in Rom. 12: 7.

H. J. Carpenter differentiates the functions of these three main groups of leaders as follows: "The apostles proclaimed the Gospel and converted people to belief in Christ; the prophet by his inspired utterance renewed and deepened conviction, repentance and hope; to the teacher fell the task of building up the daily thought and life of the local community of Christians by expounding points of belief and conduct. . . . Though the teacher did not speak with the outward marks of inspiration which were expected of the prophet, his functions implied authority; he was not expounding his own opinions, but interpreting the revelation of God in Christ".[2]

It is usually thought that the apostles, and probably also prophets exercised an itinerant ministry in the Church, moving about from

[1] A Theological Word Book of the Bible, p. 172.  [2] Ibid. p. 148.

congregation to congregation. If this were so, it would make the teachers the most important of the officials working consistently within the life of a local church.[1] In these circumstances it is easy to understand how the office would soon become not only a way of serving God, but a position that would appeal to ambitious people within the Church. Men would aspire to it, not only at the call of God and in unselfish service of His Church, but also, unhappily, from motives of pride and love of status.

These all too human motives affected Christian disciples in the earliest days, just as they are evident within the life of the Church today. Our Lord Himself had to face them in His own disciples during His earthly ministry. James and John came to Him privately asking for His assurance that in the coming Kingdom they would be assigned positions of supreme authority (Mark 10: 37), and had to be rebuked. Jesus Himself expressed His fear that the disciples might be affected by "the leaven of the Pharisees" (Mark 8: 15), and, like the Pharisees, come to love "the place of honour", "the best seats", and "to be called 'Rabbi' (teacher)" by men. He even gave precise instructions to guard against this: "You are not to be called Rabbi, for you have one teacher and you are all brethren" (Matt. 23: 6–8).

One gains the impression from James that already what our Lord feared had begun to happen in the churches which James knew and he feels it his duty to discourage some of those who are aspiring to attain to the office of teacher. So he writes: LET NOT MANY OF YOU BECOME TEACHERS. John Wesley took this to mean that only those clearly called by God should offer themselves for this post, and not any prompted by human ambition: "Let no more of you take this upon you than God thrusts out".[2]

Calvin took the word "teacher" to be used unofficially and sarcastically of such people as set themselves up to put everybody else right, self-appointed directors of other people's consciences. But this interpretation has not commended itself to other commentators.

We take the reference to "teachers", therefore, to be to a recognized office or status within the Church, and the authority and respect accorded to it had the effect of making it attractive to purely human pride and ambition. Some aspirants hankered after the privileges it

---

[1] W. Barclay in *Daily Bible Readings*, p. 53: "The Apostles and the prophets were ever on the move. Their field was the whole Church; and they did not stay long in any one congregation. But teachers worked within a congregation."
Some refer to Didache 13: 2 as evidence that teachers also travelled from church to church, but its meaning is ambiguous.
[2] Sometimes, however, at other times and in other places, a very different situation developed. People who ought to have been ready to accept the responsibility of the office of teacher shrank from it. In Heb. 5: 12, for instance, such people are rebuked. To seek position from wrong motives, or to avoid it from wrong motives are both less than Christian.

appeared to bestow—status, prominence, authority—without properly considering the immense responsibilities it involved. Those who teach are in a measure held responsible for those they teach, since any failure of the pupils may indeed be the fault of the teacher. It is a sobering thought that at the Last Judgement we who teach shall be called to give an account not only of our own lives with their failures, but of the lives of those we have taught, since some of their lapses may lie at our door. Teachers are entrusted to guide and instruct. Therefore WE WHO TEACH SHALL BE JUDGED WITH GREATER STRICTNESS.

Others may be able to plead ignorance when they have failed to reach required standards, but a teacher cannot use this plea. "Professing to have clear and full knowledge of duty he is the more bound to obey it" (Ropes, p. 227).

It has been suggested that this warning against "many teachers" implies that there had been a lack of unity in the presentation of Christian truth, and possibly angry words, animosity and rivalry between the various teachers (cf. 3: 9-10). But there is nothing in James which points to this.

It should be noted that James includes himself among the teachers. He says: *We* who teach. The severe warning is one he takes to himself.

MY BRETHREN: See 1: 2, 19, etc.

**3: 2** If verse 2 is regarded as further expounding verse 1, and continuing the warning to teachers, then the words here and in verses 2ff. are concerned primarily with the sins of the tongue to which the teacher is specially prone—cutting sarcasm to slow, careless or unpersuaded students, witty sallies at the expense of one's colleagues or rivals or Church leaders, self-display and self-commendation. Probably, however, verse 2, though not unconnected with verse 1, is in the nature of a transition, taking its start from the speaking which plays so large a part in the work of the teacher, and then proceeding to deal with the more general sins that beset all of us in connection with the words we speak. Certainly there is nothing in 3: 2-12 which applies to "teachers" more than to others.

We, therefore, understand verses 2-5 as applying to a Christian's conversation in general, rather than to a teacher's utterances in particular. As such, these verses are to be associated with many others in James which deal with the same topic: 1: 19, 26; 2: 12; 3: 6-12; 4: 11; 5: 9, 12. Clearly this power for evil (as well as good) which lies with the tongue is one which gives great concern to James. Almost certainly as a pastor in the Church he had been made sharply aware, by bitter experiences of the deep hurt that can be inflicted on others, and on the whole corporate life of the Church, when Christians do not enforce on the use of their tongues the twin controls of truth and love (as recommended in Eph. 4: 15).

Complete mastery over evil and total freedom from sin is not found in human life. If sin cannot work its way in by any other means it can gain entry into a man's spoken words. That at any rate is James's experience.

The Bible assumes the universality of sin in human life, and sometimes explicitly declares it. "All men are under the power of sin", writes Paul (Rom. 3: 9), and also "All have sinned and fall short (continually) of the glory of God" (Rom. 3: 23). "If we say we have no sin, we deceive ourselves and the truth is not in us", says John (1 John 1: 8; cf. also Eccles. 7: 20; Ecclus. 19: 16). So James here: WE ALL MAKE MANY MISTAKES. We question whether this translation adequately represents the Greek. Literally this could be translated: "We stumble again and again". The word "mistake", however, suggests an error to which blame cannot be heavily attached. This implication is not in the Greek word, and the translation of N.E.B. is to be preferred: "We all go wrong". Others translate: "fall into sin".

We all fall into sin, and at no point is this more certain than in the use of words. If we can avoid sin there, we shall probably be strong enough to withstand it anywhere. IF ANY MAN MAKES NO MISTAKES IN WHAT HE SAYS, HE IS A PERFECT MAN.

Paul does not precisely make this point, but it is noticeable that in Rom. 3: 9–18, where he has declared the universal sinfulness of man, and seeks to prove it from passages in the O.T., several of the sentences he quotes deal with the sin of speech: "They use their tongues to deceive", "The venom of asps is under their lips", "Their mouth is full of curses and bitterness".

The Wisdom Literature of the O.T. is also much concerned with the sins of speech. "Who has never sinned with his lips?" asks the son of Sirach (Ecclus. 19: 16), and continues later (28: 18): "Many have fallen by the edge of the sword, but not so many as have fallen because of the tongue" (see also Ecclus. 5: 11–6: 1; 20: 1–8; 23: 7–15; 28: 13–26). There are also many similar verses in Proverbs (e.g. 15: 1–4, 7, 23–28; 18: 21).

Ropes summarizes this verse: "All men stumble and of all faults those of the tongue are hardest to avoid". One who does avoid them must be A PERFECT MAN (i.e. blameless). With such control over so unruly a member of the body, he must be ABLE TO BRIDLE THE WHOLE BODY ALSO. Earlier at 1: 26 James has used the same word and spoken of "bridling" the tongue, by which he means holding it in check, controlling its wayward energy, as reins and harness enable a rider or driver to control a spirited horse. We may say of such a driver, that if he can control the most unruly and difficult member of his team of horses, he will be able to control them all. So James says of the members of the body, that if a man can control the wildest and most intractable of all, the tongue, he can be trusted to manage the rest as well.

Moffatt protests that this is not entirely true, since mild-speaking men have sometimes made ruin of their lives through other sins. We need not dispute this. James is making an important point, which he feels very strongly, so emphatically that he may somewhat overstate his case. All he seeks to say with all the power he can find is that the evil that comes from words can hardly be exaggerated. He speaks out of bitter experience of the hurt that can be done by careless, hasty, bitter words, and wishes to persuade all Christian readers to set a constant and careful watch over their mouths.

**3: 3** As though someone had protested that so small a member of the body as the tongue was not likely to exercise such positive influence over the whole body, James introduces three illustrations to show that in certain circumstances something very small can in fact influence decisively something else very much greater. The instances he cites are not original. Other writers had noted them too (e.g. Plutarch and Philo). But nevertheless they effectively make his point. The bit in the horse's mouth is tiny compared with the bulk of the horse itself, yet by it the horse can be controlled and directed. The rudder is insignificantly small compared with the mass of the ship itself, yet the course of the ship in the water is set by the rudder. A tiny spark can kindle a forest-fire which may destroy vast woodlands. So the tongue, only a small part of the body, can cause disasters which overwhelm the whole life.

The two analogies of the bit and the rudder are less exact than that of the spark of fire. The bit and the rudder are used to control, whereas the tongue and the fire are themselves in need of control. But James, at the moment, is seeking to illustrate only that a small cause can produce astonishingly big results.

The word here translated "BITS" comes from the same Greek word as that translated "bridle" in verse 2, and Ropes argues that here also we should translate it as "bridle" rather than "bit". But James speaks of this item of the harness as being "PUT INTO THE MOUTHS OF HORSES", and the part which goes into the mouth is known in English as the "bit". The horses in this context were probably the horses used to draw chariots rather than horses ridden by individual riders. Ropes sees a parallel in the fact that both the bit and the tongue are associated with the mouth: "It is with men as with horses: control their mouths and you are master of all their actions". It is, however, doubtful if this particular point was in James's mind.

**3: 4** Next we are invited: LOOK AT THE SHIPS ALSO. The word translated "LOOK AT" is a favourite one with James. He uses it several times. It is in Greek the same word as that from the teaching of Jesus which used to be translated: "Behold". N.E.B. translating it freely has: "Or *think* of ships". THEY ARE SO GREAT AND ARE DRIVEN BY STRONG WINDS. The Greek word translated as "and" can equally well mean "even", and several translators prefer to take it in this way, as N.E.B. does: "*even* when they are driven by strong gales". The small rudder directs the course of the great hulk of the ship, and even bends the force of the strong winds to carry the ship in the direction the rudder determines. So the ships ARE GUIDED . . . WHEREVER THE WILL OF THE PILOT DIRECTS. The word represented here by "pilot" means the man who handles the helm which turns the rudder. "Helmsman" might be better, since "pilot" can sometimes mean, not so much the helmsman himself, as one whose knowledge of the waters enables him to give advice to the helmsman, on what course to steer his ship. The word translated "will" (*hormē*) probably means "impulse", "wish", or "choice". N.E.B. agrees with R.S.V. in accepting this meaning, though its translation uses different words: "on whatever course the helmsman chooses". Another possible alternative is to take *hormē* as meaning the physical pressure of the helmsman on the helm, which moves the rudder. It would make good enough sense, but it is difficult to be sure that *hormē* could be used with this meaning.

**3: 5** The point of these two illustrations is: SO THE TONGUE IS A LITTLE MEMBER AND BOASTS GREAT THINGS. The words "boasts great things" are a literal translation of the Greek words. Some interpret them to mean (linking it up with the idea that all this is addressed to teachers) that oratory has great power to change lives and affect conduct. But this does not seem to be what James intends. Others link it with the words of Ps. 12: 3: "The tongue makes great boasts". Ropes suggests: "It has a justified though haughty sense of importance". N.E.B. follows this thought and translates: "It can make huge claims" (or, as in the footnote, "is a great boaster").

More probably, however, the word "boast" should be taken less literally, to mean: "What great achievements it can claim". So John Wesley, very sensibly, paraphrases: "hath great influence".

The paragraph is concluded with an analogy of devastating aptness (more appropriate than the examples taken from the bit and the rudder): HOW GREAT A FOREST IS SET ABLAZE BY A SMALL FIRE! The word for "forest" (*hylē*) really means "wood", whether growing live in the forest, or felled and cut and stored in the woodyard. N.E.B. prefers the second sense and translates: "a huge stack of timber", but most keep to "forest". Modern experience of catastrophic forest fires, started perhaps by a picnic fire, or a lighted cigarette end, or even a spark from a locomotive gives striking effect to this closing sally by James. What havoc the tongue can cause!—whether by false teaching in the Church, or by malicious gossip or nasty innuendo. Several of Shakespeare's plays represent latent jealousy being inflamed by poisoned words until murder is the outcome—for instance Othello, Macbeth and Julius Caesar. The tongue indeed is a fire!

3: 6–12. *And the tongue is a fire. The tongue is an unrighteous world among our members, staining the whole body, setting on fire the cycle of nature, and set on fire by hell. 7. For every kind of beast and bird, or reptile and sea creature, can be tamed and has been tamed by humankind. 8. But no human being can tame the tongue—a restless evil, full of deadly poison. 9. With it we bless the Lord and Father, and with it we curse men, who are made in the likeness of God. 10. From the same mouth come blessing and cursing. My brethren, this ought not to be so. 11. Does a spring pour forth from the same opening fresh water and brackish? 12. Can a fig tree, my brethren, yield olives, or a grapevine figs? No more can salt water yield fresh.*

This section continues James's warning in the previous one against the appalling evil the tongue may be responsible for, threatening the peace, security and well-being of a community with the same kind of disaster as a careless fire threatens to a forest parched by drought. For THE TONGUE IS A FIRE. Earlier Biblical writers had used this simile, e.g. Prov. 16: 27 ("his speech is like a scorching fire"), Ps. 120: 3–4; Ecclus. 28: 22. To make his point impressive and memorable James introduces rhetorical and high-sounding figures of speech.

**3: 6** This verse presents many problems. The text is uncertain, the punctuation doubtful, and the meaning of at least two of its important phrases far from clear. Ropes indeed claims that "as the text stands, no satisfactory interpretation is possible", and Windisch describes it as "unintelligible". Ropes is inclined to think that the text is corrupt, and Dibelius concurs in this. The R.V. in its marginal notes indicates what the main textual variants are. These are best studied from commentaries based on the Greek Text, and readers are referred to Mayor and Ropes for a detailed study of the issues, and also for a consideration of the various ways of arranging the punctuation.

For practical purposes we may here be content to accept the form of the text and method of punctuation favoured by the R.S.V. (as also by N.E.B.). Accepting this and expounding it as effectively as we may, we must leave it to readers to decide whether it is fair to describe it as "unintelligible" or "without satisfactory explanation".

The first of the picturesque phrases, which James here uses to gain effect, is that which declares: THE TONGUE IS AN UNRIGHTEOUS WORLD AMONG OUR MEMBERS. There are two points in this verse where we question the adequacy of R.S.V. translation. The verb "is" rather oversimplifies the Greek word, which is not the ordinary verb for "is", but a somewhat elaborate one (*kathistatai*). Ropes suggests for it: "presents itself as"; Hort: "acts the part of"; N.E.B.: "represents". These do more justice to the Greek word which is used.

Moreover the description of the tongue as "*an* unrighteous world" is misleading. The Greek says: "*the* unrighteous world". This is certainly a more accurate translation, and may prove a clue to tracking down the correct meaning of the phrase.

The word translated "world" is in Greek "*kosmos*". Its common meaning in the N.T. is "world" or "universe" (the English word "cosmos" is taken from it). But an earlier meaning of the word was "orderliness", and so "beauty" or "adornment". Indeed it was from the noted "orderliness" of the universe that the word came to mean "universe". Some commentators have asked whether this earlier meaning of "adornment" may not be the one James intended here. It is a use of the word found both in the LXX and in 1 Pet. 3: 3. This would give the translation: "the tongue is the adornment of evil", it is its characteristic function, by fine phrases and rhetorical devices, to dress up evil to make it appear as good, and to make what is really wicked sound pleasant, harmless and even attractive. This would provide a good meaning for the context, but not many are persuaded that James intended to use the word in this particular way.

Throughout the N.T., apart from 1 Pet. 3: 3, the word "*kosmos*" is used to mean "world" or "universe", and usually there is a note of distaste in the use of the word. It means the "world" as it has become, deeply affected with evil and ranged in enmity against God. "The ruler of this world", according to John, is not God but the Devil (12: 31). John also speaks of the "world" as hating Jesus Christ. For Paul too "the wisdom of this world" is something God must destroy (1 Cor. 1: 20), and Christians must be transformed so as not to be "conformed to this world" (Rom. 12: 2). This use of the "world" as evil is found also in James in all other contexts (1: 27; 2: 5; 4: 4).

Here he precisely calls it "the unrighteous world" (in the Greek: "the world of unrighteousness").[1] It is this meaning, as found elsewhere in James, which will probably provide the right meaning for this context also.

Before proceeding to expound the phrase on this basis, however, another possibility must be considered. It is suggested that "*kosmos*" might mean "the sum total" or "the whole gamut" of wickedness.

---

[1] This is rightly translated "unrighteous world" since it is a characteristic of Semitic languages to use the genitive case of a noun, to represent what we indicate by an adjective. N.T. Greek often reflects this Semitic idiom, as here, at Lk. 16: 9 ("Mammon of unrighteousness") and Lk. 18: 6 ("judge of unrighteousness").

That is, there is no wickedness which does not find scope and self-expression through the tongue. The great difficulty about this suggestion is that supporting evidence for such a use of *"kosmos"* cannot be provided.

The most probable interpretation of the phrase, therefore, is to understand *"kosmos"* in the typical Biblical sense, as the sinful world in its enmity against God. "In our microcosm", writes Mayor, "the tongue represents or constitutes the unrighteous world". One might say, it is the very quintessence of the evil world operating within our lives. If our lives are thought of as, by right, God's property, God's rightful Kingdom, then the tongue is the enemy agent within that Kingdom, a ready tool at the disposal of God's enemy, the ruler of this world. Blackman comments: "All the sins in the world are ones in which speech plays a part, the unrighteous world being, as it were, focused in the tongue". AMONG OUR MEMBERS, that is, of all our powers of mind and body, limbs and faculties, the tongue more than any other represents a concentration of the world's evils.

This may seem to be an exaggeration of the evil role of the tongue, but James is seeking to make his readers realize the devastation which this often under-estimated evil can cause, what Phillips calls the "vast potentialities of evil" residing in the tongue.

The evil it does STAINS THE WHOLE BODY (N.E.B. "pollutes our whole being"). Our whole personality is involved in its guilt. Once again we hear a clear echo of words of Jesus. While denying that food we eat can make us unclean in God's eyes, He adds: "What comes out of the mouth, this *defiles* a man" (Matt. 15: 11). The actual word for "defile" is not the same, but the meaning is. The same Greek word, as the one used here, occurred earlier, in its negative form, at 1: 27, where it is said to be the mark of a truly religious man that he keeps himself "unstained from the *world*". There as here it is the "world" which stains and pollutes.

Next the tongue is accused of SETTING ON FIRE THE CYCLE OF NATURE. In a footnote the R.S.V. gives, as a possible alternative, the literal translation of this striking phrase: "the wheel of birth", thus indicating a measure of uncertainty about the accuracy of the translation in the text.

This actual phrase (*ho trochos tēs geneseōs*), with its literal meaning of "the wheel of birth", is found in Greek writings produced by the Pythagorean and Orphic sects to express their characteristic belief in the reincarnation of souls and in the life of man as a long, weary sequence of recurring re-births. It was a gloomy fatalistic creed, and indeed in their writings this phrase is found linked with another which meant "the cycle of necessity" or "the round of fate". Some extreme scholars have tried to establish some kind of link between James and these schools of thought, but this is most unlikely. James, with his "robust doctrine of moral responsibility" (Ropes), would not be likely to view favourably a doctrine which inculcated a kind of fatalism.

What is possible, however, is that even in Palestine (where we now realize that Greek influences were at work far more than once was thought) these catching phrases from Greek schools of thought were having a kind of vogue. Probably they were not accurately understood, and in popular use bore a meaning very different from what was originally intended by them. This phrase for instance in common usage may have come to mean little more than "the whole range of human life" or even "the ups and downs of life" as Dibelius suggests.[1]

Others have found in the phrase a reference to the typically Greek view of life as "cyclical", life bringing back again and again the same set of circumstances as the "wheel of life" revolved. But Christians, as Jews, thought of life as moving forward to a splendid moment of culmination, to a far-off but distinct goal.

James, the Jew become Christian, would not be likely to think of life as a recurring series of pointless events, and still less as a fated sequence of reincarnations. We take it, therefore, that he uses the phrase, not in its technical meaning, but more vaguely, perhaps as he found it in popular usage, to mean: "the whole sphere of human life" or, in the words of the hymns, "all the changing scenes of life". The roundness of the wheel might suggest "the whole sphere", or its movement "the changing scenes".

The word here translated "nature" or, literally, "birth" (Greek *genesis*) is the same as that used in 1 : 23, and translated there by R.S.V. as "natural". See the note at 1 : 23. Basically it meant "birth" but could be used to mean "existence".

The tongue SETS ON FIRE the whole sphere of life. N.E.B. translates: "keeps the wheel of our existence red hot". This suggests that because of the indiscretions of the tongue the whole of our human existence is impossible to handle, inflicting injury on any who try to control it. Phillips offers a vivid, and venturesome rendering: "It can make the whole of life a blazing hell", and this is perhaps not far from the impression James intended to leave.

Phillips's introduction of the word "hell" into the earlier phrase derives justification from James's following phrase that the tongue itself is SET ON FIRE BY HELL. The word translated "hell" is literally "Gehenna". This was the Greek form of the name for a valley outside Jerusalem which was used as a refuse dump. Fires were kept constantly burning there to dispose of rubbish dangerous to health. Very aptly the name came to be used figuratively for the place of punishment

[1] Hort's attempt to derive the reference in this verse to a wheel from Ezek. 1 : 15–21 cannot be regarded as convincing.

in the after life, where those who had led evil and blameworthy lives would receive the due reward of their misdeeds. It occurs in our Lord's teaching, as a place for the punishment of the wicked, in Matt. 5: 22, 29; 18: 9.

In addition to this it appears also to have come to be regarded as the headquarters of Satan and his powers of evil. However it happened, Gehenna, beside being the place of punishment of sinners, came also to be regarded as the stronghold of evil, as it were, the base of operations of Satan himself. So it came to be used almost as a synonym of Satan himself. This appears to be the significance of the word in Matt. 23: 15, where a converted proselyte is said to become "twice as much a child of hell" as his Jewish teachers. This must mean a "child of Satan", that is an agent of the devil (cf. John 8: 44: "You are of your father the devil"). So in this context in James "hell" serves as a kind of synonym for Satan. Men's tongues all too readily yield themselves in his service. One recalls the sharp rebuke of Jesus for Peter, when, having confessed Him as the Christ, he proceeded to try to persuade Jesus that being the Christ did not imply suffering and rejection. His words became the instrument of Satan's beguiling persuasion. It must have been with shocked amazement that he heard his Lord's stinging reproof: "Get behind me, Satan" (Mark 8: 33). All too easily the tongue becomes the agent of evil; it is "set on fire by hell".

**3: 7** EVERY KIND OF BEAST AND BIRD, OF REPTILE AND SEA CREATURE, CAN BE TAMED. Man is able to control every living creature (apart from himself). The word for "KIND" is in Greek "*physis*", which strictly means "nature". It is used again later in the phrase "HUMAN KIND".

The Greek word here translated "can be tamed" literally means simply: "is being tamed", but the R.S.V. translation represents the actual meaning quite well.

The statement clearly refers to the story of the creation of man in Gen. 1: 26, where God said: "Let us make man in our image (*eikōn*), after our likeness (*homoiōsis*); and let him have dominion over the fish, birds, cattle and creeping things" (see also Gen. 1: 28). The Greek word for "have dominion" (*archō*) is different from the one used by James (*damazō*), but the meaning is roughly the same. Indeed the R.S.V. translation of the word *damazō* as "tame" is perhaps misleading. For us to "tame" an animal tends to mean to "domesticate" it, or teach it to obey our will. Many animals have been "tamed", in this sense, to take their place in the life of men, horses, dogs, cattle, elephants, camels, etc. Others can be tamed for circus shows: lions, tigers, sea-lions, snakes, etc. Even in ancient times there were fish which came to be fed at the sound of a bell. The Greek word (*damazō*) while it includes taming of this kind is not limited to this. It would

E

represent also man's power to destroy such animals as threatened human welfare, as well as to compel other animals to submit to domestic service. So N.E.B. renders "subdue", which is nearer to the meaning of the Greek, and also to the passage in Genesis. These creatures can be subdued, and indeed HAVE BEEN SUBDUED BY HUMAN KIND.

**3: 8** BUT NO HUMAN BEING CAN TAME THE TONGUE. Man's power to subdue wild animals so that they will not bring him injury, or to control them so as to make them quietly serve his need, does not extend to his tongue. It is like a demonic power that outmatches human strength. We read in Mark 5: 4 of a demoniac, named Legion, of whom it was written (before he met his master in Jesus): "No one had strength to subdue him". (It is interesting to notice that R.S.V. does use "subdue" to translate the verb *damazō* in that context.) So "no human being can subdue the tongue". It is a RESTLESS EVIL (*akatastaton kakon*).[1]

The same word, *akatastaton*, was used in 1 : 8 and was there translated "unstable". This would fit in with what is said about the tongue in verse 9 and 10, where it is shown to be notoriously "unreliable". The word could equally well indicate something which cannot be "contained" (in the military sense). It slips clear of all restrictions placed upon it. "It is always liable to break out" is the way Phillips translates it, and that gives the meaning well.

In Ps. 140: 3 we read: "Under their lips is the poison of vipers". So James describes the evil tongue: It is FULL OF DEADLY POISON. Poison makes an apt name for the evil effect of hurtful gossip. It spreads an evil atmosphere through the whole of the community, lowering morale, and destroying the character of innocent people who have no means of stopping or answering the whispered slanders. In war time it was found how despondent words could spread defeatism in a hard-pressed community. So in peace-time, depressed words of cynical detraction about, for instance, a church or a communal enterprise, can spread a poison of unbelief and lack of confidence, for which it is very difficult to find an adequate antidote, so subtly does the poison spread, and so widespread can become its effect.

**3: 9** So far it has been the *evil* effects of the tongue on which James has concentrated. Other Biblical writers note also its immense powers for good, and comment on the curious blend of good and evil achieved by it. Now James too concedes that it can "bless" as well as "curse", but even the "blessing" becomes almost an added evil, since it is so grossly inconsistent with the cursing that quickly follows—from the same tongue. In fact the acknowledgement of its words of "blessing"

---

[1] Some MSS have an alternative reading, *akatascheton*, which means "uncontrollable". There are strong MSS supporting it (C K L 33 and Syr. Sin.), though the other reading is still more strongly supported. The meaning fits the context well, in fact a little too well. On the principle that the harder reading is more likely to be correct, the one in the text is to be preferred.

amounts almost to an added accusation of bland hypocrisy. With the tongue WE BLESS THE LORD AND FATHER AND WITH IT WE CURSE MEN.

James uses "we", as elsewhere, not because he feels himself personally to be involved in this evil, but because the Christians he addresses are guilty of it, and he identifies himself with the community to which he administers his rebuke. This is a wise practice for any pastor who has to remonstrate with his people, to use "we" rather than "you" when there are hard things to be said. WE BLESS THE LORD: it was a Jewish practice (adopted also by Christians), whenever the name of God was mentioned, to add, out of reverence, the words: "Blessed be He". Echoes of this usage can be heard in Paul's writings at Rom. 1 : 25; 9 : 5, 2 Cor. 11 : 31. The famous eighteen prayers of the devout Jew each began: "Blessed be Thou, O God", and this formula was taken over by Christians, as at Eph. 1 : 3 and 1 Pet. 1 : 3.

THE LORD AND FATHER. This precise phrase is not met elsewhere in the N.T., though at 1 : 27 James refers to "the God and Father". Also in Matt. 11 : 25 our Lord combines the two names in a prayer: "Father, Lord of heaven and earth". The twofold phrase must represent a single reference to God. Perhaps James felt that "Lord" represented the truth about God derived from his Jewish upbringing, and "Father" the truth specially associated with his new insights as a Christian. Jesus is referred to as "Lord" at 2 : 1, but it is unlikely that the word refers to Jesus here. For comment on the name of "Father" as used for God see 1 : 27. The contrast between blessing God in one breath and then offending Him by cursing a fellow man reminds us of Luke 6 : 46 ("Why do you call me Lord, Lord, and not do what I tell you?").

The same tongue that piously utters reverent words of blessing upon God is that with which WE CURSE MEN. Cursing men is out of place in a Christian, even apart from the incongruity of combining cursing with blessing. Jesus told us even to "bless those who curse you" (Luke 6 : 28), and Paul reiterates it: "Bless those who persecute you; bless and curse not" (Rom. 12 : 14). "Cursing" may mean speaking words of abuse either to a person or about him; it may also mean uttering words which are believed to have potency to inflict injury on him. Here it probably refers primarily to angry words of abuse spoken to those whom we regard as subordinate to us, as well as bitter denunciation (in their absence) of others whom we do not care to criticize to their face. James protests about the careless inconsistency with which some Christians address words of praise to God in their worship, words of penitence and promised obedience and then, after sometimes only the shortest of intervals, that same tongue is pouring out words of bitter dislike and ill-will towards some one or other of our fellow men, our brothers, God's other children. Commentators note here the parallel to Peter's failure: he was at first so strong in his protestations of enduring loyalty to His Lord (Matt. 26: 33), and then so violent in denials and curses, when, only a little later, accused of such loyalty to Christ (Matt. 26: 69–75).

The sin of calling down curses on our fellow men is all the more deplorable since THEY ARE MADE IN THE LIKENESS OF GOD. The phrase is borrowed from Gen. 1: 26, a striking phrase which seeks to indicate the uniqueness of man among God's creatures, bearing a relationship to God closer than that of any other created being. It is man's near-ness (and even original likeness) to God, which makes the cursing of him a still greater offence to God who made him. Indeed God's care for His creature man led Jesus, after saying that the first commandment is to love God, to say that the second is *like unto it*, that is to love our neighbour as ourself. To obey the first of these commands in words, and in words to disobey the second, which is *like unto the first*, is gross inconsistency of conduct.

Man was at first made "in the likeness of God", but sin has dis-figured that likeness beyond recognition, almost indeed beyond repair, apart from Christ. Only in Christ Himself is that likeness of God unspoiled and clearly recognizable (2 Cor. 4: 4; Col. 1: 15: Heb. 1: 3). In Christ man can sense the kind of person God meant him to be. Seeing the true image, he comes to long for something of the broken image in himself to be repaired and restored. In Christ he finds the inspiration and the enabling power by which he can be renewed in the likeness of the image of his creator (Col. 3: 10).

James here speaks as though the image of God in man had not been completely obliterated; and indeed there is evidence of real goodness in man, as well as of gross evil. John Wesley here comments on this point: "Indeed we have now lost the likeness", but he feels compelled to add: "Yet there remains from thence an indelible nobleness, which we ought to reverence in ourselves and others". Certainly that defaced likeness of God in man is more likely to be restored by treatment which respects him as a child of God, than by ill-tempered criticism expressing itself in bitter curses.

**3: 10–12** James protests how unnatural it is for that which is bitter and offensive to come from the same source which produces what is sweet and pleasant. FROM THE SAME MOUTH COME BLESSING AND CURSING. Others before James had commented on the same incongruity. "Glory and dishonour come from speaking" (Ecclus. 5: 13). "If you blow a spark, it will glow; if you spit on it, it will be put out; and both come out of your mouth" (Ecclus. 28: 12). "Death and life are in the power of the tongue" (Prov. 18: 21). THIS OUGHT NOT TO BE. It is inappropriate and unbecoming. It is a sign that something serious is wrong—as if a tap which one moment runs with clean sweet water, good to drink, the next moment pours out filth from the drains.

James similarly asks: DOES A SPRING POUR FORTH FROM THE SAME OPENING FRESH WATER AND BRACKISH? "Brackish" water is strictly something between salt water and clear drinking water. The word James uses literally means "bitter". It is the kind of water which would make us sick if we tried to drink it. Yet the human mouth can be like that, sometimes producing what is sweet and pleasant, and then what is offensive and sickening: pious adoration of God one moment, and bitter curses of man the next.

The next illustrations are not quite so effective. Perhaps James has abbreviated them too much. He writes: CAN A FIG TREE YIELD OLIVES? OR A GRAPEVINE FIGS? A closer parallel to what he has complained about the mouth would be to say: What if a fig tree produced figs on one branch, and thistle tops on another? or figs one year and thistle tops the next? (cf. Matt. 7: 16). In nature each tree is true to itself. It produces what it is meant to produce, not now one thing, now another, without any consistency. But not so the human tongue. Sometimes, true to its origin and loyal to its creator, it can offer praises to God, and then, treacherous and rebellious, it yields itself up as an accomplice of God's enemy, and pronounces curses on man.

NO MORE SHALL SALT WATER YIELD FRESH. A fresh water lake can be relied on to contain fresh water, and a salt lake salt water (like the Dead Sea). But with the human tongue, fickle and unreliable, it is now one thing, now another.

3: 13–18. *Who is wise and understanding among you? By his good life let him show his works in the meekness of wisdom. 14. But if you have bitter jealousy and selfish ambition in your hearts do not boast and be false to the truth. 15. This wisdom is not such as comes down from above, but is earthly, unspiritual, devilish. 16. For where jealousy and selfish ambition exist, there will be disorder and every vile practice. 17. But the wisdom from above is first pure, then peaceable, gentle, open to reason, full of mercy and good fruits, without uncertainty or insincerity. 18. And the harvest of righteousness is sown in peace by those who make peace.*

This section describes the qualities of true Christian wisdom as distinguished from "the wisdom of this world".

We continue to treat this paragraph as addressed to all readers, though some commentators attach it closely to the opening verse of the chapter and interpret it as addressed in a special way to "teachers" or prospective teachers. They point out that there is a special propriety in associating the words "wise and understanding" (3: 13) with teachers. This may be true, but there is nothing in the paragraph which may not apply equally to Christians other than teachers.

**3: 13** James likes to use the device of the rhetorical question to introduce a new topic. At 2: 14 he asks: "What does it profit, my brethren, . . .?" at 4: 1: "Whence come wars . . .?" at 5: 13: "Is any among you suffering . . .?" So here he approaches his discussion of wisdom with the question: WHO IS WISE AND UNDERSTANDING AMONG YOU?

Some have suggested that James acquired this mannerism by imitating it, as he found it in the characteristic style of the diatribe, as used by Epictetus, for instance, and other Greek philosophical writers of that time. But the rhetorical question was not the monopoly of these writers. It is found also in Biblical writers of both the O.T. and the N.T. (e.g. Luke 11: 11; Rom. 11: 1–7; Prov. 8: 1; 23: 29; Isa. 50: 10). Sometimes, indeed, it is little more than a striking variant for the protasis of a conditional clause, as for instance in Ps. 34: 12. So here the same meaning could be expressed: "If anyone is wise . . . let him show his works".

In the Bible the word "wise" (*sophos*) described someone who has moral insight and skill in advising on practical issues of conduct rather than an academic knowledge of theoretical problems and their solution (cf. the earlier note on "wisdom" at 1: 5, and 1 Kings 3: 9 where Solomon's wisdom is understood to mean a power to "discern between good and evil"). It may, however, be part of James's complaint here that his readers are tending to be content with achievements in a more abstract form of knowledge such as the Greeks called "wisdom". "UNDERSTANDING" (Greek *epistēmōn*) is rendered by N.E.B. as "clever". This may represent a rather stronger emphasis on intellectual perception than on moral insight, but, in fact, these two words, "wise and understanding", are probably here used largely as synonyms to support each other (as in the LXX version of Deut. 1: 13, 15; 4: 6, etc.), rather than as distinct ideas.

James proceeds to insist that true wisdom and understanding are not to be identified with a merely intellectual cleverness. Their genuineness is proved by the quality of conduct which they produce. Just as "faith" (or what claims to be "faith") is proved not to be real faith, unless it issues in "good works" of mercy and love, so wisdom is shown to be sham and unreal unless it also leads to a good life expressed in good works. He issues his challenge to any who cherish a reputation for wisdom: "BY HIS GOOD LIFE LET HIM SHOW HIS WORKS".

The word here translated "LIFE" (*anastrophē*), not used elsewhere by James, means "life", not in the sense of "being alive" but of "conduct". Indeed where the same word occurs in 1 Pet. 1: 15 and

2: 12 R.S.V. translates it as "conduct", and in 1 Pet. 3: 1, 2, 16 as "behaviour", and in Eph. 4: 22 as "manner of life".

The word "SHOW" was also used in 2: 18, where "faith" is called upon to "show" (i.e. prove) itself by its deeds. So here wisdom is challenged to demonstrate its "WORKS", i.e. what it can do, by producing a mode of life, good in itself and of benefit to the community. A claim to wisdom which is not substantiated by good conduct is as empty as a claim to faith without good works to prove it.

James, however, hastens to make clear that he does not expect a wise man to call attention to his good conduct. Ostentation and self-display, which Jesus criticized in the Pharisees (Matt. 23: 5), is no part of wisdom. Certain things, such as ill temper and vindictiveness, for instance, prove the absence of true wisdom (just as goodwill and patience indicate its presence), and any kind of showmanship in a man, calling attention to his own good qualities, would equally demonstrate an absence of wisdom. True goodness is goodness without priggishness, goodness which is characterized by THE MEEKNESS OF WISDOM, i.e. the meekness appropriate to wisdom, and which true wisdom produces.

The meaning of "MEEKNESS" was discussed at 1: 21. It is a quality of character for which the Greeks had little regard; they equated it with weakness and lack of spirit. Our Lord, however, pronounced it one of the essential qualities of the man of God. He spoke of Himself as "meek and lowly" (Matt. 11: 29); the Gospel writers applied the word to Him through an O.T. quotation (Matt. 21: 5), and Paul appealed to it as a well known characteristic of Jesus (2 Cor. 10: 1). It is also one of the qualities of life which Christ pronounced "Blessed" (Matt. 5: 5). Here it means the complete opposite of arrogance, self-importance and self-assertion. It means "unobtrusive, self-effacing goodness". N.E.B. translates as "modesty". Meekness also implies the antithesis of resentment and the spirit of retaliation, and this meaning also is prominent here, since meekness is contrasted not only with "selfish ambition" but also with "jealousy".

Apparently among the Christians whom James knew were some who claimed to be "wise", or aspired to be thought so, who gave no evidence of "wisdom-ruled" lives, but rather of lives dominated by undisciplined human cravings and impulse, what James calls BITTER JEALOUSY AND SELFISH AMBITION.

**3: 14** The word translated "jealousy" (*zēlos*) does not necessarily, in all contexts, carry this bad meaning. It can mean "zeal" as Paul uses it of his fellow Jews in Rom. 10: 2: "They have a zeal for God, but it is not enlightened". It is a quality commended in Elijah (1 Kings 19: 10, 14; Ecclus. 48: 2). In the N.T., however, the bad meaning of the word predominates, and when it is used it usually appears in bad company. It stands, for instance, in the list of the "works of the flesh" in Gal. 5: 20, and also in a list of evil things which disfigure human life in 2 Cor. 12: 20. In modern translations it is variously rendered as "jealousy", "envy" or "rivalry".

Some take it here primarily in its religious sense of a zeal which has become extreme and fanatical, leading to bitter and relentless hostility to all who do not share every item of the zealous man's beliefs. Evil is so subtly clever in our human lives that a zeal for God and His Kingdom can all too easily become perverted into a venomous antagonism to all who do not express their love for God in precisely the same way as ourselves. So zeal for God can be distorted into strong personal dislike for others, who are different from ourselves, and jealousy and rivalry towards them.

Those who link these verses closely with the reference to teachers in 3: 1 point out that it is a common frailty of human nature for teachers in the same community to be affected by jealousy of each other, and religious teachers are not immune. In fact theological disputes have in the past so often stirred up such violent ill-will and bitterness that the phrase "odium theologicum" has, sadly enough, become almost proverbial. If we feel very deeply about the importance of a cause we believe in, it is very easy for the power of evil to pervert that deep feeling into channels of personal feeling against its opponents.

On the other hand, jealousy and rivalry are not the monopoly either of religious enthusiasts or teachers. What James has to say here is applicable to all Christians. Bitter feelings towards those who are potentially our rivals, whether in advancement or achievement, or popularity, is one of the commonest signs of human frailty. Such bitter feelings are usually rationalized by being attached to faults, real or imaginary, in the other person. There is, perhaps, no greater sign of the effective power of the grace of God in any community than when members of it live happily together, enjoying each other's company, appreciating each other's good qualities, and entirely free from "bitter jealousy". The Latin versions usually rendered this word by "aemulatio", that is, "emulation", with its longing to outdo the resented rival, to begrudge all his successes, and to add humiliation to his failures. Calvin in his commentary refers to "minds so infected with the power of malignity that they turn all things into bitterness" (p. 325).

With "bitter jealousy" goes "SELFISH AMBITION". In Greek this is a single word, *eritheia*. K.J.V. translates it as "strife", R.V. as "faction", Calvin suggested "quarrels", and no doubt something of this feeling of ill-will attaches to it. N.E.B., however, agrees with R.S.V. in the translation "selfish ambition". The meaning is clearly near to that of "jealousy", because the two words stand side by side, not only here, but also among the "works of the flesh" in Gal. 5: 20, and in the similar list in 2 Cor. 12: 20. It has been described as "the vice of the party leader, partly ambition, partly rivalry". Ropes writes that it is "the inclination to use unworthy and divisive means for promoting one's own views and interests". It is the determination to get what one wants in position and power, no matter what bitterness and ill-will are caused.

Jealousy and selfish ambition are strong, driving forces IN OUR HEARTS. They themselves do not take visible shape, but their fierce and tireless energies drive men into conduct which is arrogant and divisive. It is just these things, lurking hidden within the heart, but emerging in ugly word and act, which defile a man before God (Mark 7: 21). The meaning of the word "heart" has already been referred to at 1 : 26, and the word occurs again at 4: 8; 5: 5, 8. In the N.T. the Greek word derives much of its significance from its Hebrew antecedents in the O.T. In English usage it tends to be associated mainly with the emotional elements in our lives, but in the Bible it includes thought and will, as well as feeling. It represents "the seat of man's collective energies, the focus of personal life, the seat of the rational as well as the emotional and volitional elements in human life" (Abbott-Smith, p. 230).[1]

DO NOT BOAST: No matter how wise these people whom James rebukes may appear by certain standards, the presence in their hearts of jealousy and rivalry proves that whatever their so-called wisdom really is, it is not true Christian wisdom. As Christians therefore they have nothing to boast of, or be proud of, but rather much to be ashamed of. The same word for "boast" is used at 2:13 (as also at Rom. 11: 18). A claim to wisdom in such circumstances is discounted as "FALSE TO THE TRUTH" (N.E.B., "a defiance of the truth").

The actual Greek phrase literally means "*against* the truth", and may be attached to the verb "boast" as well as "be false".

TRUTH (already commented on at 1 : 8, and occurring again at 5: 19) is in the Bible much more than an intellectual concept. Its content is rather moral and spiritual. Sometimes in the N.T. it is equated with "the content of Christianity as the absolute truth" (as appears to be the case at 1 : 18 and 5: 19). It may, however, also mean "reality as opposed to appearance",[2] and in this present context this appears to be the predominant meaning. It is interesting to note that Paul too (in Rom. 2: 8) associates those who are guilty of selfish ambition (*eritheia*) with defiance of the truth, "they do not obey the truth".

**3: 15** THIS WISDOM (so-called) which exists side by side with jealousy and selfish ambition, which perhaps even gives rise to them, is certainly not wisdom bestowed by God. It is merely "human" wisdom.

---

[1] Cf. also Arndt and Gingrich who define "heart" in the N.T. as "the centre and source of the whole inner life with its thinking, feeling, and volition", p. 404.

[2] Arndt and Gingrich, p. 35.

Paul makes this same distinction between the two kinds of wisdom when he writes to the Corinthians. There too the context is one in which the apostle is having to rebuke quarrelling between members of the Church, who are divided from each other by a partisan preference for different human leaders. They claim to be "wise", but since their wisdom leads to ill-feeling and bitter rivalry it is not God's wisdom, he declares. He describes it variously as "human wisdom" (1 Cor. 2: 13) or "the wisdom of men" (1 Cor. 2: 5), "the wisdom of the world" (1 Cor. 1: 20), "wisdom of this age" (1 Cor. 2: 6), or "wisdom according to worldly standards" (1 Cor. 1: 26). Opposed to this is the "wisdom of God" (1 Cor. 1: 21), a wisdom "taught by the Spirit" (1 Cor. 2: 13), a wisdom which is pre-eminently disclosed in Jesus Christ. God made Him "our wisdom" (1 Cor. 1: 30). He is "the wisdom of God" (1 Cor. 1: 24; 2: 6). The wisdom of the world is here associated with cleverness and "plausible words" (1 Cor. 2: 4) as well as with strife and jealousy (1 Cor. 3: 3). God's wisdom, on the contrary, implies the subordination of self to the common good, and to the way of the Cross, which is self-denial (Mark 8: 34)—"leaving self behind" as N.E.B. translates it. This is the way which, in a community, leads to peace and co-operation, mutual appreciation and love. This "wisdom of God", to the worldly wise, looks foolish. But then too "the wisdom of the world is folly with God" (1 Cor. 3: 19).

Clearly what Paul writes to the Corinthians has much in common with this verse in James. He too asserts emphatically that this "worldly wisdom" is very different from God's wisdom; it is NOT SUCH AS COMES DOWN FROM ABOVE. This is simply a Jewish way of denying that it comes from God, without precisely using the name of God (cf. 1: 17, and John 3: 3, 7, 31; 19: 11).

It is EARTHLY, N.E.B. "earthbound", with no horizon beyond the bounds of this earth, no appreciation of values which do not lead to advantages here on earth (cf. Phil. 3: 19; Col. 3: 2). Or the word may aim at emphasizing the origin of this wisdom, as derived only from man-made cleverness. "It comes from this world" (J. B. Phillips). It is also UNSPIRITUAL (Greek *psychikē*). The word is used here as Paul used it, in contrast to "spiritual" (*pneumatikos*), to mean a "natural" man, in the sense of one who has not been awakened to the truth of God in Christ, who does not know the renewing power of God's Spirit. Paul used it in the context of 1 Corinthians, where he discusses the different kinds of wisdom, to describe the man who is content with "worldly wisdom" (1 Cor. 2: 14), who, being "unspiritual", does not receive the gifts of the Spirit of God (cf. also 1 Cor. 15: 44–46). N.E.B. translates it as "sensual" and Moffatt as "sensuous". This wordly wisdom is also DEVILISH (*daimoniōdēs*). The precise form of the word does not occur elsewhere in the N.T., but it is derived from the common word *"daimonion"* (demon or evil spirit). Ropes writes that it means "resembling or proceeding from an evil spirit". John Wesley interprets it to mean: "Such as Satan breathes into the soul". Paul too associated this "human wisdom" with "the rulers of this age" (1 Cor. 2: 8), by which he meant the demonic powers which now tyrannize over this world.

C. K. Williams in "The New Testament in Plain English" translates the three words succinctly and effectively: "earthly, animal, devilish", making the words represent an ascending scale of wickedness.

**3: 16** FOR WHERE JEALOUSY AND SELFISH AMBITION EXIST, there we see clear evidence of unredeemed human nature at work, and devilish influences in control, seeking to further their own ends. The evil consequences of jealousy and selfish ambition are DISORDER AND EVERY VILE PRACTICE. The Greek word for DISORDER is *akatastasia*, which is the noun associated with the adjective (*akatastatos*), translated as "unstable" at 1: 8 and as "restless" at 3: 8. R.S.V. translates the same word in 1 Cor. 14: 33 as "confusion". This word also is found in the list of evil things in 2 Cor. 12: 20, along with "jealousy" and "selfish ambition". True wisdom, as God gives it, has the effect of drawing people together and building them up into a stable and enduring society. But earthly wisdom separates them in rivalry and antagonism, and produces "disorder" or "disharmony". In such circumstances where disharmony exists, created by jealousy and rivalry, EVERY VILE PRACTICE battens and thrives. Under the stress and strain of such lack of stability, all the controls that normally hold human wickedness in check are loosened, and "evil of every kind" (as N.E.B. translates) breaks out.

**3: 17** In contrast we now turn to THE WISDOM FROM ABOVE, God's gift to His people. For a discussion of "wisdom" see 1: 5. This kind of wisdom it is not in man's power to achieve by his own endeavours and devices. The wisdom of this world he may acquire by his own wit and perseverance. But God's wisdom comes only as God's gift, to be received humbly and gratefully. "God has revealed it to us through the Spirit", declared Paul (1 Cor. 2: 10). Its only source is in God, a truth emphasized also by the Wisdom writers of the O.T. "The Lord gives wisdom" says the writer of Proverbs (at 2: 6; cf. 8: 22–31). "Wisdom is the breath of the power of God" (Wisd. of Sol. 7: 25, cf. 9: 4, 9f.). "All wisdom comes from the Lord" (Ecclus. 1: 1, cf. 24: 3). In 1 Kings 3: 5 and 9 it is clearly stated that Solomon's wisdom came to him only as a gift from God.

This true Wisdom, which only God can bestow on man, is now described in a sequence of lovely words. Similar lists are found in the "fruit of the Spirit" in Gal. 5: 22, in the characterization of Christian love (*agapē*) in 1 Cor. 13: 4–7, in the words which portray the "new nature" in Col. 3: 12ff. Not unexpectedly there are many similarities between these lists, since they all describe qualities awakened in the life of the Christian by the renewing touch of God, through His Spirit, through His love, through His gift of Wisdom, through the power of the Living Christ. They are indeed the qualities of Christ Himself who is the Wisdom of God (1 Cor. 1: 24), who is the Love of God incarnate, who is under God the lifegiving Spirit, the Second Adam, the New Man (1 Cor. 15: 45–47).

God's wisdom as bestowed on man reveals itself in conduct which is PURE (*hagnē*). This means that it is free from self-interest and selfish ambition. It is single-minded (Matt. 6: 22, Luke 11: 34; cf. Acts 2: 46, Eph. 6: 5, Col. 3: 22), though the Greek word is not the same. It means that one who claims to be serving God is wholly serving Him and not, at the same time, seeking to further some private interest of his own; if he aims to render some service to his fellow man, he does so without ulterior thoughts of the praise and approval that will come to him as a result. He is not "double-minded", to use James's own word from 1: 7.

The second characteristic of true wisdom is that he who has it is PEACEABLE. Worldly wisdom, as we have seen, makes for contention and strife. It divides and alienates. True wisdom conciliates and unites. It is peace-loving, it promotes peace. This means that it is not just inoffensive, but it is also actively peace-making (a quality commended by our Lord in Matt. 5: 9). This means that it is active in seeking to remove all causes of ill-will, and to bring into being circumstances that favour harmonious co-operation. It not only patches up quarrels, but sees in advance the possible causes of quarrels and seeks to remove them before they become the occasion of strife.

It is also GENTLE (*epieikēs*). Translators vary very much in their choice of an English word to represent this Greek word. Calvin suggested "humane", as a suitable word to describe that quality which is "far away from that immoderate austerity which tolerates nothing in our brethren". Others suggest: considerate, reasonable, forbearing, forgiving. Barclay seeks to determine its meaning from a definition found in Aristotle: "The man who is *epieikēs* is the man who knows when it is actually wrong to apply the strict letter of the law". He does not stand on his own rights, he is forgiving and merciful. In 2 Cor. 10: 1 it is combined with meekness as a recognized characteristic of Christ.

OPEN TO REASON (*eupeithēs*) is a word which does not occur elsewhere in the N.T. It could mean "ready to obey", and so eagerly obedient to God; but more probably here it carries the meaning of "easy to persuade". As such it describes a character which is the opposite of stubborn, self-opinionated, impervious to persuasion or appeal. Other translators have used for it "amenable", "conciliatory".

FULL OF MERCY means compassionate to those in trouble, even if their trouble is of their own foolish making. Mercy is one of the qualities of God Himself (see Ps. 86: 5; 100: 5; etc.). According to Jesus, it is also what God most of all looks for in men (see Matt. 9: 13; 12: 7; 23: 23). The practice of it was precisely commanded by Jesus (Luke 10: 37). See note at 2: 13.

It is also FULL OF GOOD FRUITS, and it is by their fruits that we determine the real quality of both trees and men (Matt. 7: 17–20). The Holy Spirit in man bears rich fruit (Gal. 5: 22), and so too does the wisdom which God bestows, "the wisdom that is from above". Good fruits here mean deeds of practical usefulness to others in their need, deeds prompted by mercy and compassion. The emphasis on deeds reaffirms that mercy, to be real mercy, does not consist of nice feelings and tender sympathy over other people's troubles. It also leads on to good fruits, to practical action for their relief.

The next word (adiakritos—R.S.V. "without uncertainty") is more difficult to define. It does not occur elsewhere in the N.T., and so there is no other context to help us to determine its meaning. Moffatt suggests "unambiguous", and N.E.B. "straightforward". Barclay says it is the opposite of "wavering, hesitant, vacillating". It means "to choose one's course and continue in it". Whatever such a man undertakes he does wholeheartedly. None of these, however, is particularly appropriate in this context. A second alternative, more suitable to the context, therefore has its appeal. The verb, from which this adjective is derived, is diakrinō. It is the word used in Acts 11: 12. There Peter is giving an account of his vision at Joppa to the Christian leaders at Jerusalem, in consequence of which he felt assured by God that Gentiles as well as Jews must be allowed to hear and accept the Gospel. In consequence of the vision, he says that he went into a Gentile house and shared its hospitality, "making no distinction" (diakrinō). That is how the R.V. translated it. It is true that R.S.V. abandons this and translates Acts 11: 12: "The Spirit told me to go with them, without hesitation". N.E.B., however, recognizes in a footnote the possibility of translating as R.V.: "making no distinctions". Blackman favours this meaning for the word adiakritos in this context in James, and translates "without partiality". Such a meaning suits what we know of James. He has already insisted on the need for "no partiality" at 2: 1. Phillips agrees with Blackman and suggests: "with no breath of favouritism". This meaning seems the better one in this context.

WITHOUT INSINCERITY translates the Greek word anhypokritos, which literally means "without hypocrisy", and so "sincere", "without affectation", "free from posing or attempting to make a good impression". It is the word Paul uses at Rom. 12: 9 when he pleads: "Let love be *genuine*" (cf. also 2 Cor. 6: 6; 1 Pet. 1: 22, where it is also used to describe true Christian love).

**3: 18** THE HARVEST OF RIGHTEOUSNESS IS SOWN IN PEACE. This verse presents a problem of interpretation. The key words in it are the two words, RIGHTEOUSNESS and PEACE. They are frequently associated in the Bible. Both righteousness and peace are God's will for His people, and when both are present they represent the fulness of His bounty. "Righteousness and peace will kiss each other", declared the Psalmist (85: 10), as he interpreted what he understood as the meaning of God's salvation and His glory.

Usually the relationship of the two is understood as one of base and superstructure, or seed and fruit, righteousness being the cause, and peace the effect which results from it. Isaiah expresses this with perfect clarity: "The effect of righteousness will be peace, and the result of righteousness quietness and trust for ever" (Isa. 32: 17). In a community it is only when fair dealing prevails, and legitimate grievances are quickly remedied that peace can be maintained. Within the human heart also true and lasting peace can only be built upon a foundation of righteousness, that is, obedience to the known will of God. Probably this thought lies behind the phrase in Heb. 12: 11, "the peaceable fruit of righteousness".

On the basis of this clear understanding of the relationship between righteousness and peace, one might assume that what James was aiming to say in this verse would be: "Peace is the harvest which grows when righteousness is sown. Righteousness is the seed which is sown by those who make peace". It is just possible that James does here mean something like that, but probability is in fact against it. James appears rather to reverse the usual relationship and to declare that peace is the pre-requisite of righteousness.

The link between this verse and the preceding verses is clearly the idea of "peace". Worldly wisdom, James has insisted, leads to strife and disorder; heavenly wisdom brings peace and harmony. So this further saying about peace follows. Blackman argues that originally it was an isolated aphorism, which came to be attached to the preceding verse because both dealt with the thought of "peace". Whether this is so or not, it must be admitted that apart from the word "peace" there is no obvious continuity of thought between verses 17 and 18.

The phrase "THE HARVEST OF RIGHTEOUSNESS" (literally "the fruit of righteousness") may be interpreted in two ways. (a) If "of righteousness" is a genitive of origin, then it means the "fruit which grows from righteousness" (as in the similar phrase, "the fruit of the Spirit" in Gal. 5: 22). (b). If on the other hand this genitive case is one of "definition", then the phrase means "the fruit which consists of righteousness" (just as we may say "the city of London" meaning the city which is London), and reference to the seed which produces the fruit must be sought elsewhere. Interpretation (a) is better suited to the relationship between righteousness and peace so clearly defined in Isa. 32: 17, but (b) seems to fit in better with the rest of the verse, and also falls into line with the thought also expressed in Jas. 1: 20. There we read that "the anger of man does not work the righteousness of God", the corollary of which might be that when man has a quiet mind and composed spirit he may be able to achieve righteousness. In that case peacemakers and the peace they produce may be regarded as the needed condition in which righteousness may flourish.

Rather oddly, James writes that this harvest IS SOWN. Strictly speaking, of course, it is seed which is sown, and the harvest is reaped and gathered. It must be that here the phrase is used loosely. We sometimes do this with the word "crop". This means the yield of a field which has been sown with seed, but carelessly sometimes people may speak of a crop as having been sown. It is inaccurate, but we know what it means—"the seed, which will produce the later crop, has been sown".

The seed which will produce righteousness as its harvest is sown IN PEACE, that is in an atmosphere of solid friendship and goodwill. So John Wesley comments: "The principle productive of this righteousness is sown, like good seed, in the peace of a believer's mind, and yields a plentiful harvest of happiness (the fruit of righteousness) for them that make peace—that labour to produce this holy peace among all men". Wesley interprets these words as applying primarily to the inner experience of the individual Christian so that peace becomes "peace of mind". We should not wish to exclude this as part of the meaning of James, but the main emphasis seems to be on peace within a community, which has been disturbed by jealousy and rivalry. If, of course, verse 18 is treated as independent of the verses preceding, it could be argued that Wesley's individualistic interpretation is the one James intended.

The R.S.V. translates as though the phrase "in peace" belongs closely to the verb "is sown", and this is probably correct. But it stands, in the Greek, before the verb and it may be argued that it should be attached to the preceding phrase "the harvest of righteousness". In this case we could translate: "the harvest of righteousness which consists of peace". This would favour the interpretation (a) above. This translation is just possible but the Greek words would have to be somewhat forced to produce it, or else we should have to assume that James here expressed himself rather carelessly.

BY THOSE WHO MAKE PEACE: This also is an ambiguous phrase. In Greek it stands in the dative case, and its normal meaning would be "*for* those who make peace" (as in R.V.). Occasionally, however, though it is a departure from normal practice, a dative of the person can be translated as if it were an agent, and so here could mean "*by* those who make peace". Hort objects to this explanation writing that the phrase does "not denote pure agency, but also what redounds *to* them". Blackman, on the other hand, while conceding that a dative of advantage is more normal Greek, adds: "We prefer to take it as a dative of the agent after a passive verb".[1]

Those who MAKE PEACE, "the peacemakers" are commended by our Lord in His Beatitudes (Matt. 5: 9), and Christ Himself is described as the great Peacemaker in Eph. 2: 15 and Col. 1: 20.

If, then, (i) "the fruit of righteousness" means "the product which consists of righteousness", and (ii) if "in peace" can be understood as attached to "is sown", and (iii) if the dative "for those who make peace" can here be understood to mean "*by* those who make peace", then the meaning of the sentence is that peace is a field or a garden plot where peacemakers sow their actions (of meekness and unselfish consideration for others), and the fruit which grows from such seed is righteousness. Barclay appears to favour some such interpretation as this and adds the comment: "Nothing good can ever grow in an atmosphere where we are at variance with each other". This is undoubtedly true: where the atmosphere is poisoned by ill-will and jealous strife, it is cruelly difficult for anyone, even with the best intentions, to keep his mind clear and his judgement unclouded, and his feelings unaffected by the prevailing bitterness and resentment. His best attempts to be fair to all parties are defeated. Where, however, happy personal relationships exist, it is correspondingly easy to be fair and honourable in our dealings with each other.

It is probable therefore that this is the interpretation to be accepted here. R.S.V. translation seems to favour this, and so does N.E.B.: "True justice is the harvest reaped by peacemakers from seeds sown in a spirit of peace".

If, however, "the fruit of righteousness in peace" could mean "the fruit of righteousness which consists in peace" (i.e. peace which is the product of righteousness), then the meaning might just possibly be: "Peace is a harvest which grows where righteousness is sown, and peacemakers enjoy its benefits".

[1] An instance of such a dative of the agent is found at Luke 23: 15, "Nothing deserving of death has been done *by* him". "By him" in the Greek is a simple dative. Jas. 3: 7 may also be quoted, since "by humankind" represents a Greek dative.

# CHAPTER FOUR

**4: 1–3:** *What causes wars, and what causes fightings among you? Is it not your passions that are at war in your members? 2. You desire and do not have; so you kill. And you covet and cannot obtain; so you fight and wage war. You do not have, because you do not ask. 3. You ask and do not receive, because you ask wrongly, to spend it on your passions.*

These verses are a sharp exposure of those impulses and attitudes in human life which inevitably cause strife and unrest in the community.

The reference to "peace" in the preceding verse suggests this consideration of elements in human nature which so easily and often disrupt peace, and lead to lasting feuds and painful quarrels.

**4: 1** Characteristically James introduces this new section with a question, which he proceeds to answer himself: WHAT CAUSES WARS, AND WHAT CAUSES FIGHTINGS AMONG YOU? This is a question which has concerned moralists at all times. Ropes cites from Philo, De Gig. 11, the following passage: "Consider the continual war which prevails among men even in time of peace, and which exists not merely between nations and countries and cities, but between private houses, or, I might rather say, is present in every individual man; observe the unspeakable raging storm in men's souls".

This quotation serves to show, not only that others besides James in these ancient times were asking this same question which so fills the thoughts of modern sociologists, but also makes it clear that the word "war" (*polemos*), besides meaning war between nations, can also be used of feuds and vendettas between families and individuals. It can even describe the conflicting impulses within a man's own life. Here in James its main reference must be to conflicts of a personal type, rather than to what we normally mean by "war", and most modern translators use some such word as "conflict", "antagonism", or "feud" rather than "war". Similarly the word translated "fightings" (*machai*) literally means "battles", but must mean what we should normally call "quarrels".[1]

It may be that "wars" and "fightings" are here used roughly as synonyms, and no real distinction between them is in the writer's mind.

---

[1] The same Greek word is used, also in the sense of a personal quarrel, at 2 Cor. 7: 5, 2 Tim. 2: 23–24, and Tit. 3: 9.

If, however, a distinction is to be made, "war" represents a continuing state of hostility, and "battle" a specific outburst of active antagonism. In terms of personal rather than national conflict, "war" would stand for an enduring feud or persistent antagonism, and "battle" for one of the quarrels which flare up from time to time out of that antagonism.

James writes as one who assumes the prevalence of "strife" and "quarrelling" in the community. "AMONG YOU" need not be taken to mean Christians, even though the letter is addressed to Christians. It may be used generally of all human life, but what is characteristic of human life is always likely to assert itself even within the Church, since the frailty of our human nature persists among the members of the Church, and betrays itself in the existence of strife and ill-will.

Sometimes we tend to think that peace is the natural state of man, and that strife is the unnatural element which disturbs it. Quite the reverse is true. Strife is characteristic of human life, and where lasting peace exists in a community, it is the mark of a great work of God's grace. Peace represents a notable achievement, and is possible only when individuals are ready to subordinate personal feelings to the common good. It does not just "happen" but has to be "striven for" (Eph. 4: 3). It is like a garden with beautiful flowers. It does not just "happen" by accident. Quarrels are like weeds; they flourish everywhere.

In the statement which outlines the purposes of U.N.E.S.C.O. we read: "Since wars begin in the mind of men, it is in the minds of men that the defence of peace must be constructed". This corresponds to what James is saying here. The work for peace must begin within the hearts of men, since it is there that the seeds of strife are to be found. These seeds are, in the R.S.V. translation, called "PASSIONS".

The Greek word so translated is *hedonai*, which is usually translated pleasures, and which is the root from which the word "hedonism" comes. Ropes interprets it as "the pursuit of pleasure", and N.E.B. has "bodily desires". The same word is used at Luke 8: 14 of "the pleasures of life" which help to choke the good seed of God after it has been sown in the human heart. It occurs also in Titus 3: 3 for the "pleasures" which can enslave a man.

Some try to distinguish the meaning of this word from that of the verb "desire" (*epithymeō*) which follows in verse 2, but it is doubtful whether James intended any precise difference. The "passions" here are desires and wishes for any personal satisfaction of our own, for money, fame, revenge or pleasure, which resent any kind of restraint, and refuse to submit themselves to the will of God. If men follow their "passions", chaos is inevitable, for different men desire the same things, or else conflicting things. Peace is possible only when all concerned are ready to subordinate personal wishes to one controlling purpose. For the Christian community this is the will of God.

Commentators quote similar statements from other writers on ethical subjects, especially Plato. In Phaedo 66, for instance, he wrote: "The sole cause of wars and revolutions and battles is nothing other than the body and its desires", and in Laws 626 D: "To conquer oneself is of all victories the first and the best, but to be defeated by oneself is at once the most shameful and worst of all. It simply signifies that in each of us there is a war on against ourselves".

So James writes: The PASSIONS ARE AT WAR IN YOUR MEMBERS, that is, they are conducting a campaign in human lives and in communities. A similar passage in 1 Pet. 2: 11 speaks about "passions of the flesh that wage war against the soul". Possibly when James writes about the passions at war, he also means that they are at war with the soul of man, though he does not precisely say so. Alternatively, he may think of the war as one against God, or he may have in mind the confusion as one passion conflicts with another, and man's life becomes a battle-field of warring desires. In Rom. 7: 23 Paul uses what is substantially the same word to describe the war in man's inner life between the "law of his mind" and his "lower nature".

The "passions" at any rate are here campaigning to establish their right to rule in man's life and to displace the rightful ruler. Tasker writes: "Human nature has been invaded by an alien army which is always campaigning within it", and describes the invaders as "an overwhelming army of occupation". The "passions" are rebels, aggressively seeking to usurp the place of the proper authority.

"IN YOUR MEMBERS" may mean in the personal life of the individual, or among the various members of the community. But if it means the second, it will also include the first, since individuals in a community become the centre of strife and ill-will, when these things have gained a measure of dominance within their hearts.

**4: 2** This verse raises problems. One has to do with punctuation. The earliest manuscripts do not help us here, since they do not use punctuation marks. Each editor has to insert these as he thinks best. The R.V. (following K.J.V.) punctuated as follows: "Ye lust, and have not: ye kill, and covet, and cannot obtain: ye fight and war". This does not make satisfactory sense, mainly perhaps because "covet" coming after "kill" in the same sentence, is something of an anti-climax. If this punctuation is right, one would expect, "ye covet and kill", the more extreme word following the less extreme one. If, therefore, we accept the text as we find it in the MSS, it is better to punctuate as R.S.V. does, which along with most modern translators, follows a suggestion first made by Westcott and Hort. This gives us two parallel statements which neatly balance each other.

Even the improvement of the punctuation, however, does not remove all difficulties. What are we to make of the word "kill" in a context like this? Did the people to whom James wrote actually go to the extent of killing other people?

The "killing", says James, is the result of thwarted desire. YOU DESIRE AND DO NOT HAVE. Men want something very badly. They find that someone else stands between them and the fulfilment of their longing. The fierceness of their desire and the violence of their resentment against interference with it actually culminates in murder. This is not other than our Lord warned us to be prepared for. He said: "For within, out of the heart of man, comes . . . murder" (Mark 7: 21). The Old Testament bears witness to the same grim truth. Bitter jealousy led Cain to kill Abel. Thwarted covetousness led to Naboth's death at the hands of Ahab and Jezebel. Uriah the Hittite was sent to his death to make way for David's lust.

James may have such instances in mind, and when he writes "*you* kill", does not mean precisely the people to whom he writes, but "men in general". He is describing what can happen, and indeed does happen in human communities. The rich people, for instance, are denounced in 5: 6 because their hostility to the righteous man does not stop short even of murder.

Those who feel that "*you* kill" cannot be taken in this general sense, but must mean the very people to whom James writes, point to a similar unexpected reference to murder in relation to Christian people in 1 Pet. 4: 15: "Let none of you suffer as a murderer". There are also these words in the Didache, 3: 2: "Be not angry, for anger leads to murder, nor jealous, nor quarrelsome, nor quicktempered, for from all these come murders". It is pointed out also that Jews could be very violent against anyone whom they regarded as endangering their faith. They plotted, as a religious duty, to kill Paul (Acts 9: 23; 20: 3). Jewish Christians also seem to have exhibited this same extreme of violence in what they thought to be the service of their religion. To conciliate them Paul had to be urged to make special concessions of a kind that must have been very distasteful to him, and it is quite clear from his letters that he was aware that their hostility would not stop short of extreme measures. In 2 Cor. 11: 26 he equates the danger he has to fear from "false brethren" with "danger from my own people" and with "danger at sea".

In spite of these arguments, however, it is still very difficult to take the word "kill" literally, if it is addressed to Christian people, and other possibilities must be sought. One is to assume that James, as he used it, was making a deliberate reference to the known words of Jesus Himself, as recorded, for instance, in Matt. 5: 21ff., where continuing resentment is condemned as a kind of incipient murder. Certainly John took this saying of Jesus very seriously, for he wrote: "Anyone who hates his brother is a murderer" (1 John 3: 15). So when James writes "kill" it may be that he knows his readers are aware that for the Christian hatred is to be regarded as if it were murder. John Wesley in his commentary understood it in this way and in expounding the word "kill" adds "in your heart".

Some scholars find all these attempts to make sense of the word "kill" in this context unconvincing, and take refuge in a "*tour de force*". They argue that the word "kill" is a copyist's error, and that originally a word, similar in appearance and sound, but very different in meaning, had been used. The Greek word here for "kill" is *phoneuete*, and there is a word *phthoneite*, which means "envy". It is suggested that James originally wrote "envy" and this was somehow changed in transmission to "kill". In support of this it is argued that the meaning "envy" is eminently suitable to the context. The sentence would then read: "You envy and covet . . ." It must be insisted that this is wholly a conjecture, and that there is no manuscript evidence for any such reading. Nevertheless, it is claimed, similar errors are known to have occurred in other contexts. At Gal. 5: 21, for instance, the MSS reveal a state of confusion about the correct reading, some favouring *phthonoi* and others *phonoi*, which are the nouns corresponding to the two verbs under discussion. Moreover at 1 Pet. 2: 1 Dibelius is able to cite two MSS[1] which read *phonoi* for *phthonoi*. It is, therefore, the kind of error that was made sometimes, and it cannot be denied that famous names in New Testament scholarship have declared in favour of "envy" here. Erasmus appears to have been the first to put forward the conjecture, but Calvin, Luther and Tyndale all adopted it. Moffatt was so certain it was right that he incorporated it in his translation of the New Testament, and Dibelius accepts it confidently, quoting the names of other modern scholars who agree.[2]

Undoubtedly this conjecture makes good sense, as can be seen by the translation of Phillips, who also accepts it: "You crave for something and don't get it, you are jealous and envious of what others have got and you don't possess it yourselves. Consequently, in your exasperated frustration you struggle and fight with one another".[3]

It is, however, a recognized principle of Textual Criticism that a conjecture with no MSS support is a very desperate expedient, only

[1] B and 1175.
[2] "So ist denn die schon von Erasmus vorgeschlagene und von vielen Neueren (Spitta, Mayor, Belser, Windisch) angenommene Konjektur *phthoneite* eigentlich selbstverständlich" (p. 200). He argues that the nearness of the words "war" and "battle" led to the introduction of the word "kill", instead of the original one meaning "envy".
[3] Phillips follows the older punctuation of R.V. and K.J.V., which makes good sense if Erasmus's conjecture is adopted.

admissible as a very last resort. Since then the MSS unanimously support "kill", and since there are admissible explanations of what is undoubtedly a very difficult word, we are well advised to choose the best of these rather than accept a conjecture, however attractive.

YOU COVET AND CANNOT OBTAIN: this is parallel to the clause, "You desire and do not have" in the previous sentence. The word for covet is Greek *zēlō*, from the same root as the noun *zēlos* which is translated "jealousy" in 3: 14. Like the noun it may bear a good meaning, and the object of desire may be something worthy, as in 1 Cor. 12: 31; 14: 1, but usually it carries a bad meaning, as in 1 Cor. 13: 4, Acts 7: 9, and here. It may mean a desire either to possess something or to get the better of someone else. When the desire is not satisfied, the outcome is that YOU FIGHT AND WAGE WAR, that is, use every available means to seize forcibly what you want, or remove the offending person.

Very appositely Ropes quotes Philo, De Decal. 28: "Wars famous in tragedy have all flowed from one source: desire either for money or glory or pleasure. Over these things the human race goes mad".

Suddenly there is an abrupt change of mood. James has been denouncing the wicked causes of strife in human communities—the aggressive self-seeking of corrupt human nature, concerned only to find satisfaction for its own desires without regard for the evil things it brings to others and the community as a whole. Now he turns from the causes of this ugly evil, and points us to the neglected cure of it. The cure lies in the completely opposite approach to life, not greedy self-seeking, but a readiness to submit the whole of life in meek obedience to the will of God, a humble desire to learn that will, and a glad acceptance of it as the one rule of life, once it is known. This is the way that leads to peace and good will in the community, and it is the refusal of this which provokes bitter hatred and illwill.

YOU DO NOT HAVE, BECAUSE YOU DO NOT ASK. It is as though James says: You hunger for satisfaction, but are seeking it in the wrong place. Why not try prayer to God? If they reply that they do pray, since they are conventionally religious people, he replies, "YOU ASK WRONGLY": you must be praying in the wrong way, selfishly and with worldly aims and with wrongs done to your fellows unrepented (Matt. 5: 23–24), and therefore God cannot answer your prayers.

The change is so abrupt that some have asked whether this sentence does not in fact introduce a new topic, unrelated to the fore-going, but the two can be related to each other. James writes that the way for a Christian to get what his heart is set upon is to ask God for it, not to pursue it ruthlessly and without regard for others. Jesus had said: "Ask and it shall be given unto you" (Matt. 7: 7), and "Whatsoever you ask in prayer, you will receive, if you have faith" (Matt. 21: 22; cf. John 14: 13, etc.). True satisfaction is to be found only when we want the right things, and these God readily grants to those who ask for them in prayer.

The trouble with the people rebuked in verses 1 and 2 is that what they are seeking is not God's will for them. Only people utterly blind to God's nature could ask God to give what they hungered to have. True prayer begins with a willingness to learn God's will, and a readiness to submit our hearts to God to have them made to want His will. "If we ask anything according to His will, He hears us" (1 John 5: 14). The essence of prayer is not to get what we want out of God, but to have ourselves so changed by God that we come to want what He wants for us, to "love what God commands and to desire what He promises".

**4: 3** The only things really worth having are those we can ask God for, and if we ask for them completely "in Christ's name", God will grant our prayer. If we ASK AND DO NOT RECEIVE it is BECAUSE WE ASK WRONGLY. Either we ask for the wrong things, misunderstanding God's will for us, or we ask for things, good in themselves, but we want them for the wrong motives. Paul, for instance, three times asked God to remove some trouble from his life, but God's answer was "No", but "My grace is sufficient for you" (2 Cor. 12: 8–9). He wanted freedom from trouble; God wanted for him the experience of finding God's help sufficient to enable him to bear that trouble. He was asking for the wrong thing. Other people ask for things God might well be ready to give, except that they ask for them for wrong reasons—not to please God better or be more effective in His service, but to gain status over others, comfort, ease, praise. They want to use what God grants, money, leisure, health, strength, or friends, not for the greater glory of God, but to SPEND IT ON YOUR PASSIONS, to use it for their own personal ends, and the satisfaction of their own desires. That is why God must say "No" to their pleas.

Let Calvin provide the summary of this section: "James meant briefly this—that our desires ought to be bridled; and the way of bridling them is to subject them to the will of God. And he also teaches us, that what we in moderation wish, we ought to seek from God Himself; which, if it be done, we shall be preserved from wicked contentions."

*4: 4–6. Unfaithful creatures! Do you not know that friendship with the world is enmity with God? Therefore whoever wishes to be a friend of the world makes himself an enemy of God? 5. Or do you suppose it is in vain that the scripture says, "He yearns jealously over the spirit which he has made to dwell in us"?* 6. *But he gives more grace; therefore it says, "God opposes the proud, but gives grace to the humble".*

These verses administer a sharp rebuke to those who are so attracted by the pleasures, profits or praises of the world that they become unfaithful to God.

**4: 4** The verses are addressed to "UNFAITHFUL CREATURES". This is a good translation for the Greek word and avoids difficulties created by more literal translations. The Greek word actually means "adulteresses". Some manuscripts (perhaps because the copyists were puzzled at the exclusively feminine word for the wrongdoers) add "adulterers", and this reading is represented in K.J.V. The best MSS, however, have only the single word.

It is true that "adulteresses" is a feminine word, but probably there is no intention of excluding men from the rebuke, nor yet of confining the rebuke to disloyalty to the marriage bond. In the O.T. the people of Israel are called the "bride" or "wife" of God (Deut. 31: 16; Isa. 54: 5; Jer. 3: 20), and within the context of this metaphor any disloyalty on the part of Israel to their covenant with God could be described as "adultery". So any group within Israel, who were carelessly disobedient to God's laws, could be denounced, as in the words of Jesus, as "an evil and adulterous generation" (Matt. 12: 39). Such a description implies general disobedience to the God whom they had promised to obey, and this may or may not include the precise sin of adultery.

Those who by their disobedience thus "forsook God", in spite of their pledged covenant with Him, may be said to be "playing the harlot" against Him (Hos. 9: 1). This usually applies to the nation as a whole but may be used of individuals within the nation. The phrase rightly translated in Ps. 73: 27 as "all who are false to God" could more literally be translated: "all who have committed fornication against Him". "In the O.T.", writes Hort, "all sin and apostasy are spoken of as adultery". Perhaps at first this scornful word was applied mainly to those Jews who tried to combine deference to a heathen god with a show of loyalty to Jehovah, but more generally it could be used of any disloyalty to their vow of obedience to God.

Disobedience to God is often provoked by a longing for the pleasure of or FRIENDSHIP WITH THE WORLD. Here, as elsewhere in James, this means the world in its hostility to God. James has already pleaded with his readers to "keep themselves unstained from the world" (1: 27) and to be content to be "poor in the world" (2: 5) provided they can be "rich in faith". In 1 John 2: 16 the "world" is explained as meaning "the lust of the flesh, and the lust of the eyes, and the pride of life". In 2 Tim. 3: 4 men who turn from God are described as "lovers of self, lovers of money, . . . lovers of pleasure rather than lovers of God". Demas, of whose desertion Paul speaks so sadly (2 Tim. 4: 10), acted so because he was "in love with this present world". It is in this sense that James uses "world".

To be friendly with the world means to cherish a relationship of mutual appreciation with those who exclude God and God's will from their lives, to value their approval and goodwill, and to be ready to disguise or forego our loyalty to God in consequence. Inevitably, therefore, such FRIENDSHIP WITH THE WORLD involves ENMITY WITH GOD. It refuses utterly "to be hated by all men for his name's sake" (Matt. 10: 22), which our Lord said would often be the lot of His disciples. Paul too speaks of "enmity to God" (Rom. 8: 7) and equates it with a refusal to "submit to God's law" and an inability to "please God". The Christian who tries to "keep in with" the world cannot but fail to please God. A choice must be made. We cannot gain the approval both of "the god of this world" (2 Cor. 4: 4) and of the true God, who is the Father of our Lord Jesus Christ. We cannot serve God and Mammon (Matt. 6: 24).

THEREFORE WHOEVER WISHES TO BE A FRIEND OF THE WORLD MAKES HIMSELF AN ENEMY OF GOD. The Christian is called upon to claim his privilege of being, like Abraham, a friend of God (2: 23). Lest we should think this implies an easy-going familiarity, it is well to recall the words of Jesus: "You are my friends, if you do what I command you" (John 15: 14). This would not serve as a basis for a purely human friendship, but it is the only basis for friendship between God and man. To enjoy the high privilege of God's "friendship" means that we do His commands. Since these are incompatible with pleasing "the world", we must make our choice. To choose the advantages that come from "pleasing the world" means to choose that which ranges us against God and His holy law.

**4: 5** This verse presents real difficulties. Hort links it with 3: 6 and calls these two verses the most perplexing in the whole of the epistle.

It begins by insisting that a verse from Scripture cannot be spoken IN VAIN, that is, it must mean just what it says, and what it says is unquestionably true.

The first problem arises from the fact that the following words, quoted as from Scripture, do not in fact come from the Scriptures of the Old Testament, as they are known to us. Calvin tried to evade this difficulty by arguing that the reference to a quotation from Scripture applies not to what follows, but to the verse which precedes, which condemns friendship with the world, since this could be taken as giving the sense of many passages in the O.T. Most scholars, however, feel unable to take up this suggestion, and assume that the reference to scripture must be to what follows.

Since these words cannot be traced in the O.T., some have suggested that they occurred in some other sacred book, which the author either regarded as Scripture, or mistakenly ascribed to Scripture. Dibelius appears to favour this explanation. He points out that there are in the Shepherd of Hermas close similarities to this quoted passage, and this may imply that elsewhere an exact parallel might be found. Another suggestion is that the quotation may come from some unknown Greek translation of the O.T., which differs at this point from those known to us.

A more probable explanation is that James is not quoting any single passage from the O.T., but giving the general sense of much of its teaching. John Wesley's judgement, for instance, was: "St. James seems to refer to many, not any one particular Scripture".

Even if this explanation is regarded as satisfactory, our difficulties are not ended, for it is impossible to say with complete confidence what the quotation itself really means. The Greek words are so ambiguous that several varying translations are possible, and there may be different ways of expounding the same translation. Erasmus comments: "There are waggon-loads of interpretations of this passage".

It would be inappropriate here to attempt to enumerate all the suggestions that have been made. Many of them depend on fine differences in the understanding of Greek words and phrases. Students who wish to have these set out and discussed should consult commentaries based on the Greek text, such as those by Ropes and Mayor. Here it must suffice to indicate the chief sources of the ambiguity and to note those three of the possible translations which appear to have the strongest scholarly support.

The chief causes of ambiguity are three:
(i) In the Greek the word "spirit" may be either (a) subject of the verb: "The spirit yearns over . . ." or (b) object: "God yearns over the spirit. . . .".
(ii) The spirit may be either (a) God's Holy Spirit, or (b) the spirit which God breathed into man at his creation, what normally we might call the "soul".
(iii) The word "jealously" may be used either (a) in a good sense of that in God which requires complete and unshared devotion from His creature man, or (b) in the bad sense, to mean the evil quality which so often infects the human heart, but should have no place in the life of the Christian.

Out of these ambiguities variant translations arise. We record the three which appear to have most claim to consideration:

(1) R.S.V. (supported by Moffatt and Dibelius) accepts from the above alternatives 1 (b), 2 (b), and 3 (a), and translates: "He (God) yearns jealously over the spirit which He has made to dwell in us".

(2) Mayor (followed substantially by Weymouth and C. K. Williams) accepts the alternatives 1 (a), 2 (a), and 3 (a), and translates: "The Spirit which God has made to dwell within us jealously yearns for the full devotion of our hearts".

(3) N.E.B., choosing from the alternatives 1 (a), 2 (b), and 3 (b) translates: "The spirit which God implanted in man turns towards envious desires".

The second of these makes James refer explicitly to the Holy Spirit whom God has given to believers. Apart from this there is no other clear reference to the Holy Spirit in the epistle. Many, therefore, object that this casts doubt upon an interpretation which finds reference to the Holy Spirit here. It would, on the other hand, have the advantage of bringing James more fully into line with the rest of the N.T.

The third has the advantage over the other two of preparing the way more satisfactorily for the sentence which follows since, if this verse is an affirmation of the corruption which infests the human heart, the reference to God's still more abundant supply of grace to counter this prevalent evil (in verse 6) is very appropriate.

With these brief comments on (2) and (3), we confine our attention to (1), which is the translation used by R.S.V.

The translation "YEARN OVER" well represents the Greek word, which occurs also at other places in the N.T. (e.g. at Phil. 1: 8 and 1 Pet. 2: 2). It suggests a strong, loving concern for someone, such as a mother may feel for an ailing or suffering child. So God yearns over THE SPIRIT WHICH HE HAS MADE TO DWELL IN US. This is a reference to the story of man's creation in Gen. 2: 7 (cf. Isa. 42: 5). God longs to see this spirit, which He breathed into man, set free from those evil things which have begun to rob it of happiness and goodness, undermining its true welfare, and even destroying its very life.

God is described as yearning JEALOUSLY. This is probably the correct meaning of the Greek phrase (*pros phthonon*) though no precise parallel of the expression can be found elsewhere. Arndt and Gingrich record this as the probable meaning, but add that the words are "perhaps textually damaged", indicating that the oddity of the Greek phrase rouses their suspicions.[1]

[1] Some quote similar Greek phrases to argue that the translation here should be "*against* envy", as though the envy (or jealousy) were the evil quality which destroys all that is good in human life. Therefore God yearns "against envy". John Wesley prefers this, and translates: "The Spirit that dwelleth in us lusteth *against* envy", and explains that this means that the Spirit "is directly opposite to all those unloving tempers which flow from friendship with the world".

The modern mind shrinks from ascribing jealousy to God, since, in human life, jealousy is an ugly thing. But the Bible has no such qualms, and often we read: "I the Lord thy God am a jealous God" (Exod. 20: 5, etc.). It means that God longs for the entire, undivided devotion of every human heart. He made it for Himself, He has redeemed it in Christ, and He will not be content so long as any part of it is handed over to evil. Being God, He cannot and should not be satisfied with only a fragment. He must have all. "To yearn jealously" means, as Mayor indicates, "to yearn for the full devotion of our hearts".

In place of "the spirit which He made to dwell in us" some MSS have (less accurately) "the spirit which dwelt in us".

**4: 6** BUT GOD GIVES MORE GRACE: Here "GRACE" appears to be used in a sense similar to that which is characteristically Pauline, of God's generous, active, effective help to man, far beyond anything the man deserves or can rightly expect. We recall, for instance, the word of Christ to Paul as he cries in his distress for some act of deliverance: "My grace is sufficient for you" (2 Cor. 12: 9), or the more general affirmation: "Where sin increased, grace abounded all the more" (Rom. 5: 20).

The use of the phrase "*more* grace" is peculiar. The comparative "more" may be loosely used to mean "more and more grace" or "abundant grace". If, however, it is to be taken literally, then this sentence would follow more naturally, as was stated earlier, after the form of translation of the earlier verse as given in N.E.B. "The spirit which God implanted in man turns towards envious desires", but God gives more grace, that is, more even than the violent strength of the envious desires, and sufficient to hold them in restraint.

If, however, we interpret the phrase in the context of the R.S.V. translation it must mean that though God's "jealous" concern for complete obedience is a most pressing concern, yet His grace is even "more"; His mercy outstrips even His righteousness. Man's sin puts him under the just condemnation of God, but his penitent need can confidently appeal to God's mercy over against His judgement.[1]

Since "grace" is no less characteristic of God than His "jealous" requirement of man's complete obedience, James pauses to indicate the circumstances in which man may find himself confronted by one or the other. If our rejection of His claim for our full devotion is high-handed, arrogant and careless, as though we have a perfect right to run our lives just as we wish, then we shall be made to learn the painful truth declared in Scripture (in Prov. 3: 34) that GOD OPPOSES THE

---

[1] A less probable suggestion is that "grace" here has the pre-Pauline meaning of "favour", so that the sentence could be rendered: "The Lord gives greater favour (than the world's friendship does)".

PROUD. If, however, our failure to give God His due springs not from arrogant defiance and stubborn unconcern for His claims, but from our human frailty and weakness, so that we come before Him penitent and ashamed, we shall find that "there is forgiveness with Him": HE GIVES GRACE TO THE HUMBLE, that is, forgiveness for the past and delivering power for the future.

4: 7–10. *Submit yourselves therefore to God. Resist the devil and he will flee from you. 8. Draw near to God and he will draw near to you. Cleanse your hands, you sinners, and purify your hearts, you men of double mind. 9. Be wretched and mourn and weep. Let your laughter be turned to mourning and your joy to dejection. 10. Humble yourselves before the Lord and he will exalt you.*

This section consists of brief exhortations, which could be understood as originally independent sayings, which are here somewhat loosely associated together. Some scholars interpret them in this way, and do not seek for any clearly discernible continuity of thought. This may be the best way, but we shall try to suggest where the continuity of thought may be found.

Verse 10 would have followed verse 6 admirably. Verse 6 ends: "God gives grace to the humble", and verse 10 begins: "Humble yourselves therefore before God". Several other terse injunctions, however, are inserted between these two verses.

**4: 7** The word "SUBMIT YOURSELVES" (from Greek *hypotassō*) might be rendered "subordinate yourselves". It is a word which occurs frequently in the epistles. A Christian is one who must learn to subordinate his own wishes, not only to God but also to others within the Christian community, and even to secular authorities "for Christ's sake" (Rom. 13: 1–5; 1 Pet. 2: 13). Wives are to subordinate themselves to their husbands (Col. 3: 18; Eph. 5: 22; Titus 2: 5; 1 Pet 3: 1; cf. 1 Cor. 14: 34), servants to their masters (Titus 2: 9; 1 Pet. 2: 18), younger people to those who are older (1 Pet. 5: 5). The Corinthians are urged to subordinate themselves to those leaders among them who have proved themselves men of Christian quality (1 Cor. 16: 16), and in Eph. 5: 21 the instruction is to subordinate ourselves to "one another".

The day will come when all things will be made subordinate to God (1 Cor. 15: 27). The Kingdom of God will then come with power. The rule of God, which will be fully realised on some future day, is, however, already partially realized within the lives of true believers. So it is characteristic of them even now that their lives are "subordinated to God" (see Heb. 12: 9). It means that their own will is completely obedient to the will of God. God's will, not their own, is the effective power in their lives.

If the Christian is one who yields or surrenders his will to God, his attitude towards God's arch-enemy is quite the reverse. Indeed it is the measure of our obedience to God that His enemies become our enemies. Satan, the power of evil, is not treated with timid and misguided courtesy, nor yet with neutral indifference, but with determined defiance. The Christian is to RESIST THE DEVIL. The same word "resist" (*antistēte*) is used in Eph. 6: 13, where we are bidden to "withstand" in the evil day all the embattled forces of evil. The same word occurs again in 1 Pet. 5: 9, where also we are called upon to "resist" the devil.

It was thus that Jesus Himself confronted Satan in the wilderness neither deceived by his subtleties nor daunted by his threats. So too the Christian is instructed to recognize evil for what it is, and neither to shrink from the Evil One when he comes as a "raging lion" (1 Pet. 5: 8), nor be tricked by him into compliance when he seeks to disarm our watchfulness by approaching us as "an angel of light" (2 Cor. 11: 14). Watchfulness against "the wiles of the devil" (Eph. 6: 11) and bold defiance against his attacks is the correct attitude of the Christian. We are to love our enemies, but to hate evil (Rom. 12: 9).

James calls "Satan" the "devil". The Greek word for "devil" originally meant "slanderer", and some have tried to find here a particular reference to slandering. It is better, however, to understand it simply as a variant for Satan. It is used in this way in the Septuagint and also in several books of the New Testament.

The command is followed by a promise. If instead of hesitation and misgiving we confront the Devil with resolute will HE WILL FLEE FROM YOU. Jesus exerted this power to turn evil spirits to flight (e.g. Mark 1: 25; 5: 8, etc.), and even during His earthly life His disciples sometimes shared it with Him: "Lord, even the demons are subject to us in your name", they said (Luke 10: 17). Similarly Paul, in the name of Jesus, could exercise this authority over evil spirits (Acts 16: 18).

**4:8** As we yield our wills in obedience to God, it is not as servants to a master, however, so much as children to a loved parent. A servant is one who does the master's will, but does not enjoy his intimate friendship and companionship. A child in the home, however, is happy in the father's company. So the Christian is invited, as a child in God's family, to DRAW NEAR TO GOD, to draw strength and comfort from the sense of His nearness. And if we come to God, we shall never be turned away (cf. John 6: 37). Rather God WILL DRAW NEAR TO US.

This does not mean that in our relations with God, the initiative lies with us, and He comes to us only if we make the first approach.

God is always drawing near to us in many different ways, and often we are unaware of His gracious presence, or else unwilling to acknowledge it. It would be nothing more than we deserve, if, when we did turn to Him in some special need, God withdrew from us, as we had done from Him. But that is not God's way: if we turn to Him in humble penitence, and confessed need, coming as a disobedient child to his father, we always find Him waiting to receive us, just as the returning Prodigal found, though he had done nothing to deserve such fatherly love. As Calvin put it: "James meant no other thing in this passage than that God is never wanting to us, except when we alienate ourselves from Him".

Some commentators point out that the phrase "draw near to God" is sometimes used in the Bible of the special function of the priest (e.g. Exod. 19: 22, Ezek 44: 13), and they discern here a veiled suggestion that it is a privilege of believing Christians to be "priests to God" (Rev. 1: 6; 5: 10; 20: 6), "a holy priesthood" (1 Pet. 2: 5, 9), as though all Christians now exercised the right which in Judaism was the exclusive privilege of a few. Though "the Priesthood of all Believers" is certainly emphasized in Scripture, it is doubtful if we can find it here. The word "draw near" (*engizō*) is a common one in Greek, and is used very widely without any reference to the special privilege of the priest. It is noticeable, however, that where the word is used of "drawing near" *to God* in Heb. 4: 16 and 7: 19 it describes the privilege of Christians as it has been made theirs by the great High Priest, Jesus.

Here, however, it appears to be an affirmation of the general privilege of Christians that they have at all times through Christ "access to God" (Rom. 5: 2, Eph. 2: 18; 3: 12).

If a man draws near to God, he must, as far as he can, prepare himself. He must CLEANSE HIS HANDS AND PURIFY HIS HEART. We are reminded of Ps. 24: 4: "Who shall ascend the hill of the Lord? . . . He who has *clean hands* and a *pure heart*" (cf. also Isa. 1: 16).

It is not, of course, that our lives have to be made entirely satisfactory, before we may draw near to God. Otherwise, who would ever be able to come? Often it is the very act of drawing near which first awakens the desire to have things put right, and then bestows the means for this to be done. But he who comes to God must be *willing* to be put right. Faith is not identical with obedience, but it must imply the readiness to be obedient, if only the power to obey is granted to us. Genuine faith, therefore, while fully aware that only God can really heal a sick soul will at the same time want to put right immediately those things which lie within its own power. That is the assumption behind the demand of John the Baptist upon those who professed penitence: "Bear fruits that befit repentance" (Luke 3: 8). It is not true repentance, if we are still hoping to keep in our lives the very things we are repenting of. True repentance implies the readiness to discard everything that provides facilities for further sinning; it implies also a readiness to make what amends we can for wrongs already committed. So Jesus insisted that true worship can be offered to God only when wrongs done to others have been, so far as is possible, remedied (Matt. 5: 23).

Those who come to God, therefore, must come in penitence, ready to be healed of those things in them which displease Him, and to put right themselves those outward things which it is in their power to deal with. Therefore we must CLEANSE OUR HANDS. "HANDS" here are contrasted with "heart". The word symbolically includes all *outward* acts of wrongdoing, acts known to others as well as ourselves. But this is not enough. Mere outward conformity is not all that God asks. So we are bidden to cleanse the inward springs of life and action, and PURIFY OUR HEARTS (for the meaning of "heart" see comments at 1: 26 and 3: 14). "We hence learn", writes Calvin, "what is the true character of repentance. It is not only an outward amendment of life, but its beginning is the cleansing of the heart."

Purity of heart is much insisted on in the New Testament. Our Lord pronounced the pure in heart blessed, "for they shall see God" (Matt. 5: 8). It is with the same emphasis that James asks purity of heart from those who "draw near to God". It is out of the inward places of the heart that outward acts of wrong-doing proceed, and it is the evil things which come from the heart which "defile a man" (Mark 7: 21–23; see also I Pet. 1: 22 and I John 3: 3).

Those who sensed some indirect reference to the priesthood in the words "draw near to God", find it also in the insistence on cleansing and purification. These were required of the priests before they entered upon their duties (Exod. 30: 20–21). It is, however, clear beyond any doubt that what James is requiring here is not any ceremonial cleansing (as, for instance, in John 11: 55) but moral purity.

Those who are being exhorted are addressed as "SINNERS", even though they are within the Church. But James has already made it plain how greatly he is disturbed by the presence of grossly un-Christian conduct in those who profess faith in Christ.

They are also called "DOUBLE-MINDED", as in 1: 8 (see comment there). Their friendship with the world (4: 4) is undermining their loyalty to God. They are trying to reconcile two quite incompatible aims. They are trying to serve two masters (Matt. 6: 24)—wordly success and the service of God. Since "hands" and "hearts" have been mentioned in this connection, there may be in "double-minded" here a further suggestion that the people addressed may be in danger of arguing: "It does not matter what goes on in my thoughts, provided that my outward acts are respectable". This disastrous attitude could be described as a kind of double-mindedness, that is a lack of integration within the personality.[1]

**4: 9** This demand for deep repentance as we approach God is treated very seriously. Such an approach cannot be reconciled with any attitude of casualness or light-heartedness. Rather the readers are commanded: BE WRETCHED, MOURN AND WEEP. The lack of purity in outward act and inward thought should utterly destroy any attitude of carefree unconcern. Ropes translates the first word of the phrase as "Make yourselves wretched", as though implying some acts of self-castigation (the Greek imperative, in the aorist tense, suggests a decisive action), but probably the N.E.B. is nearer to James's meaning with "Be sorrowful". The realization of continuing evil within their lives should make them feel wretched, without any further self-imposed discomfort. The Greek word for "Be wretched" (*talaipōreō*) is basically the same word which Paul uses in Rom. 7: 24 to describe the "double-minded" man who sees what is right and tries to do it, only to find he is not able to. He cries: "O wretched (*talaipōros*) man that I am". In Paul, however, the continuing evil in his life is not due to carelessness, but to his human helplessness in face of the insidious power of evil.

Other commentators, however, as well as Ropes, understand the word as a summons to some special act of self-affliction or deprivation. Mayor suggests that it is a demand for some "voluntary abstinence from comforts and luxuries"; and Blackman wonders if it is a call to a discipline of fasting, "a day for a man to afflict his soul" (Isa. 58: 5, R.V.). But it is probable that James would have indicated it more precisely, had he intended this meaning. It is, rather, an urgent call to them to awaken to the spiritual need and peril in which they stand, and to feel the sharp concern which their plight merits.

Similarly he calls on them to MOURN AND WEEP. These same two words (*pentheō* and *klaiō*) are used together in Luke 6: 25, but curiously enough, in the beatitudes, Matthew has "Blessed are those who mourn" (*pentheō*), and Luke has "those who weep" (*klaiō*) (Matt. 5: 4, Luke 6: 21). The words, therefore, are roughly synonymous, "mourning" being the inward state of mind, and "weeping" the outward expression of it. The distress they symbolize here primarily refers to the realization of their own spiritual poverty and peril. It signifies their sense of shame at their failure to please God; it is what, in 2 Cor. 7: 10, is called "godly grief".

The word "MOURN" may also mean distress for someone else's

---

[1] For a discussion of the word "double-minded" (*dipsychos*) as it occurs in *The Shepherd of Hermas* and in the literature of the Qumran Community, see in *New Testament Studies*, Vol. 4, No. 4, pp. 327-334, an article by O. J. F. Seitz.

sorrows rather than our own. Since James has already administered sharp rebukes to those who show a callous disregard for the crying needs of others (e.g. at 2: 15–16), it may be that here too he is summoning his readers to a more sympathetic attitude to others' distresses, even to the point of feeling those distresses as if they were their own. This would be in accord with the plea of Paul that we should be ready to "weep with those who weep" (Rom. 12: 15). It was the plight of others that brought tears to the eyes of Jesus (John 11: 33; Luke 19: 41).

Ropes writes of this verse: "James is not giving a complete directory for conduct at all times, but is trying by the unexpected intensity of his language to startle half-hearted Christians into a searching of heart and a self-consecration which he believes essential to their eternal salvation".

LET YOUR LAUGHTER BE TURNED TO MOURNING. Apparently their friendship with the world has provided occasions for hilarity and merry-making which is quite out of keeping both with the spiritual peril in which they are living, and the urgent needs of those about them. Perhaps James is recalling the word of Jesus: "Woe to you who laugh now, for you shall mourn and weep" (Luke 6: 25).

This is not a condemnation of all laughter, but of thoughtless laughter in a situation which should rather provoke sadness and a sense of concern. Laughter can have great healing powers, to relieve inward stress and tension, and to ease strained personal relationships. It can be a blessing to thank God for. But very easily laughter can become poisoned with bitterness and uncleanness. It becomes a vehicle of indecency, so that a comedian who can create laughter without vulgarity is something of a rarity. Very often, also, it becomes an instrument of cruelty, so that while others laugh someone who is the butt of the joke is embarrassed and humiliated.

The associations of laughter in the Bible are not very pleasant ones. It is commonly linked with ridicule; "laugh to scorn" is a frequent phrase. It does not usually appear as a sweet or gracious thing. There is, however, the laughter of glad relief and spontaneous gaiety, which springs from the joy of an unexpected deliverance from trouble (Ps. 126: 2).

Here the laughter which is rebuked is not indecent or cruel laughter, but the flippant laughter of careless unconcern in the presence of facts which more properly should induce grief and remorse.

Similarly their frivolous and superficial JOY should be turned into DEJECTION. True joy is one element in the fruit of the Spirit, but here the word is used not in its Christian meaning, but simply of irresponsible happiness, unconcerned about the world's griefs and sins. The word DEJECTION has no necessarily moral significance, but in the context it signifies something related to penitence, and some commentators have likened it to the downcast look of penitence with which the taxgatherer came before God in Luke 18: 13.

**4: 10** This verse takes up the thought of verse 6, which ends with the promise that God "gives grace to the humble". Since this is so, we are here exhorted: "HUMBLE YOURSELVES BEFORE GOD". Micah in his memorable words (6: 8) had declared that one of the basic requirements of God is that man should "walk humbly with" his God. To be humble before God means to be sharply aware of His unapproachable majesty, and of our utter unworthiness, even at our best, to be received by Him. It means to acknowledge His right to command and order our lives, and our readiness to submit our wills to His perfect will. To be humble before God also implies a willingness to be humble in our treatment of others, to follow ways of unnoticed service (Luke 22: 26), without seeking prominence over or deference from others. 1 Pet. 5: 6 also bids us, "Humble yourselves under the mighty hand of God". This word, as well as the one in James, echoes the word of Jesus in Matt. 18: 4.

Words of Jesus also link present "humbling of ourselves" with future "exaltation": "Whoever humbles himself will be exalted" (Matt. 23: 12; Luke 14: 11; 18: 14). James, therefore, with the full authority of Jesus adds: "HE WILL EXALT YOU".

Many New Testament words associate in this way obedience with reward (as, for example, in 4: 8). It is not that God seeks to entice us into right conduct by the offer of reward, but rather it is an affirmation about the structure of life itself, as made by God, that obedience to His will normally leads to great spiritual blessings (even though temporal loss and persecutions may also be suffered; cf. Mark 10: 30). All the commands of God are indeed "for our good" (Deut. 10: 13).

So here, if we submit personal wishes to the will of God, and take the humble path of Christian service in the community (rather than seek that eminence which gives the impression of superiority over others) the promise is that GOD WILL EXALT YOU. He will confer on us a position of privilege (not in this world, nor as this world counts privilege) but in that future Kingdom of God, where righteousness, peace and joy are the qualities of life that God's people are being trained to enjoy.

4: 11–12. *Do not speak evil against one another, brethren. He that speaks evil against a brother or judges his brother, speaks evil against the law and judges the law. But if you judge the law, you are not a doer of the law but a judge. 12. There is one lawgiver and judge, he who is able to save and to destroy. But who are you that you judge your neighbour?*

James had already made emphatic protest against the sins which intrude their way into our speech. One who does not fall into sin in the words he speaks can be described as a "perfect man" (3: 2). Since the tongue is so prone to evil, we are advised to be "slow to speak" (1: 19). The tongue, we are warned, is a "fire", "a restless evil", "full of deadly poison" (3: 5–12). Elsewhere it is regarded as an untamed horse, whose every movement is unpredictable and dangerous, which we must learn to "bridle". (See notes at 1: 26 and 3: 5–12.)

**4: 11** Of the many sins of which the tongue is guilty, the one here particularly condemned is that of fault-finding, of disparaging what others do and are. The Greek word here translated "SPEAK EVIL AGAINST" (*katalaleō*) means literally "to talk somebody down", "to disparage". It means speaking of others in a way calculated to lower them in other people's estimation, and speaking of them in their absence, when they have no opportunity to defend themselves or correct untrue statements. That is why in the older translations this word was often translated "backbite", with its suggestion of a hurtful injury inflicted on a man behind his back.

This evil behaviour, though indeed it is so common that we are inclined to overlook the wickedness of it, is frequently condemned in Scripture (see, for instance, Ps. 15: 13; 50: 20; 101: 5; Prov. 16: 28; 26: 20; Wisd. of Sol. 1: 11). Indeed Prof. W. Barclay, writing on this verse, comments: "There are few sins which the Bible so unsparingly condemns as the sin of irresponsible and malicious gossip. To tell and listen to a slanderous story, especially about a distinguished person, is for all people a fascinating activity."

The same word (*katalaleō*) is used twice in 1 Peter (2: 12; 3: 16) of the slander and misrepresentation which Christians have often to suffer at the hands of non-Christians. That non-Christians treat those they dislike in this way is not to be wondered at. Paul also lists it a vice commonly found among the unconverted (Rom. 1: 30). But it is a wrong no Christian should allow himself to be guilty of, and certainly it is a wrong he should not inflict on a fellow-Christian. 1 Peter 2: 1 firmly insists that all who have become Christians discard this type of conduct, along with every other evil thing; and it is with shame and sorrow that Paul writes to the Church members at Corinth that he has reason to fear that this ugly sin is prevalent among them (2 Cor. 12: 20).

This hinting at other people's faults and suggesting bad motives for apparently praiseworthy acts is a mean sin. It springs very often from pride, since to refer to the fault of another seems to imply that we are free from it ourselves. Calvin refers to this sin as "fondly exalting ourselves by calumniating others". Few things so lower the moral temperature, and so conclusively destroy harmony and goodwill within a community. John Wesley's comment on it is: "This is a great hindrance to peace. O who is sufficiently aware of it."

It is perhaps this association between disparagement of others and pride in ourselves which forms the link between this verse and the preceding one. If we are humble before God and towards men, not wishing to exalt ourselves above them, by representing them as poorer Christians than we ourselves are, then we shall have no heart for "talking them down".

Moffatt, however, finds it so difficult to establish a connection between verses 10 and 11 that, in his translation, he transfers verses 11 and 12 to follow 2: 13. Certainly that context is also dealing with the topic of the sins of the tongue, but there is no manuscript evidence for so drastic a rearrangement.

James reinforces his plea for the kind of conduct one would expect among members of a Christian congregation by reminding them that they are indeed members of one and the same family. He addresses them again as "BROTHERS". The thought of their loyalty to the family solidarity, if nothing else, should restrain them from disparaging other members in the family. This appeal to their loyalty to the "brotherhood" is further underlined by the introduction of the word "brother" twice more in this same verse. That brother for whose sake we are not willing even to refrain our tongue from biting words, by imposing on it the twofold bridle of truth and love, is the "brother for whom Christ died" (Rom. 14: 15).

To disparage a person is, in effect, to pass judgement on him or on some action of his as being in some way discreditable. The sin of disparagement is, therefore, forbidden by our Lord in his precise words: "Judge not, that you be not judged" (Matt. 7: 1 and Luke 6: 37), and by Paul, "Let us no more pass judgement on one another" (Rom. 14: 13). It is not surprising, therefore, that James here equates "speaking evil against one's brother" with "JUDGING ONE'S BROTHER".

To set oneself up as judge over a brother's conduct is for us arrogantly to usurp God's prerogative. Judgement and punishment of wrongdoers rightly belong to God. It is wrong for ignorant and misinformed man to assume to himself a right which belongs only to One who knows all the facts, and reads the heart as well as the overt action. "Justice is mine, says the Lord, I will repay" (Rom. 12: 19, N.E.B.). Our task is mercy, not judgement.

Some of our Lord's parables also make the point that Christians are not to spend their time trying to discover those in their midst who are not perfect. Many fail to reach that standard, but to become censorious of fellow-Christians is usually to fall into a fault more grievous than the one which we criticize in them. The parables of the Tares and the Dragnet (Matt. 13: 24ff., and 47ff.) seem to point this lesson. Judgement is to be left to God, not snatched by us out of His hands. The precise words of Jesus about the speck and the log in Matt. 7: 3-5 warn us how blind we can be to our own grievous faults, even while we strive to put right unimportant frailties in another. Censoriousness is one of the besetting sins of the saintly; but the true saint is one who neither judges nor disparages another, about whom those who know him best can say: "I do not remember him ever saying an unkind word about anyone".

James now makes a further point: to speak evil against one's brother or to judge him is to SPEAK EVIL AGAINST THE LAW. This English translation is ambiguous. It could mean simply that by disparaging another we are breaking the law. The original Greek, however, makes it clear that this is not the meaning of the phrase. The N.E.B. brings out the true meaning unmistakably: "He who disparages his brother disparages the law".

The "law" here may mean the Jewish Law, but more probably James is thinking of what he has already called "the Royal Law" (2: 8) and "the law of freedom" (2: 12). This means the Jewish Law as fulfilled by Jesus in his life and teaching (Matt. 5: 17), its imperfections removed or corrected, so that it represents the complete will of God. It is made clear in 2: 8 that the basis of this new moral law of the Christian is that single commandment out of the Old Testament which our Lord Himself selected from among the great mass of commandments to serve as the summary of God's will for us in all our relationships with our fellows: "You shall love your neighbour as yourself" (Lev. 19: 18; Mark 12: 31).

To love one's neighbour as oneself clearly rules out all talk about his supposed faults and weaknesses, since we certainly should not like to think that others were doing this to us. Indeed in the original context in Leviticus, the commandment is directed against this very fault. Lev. 19: 16 reads: "You shall not go up and down as a slanderer (R.V. has 'tale-bearer') among your people", and Lev. 19: 18 has: "You shall not bear any grudge against the sons of your own people, but" (what is indeed the very opposite) "you shall love your neighbour as yourself".

Disparaging and judging a brother, therefore, clearly breaks the law of love toward one's neighbour. But James says further that it is to "speak against the law" itself. This must mean that to slight and ignore a law deliberately is to set oneself above the law, and by our act, if not in precise word, to declare it a bad law, not worthy to be obeyed. Every time we break the law we undermine its authority both in our own lives and in the lives of others. So by disregarding this law of love we are undermining its validity, we are disparaging it. We are also guilty of JUDGING THE LAW, since by our conduct we are setting ourselves up as superior to it, with a right to abrogate it when we think it inapplicable to ourselves.

If, however, you act as though you knew better than the law, writes James, IF YOU JUDGE THE LAW, YOU ARE NOT A DOER OF THE LAW. God gave the law for it to be obeyed in real life, not merely listened to in the formal worship of the Church. He expects His people to be not merely "hearers of the law", but "doers" of it (Rom. 2: 13). Still less does He expect them to become critics of the law (i.e. judges of it), as they do when they set their own judgement above that of the law.

**4: 12** THERE IS only ONE LAWGIVER: that is, God. He gave the law. He is above the law. He alone has the right to modify or overrule it. If a man presumes to interfere with the law, which is the declared will of God to man through Christ, he is usurping the prerogative of God. Man should obey God's law, not aim at setting up a different law more congenial to his human weaknesses.

God is not only lawgiver, but JUDGE, in the sense that it is His responsibility to enforce the law, once it has been given. He declares what is right, and also upholds it.

The strong note of Jewish monotheism is heard in the word "ONE". It reminds us of a similar emphasis on the "one" who alone can rightly be called "good" (Mark 10: 18). To Him alone belongs the verdict, "Well done", or "Depart from me", as he assesses those whose lives should be controlled by the law He has given. HE IS ABLE TO SAVE AND TO DESTROY. This twofold power in God is constantly affirmed in the Old Testament: "I kill and I make alive" (Deut. 32: 39, cf. 1 Sam. 2: 6–7; 2 Kings 5: 7; Ps. 68: 20).

"He is able" is a recurring phrase in the New Testament, and very often what He is able to do is to "save", or to offer some kind of effective aid (Matt. 3: 9; Rom. 14: 4; 2 Cor. 9: 8 ; Eph. 3: 20; Phil. 3: 21; 2 Tim. 1: 12; Heb. 2: 18; 7: 25; Jude 24). It can, in the New Testament as well as in the Old, also be associated, as here, with the power to destroy as well as to save (cf. Matt. 10: 28: "Fear him who can destroy both soul and body in hell").

"Save" and "destroy" are words which may have a *present* spiritual meaning, or a *future* eschatological meaning. Salvation can mean the restoration of the human personality (body and soul) to what God intended it to be; and death can be that separation from God, even in this life, which sin has caused. Paul can speak of those who are "dead in trespasses", and of the triumph of sin over a living man as "death" (Rom. 7: 9–10). Here, however, the reference appears to be largely to the *future* verdict of God as Judge.

Having rebuked those who by their criticism of others show that they flout the law of love and take to themselves rights which belong only to God, James concludes with a devastating shaft of withering frankness: BUT WHO ARE YOU THAT YOU JUDGE YOUR NEIGHBOUR? Are you so much better than others that you can set yourself up as their judge. Who do you think you are, assuming to yourself the authority to act in God's place? John Wesley in his commentary supplies the answer which the form of the question implies: "A poor, weak, dying worm".

The use of the word NEIGHBOUR (replacing "brother" of verse 11) makes it clear that all along it has been the "royal law" (2: 8) of love for neighbour which has been the law under discussion in this section.

> 4: 13–17. *Come now, you who say, "Today or tomorrow we will go into such and such a town and spend a year there and trade and get gain"; 14. whereas you do not know about tomorrow. What is your life? For you are a mist that appears for a little time and then vanishes. 15. Instead you ought to say, "If the Lord wills, we shall live and we shall do this or that". 16. As it is, you boast in your arrogance. All such boasting is evil.*
>
> 17. *Whoever knows what is right to do and fails to do it, for him it is sin.*

Verses 13–16 are a further rebuke to man's arrogance and self-sufficiency. In the previous section James has condemned the sinful act of the man who assumes to himself God's function as Judge, and finds fault with his fellows, subjecting their conduct to disparaging criticism. Here another aspect of man's presumptuous self-confidence is exposed—his assumption that he is the final arbiter of his own life. He plans for the future without any recognition that our times are in God's hands, and not in our own. To walk humbly with God, as we are required to do, implies a recognition that it is only in God's merciful providence that we shall be alive next year or even tomorrow. No man knows what a day may bring. The proper attitude to life is to acknowledge humbly this dependence on God, and when plans for the future have to be made, to make them in a humble spirit which knows that though "man proposes, God disposes".

Verse 17 states a most important truth about what is included within the word "sin". It appears to be only loosely attached to the preceding verses.

**4: 13** The opening words of 4: 13 are the same as those of 5: 1: "COME NOW". It is a colloquial phrase which indicates that James is addressing himself to a different group of people, and asking for their attention. N.E.B. happily translates the phrase as: "A word with you, you who say . . ."

The people addressed are those who have prospered in their business and commerce. As the result of past success they are full of confidence in their powers to TRADE AND GET further GAIN. They say, as they discuss their plans: TODAY OR TOMORROW WE WILL GO INTO SUCH AND SUCH A TOWN AND SPEND A YEAR THERE. Not only is the next day confidently treated as their own inalienable property, but the next year also.

James's rebuke is not a condemnation of wise planning in advance. Efficient community life requires such planning, as Joseph as "prime minister" in Egypt proved. What is condemned is the attitude of mind which enters into such planning without a humble recognition that it is God, not we ourselves, with whom lies the authority to determine whether we are alive this time next year or even tomorrow. They ignore the wise words of Prov. 27: 1: "Boast not about tomorrow, for we never know what a day will bring".

Even outside the Bible wise men have commended this attitude of humility towards the future. Seneca, for instance wrote: "No man has such rich friends that he can promise himself tomorrow". Our Lord Himself forcefully commended it too in the parable of the Rich Fool, where He exposes the utter folly of assuming that the unknown future is at our disposal. Like those whom James addresses, the Rich Man had prospered. He had stored up resources sufficient to provide him with comfort and luxury for many years to come. He was full of self-congratulation and complacency. But the future is God's, not man's and God said to him: "Fool! This night your soul is required of you" (Luke 12: 16ff.; cf. Ecclus. 11: 18–19). A humbler man would have acknowledged his gratitude to God for the past, and his dependence on God for the future; perhaps also, with such material wealth at his disposal he would have remembered the needs of so many of his less fortunate fellow men and women. (This failure in charity is particularly the theme of the next section, see 5: 1ff.) This rich man, however, congratulates himself on "many years" of affluence in front of him. Those whom James reprimands do not look further ahead than one year, but the offence is the same. Calvin comments: "They claimed for themselves a whole year, though they had not a single moment in their own power. . . . We are sure, no not even of one moment". As James says simply: "YOU DO NOT KNOW ABOUT TO-MORROW".

**4: 14** WHAT IS YOUR LIFE? What is its nature, its quality? What does it most remind you of? What the Bible calls the "everlasting hills"? Certainly not. The things to which life is likened in the Bible are those things which are most transient, short-lived and insecure. It is like "an evening shadow" (Ps. 102: 11), "the wind" (Job 7: 7), "a cloud" (Job 7: 9), or "grass" (Ps. 103: 15), which in Palestine is green for a few brief days, and then is scorched up by the searing wind (cf. also James 1: 10–11). So here James calls it "a mist". The word could also be translated as "steam", or "vapour", or "a puff of smoke"—something which is there for a passing moment, and then has gone, with no kind of permanence in itself. So is our life: it APPEARS FOR A LITTLE TIME, AND THEN VANISHES.

**4: 15** This uncertainty of human life is used in Wisdom 2: 4 by evildoers as an excuse for snatching all the pleasure out of it while there is time. Others use it as an excuse for attempting nothing. Here James refers to it as a reason why men should be humble before God, and in all their future planning acknowledge that all we intend is subject to the will of God. INSTEAD YOU OUGHT TO SAY: IF THE LORD WILLS.

Even before the time of Christ, there was a conventional piety, which was accustomed to use this or some similar phrase. In such writers, for instance, as Xenophon, Plato, Plautus, Ennius, Livy, we meet the words, "if God wills", or "if the gods will". It is true that sometimes they represent little more than a superstitious formula, used as an attempt to propitiate the anger of any god who might bring ill upon them, if they do not properly acknowledge him. In some cases, how-ever, it may have represented an attitude of genuine piety and a recognition that human life did not possess in itself the power to deter-mine its own future. In Latin this acknowledgement of God's due rights sometimes took the form of "deo volente" ("God willing"), whose initial letters form the convential phrase "D.V.".

At first we may be surprised to find that phrases such as this do not, however, commonly occur in the Bible. This is certainly not because the Biblical writers overlooked the truth about our utter dependence on God, but rather because this thought is so basic to their whole attitude that it is assumed rather than precisely expressed. It is used, however, sometimes when a writer finds himself compelled to refer to his own future plans. Paul, for instance, as he passes through Ephesus on his way to Palestine, hoping to call in to see the Christians there on his way back to Europe, says: "I will return to you, if God wills" (Acts 18: 21). To the Corinthians he writes: "I will come to you soon, if the Lord wills" (1 Cor. 4: 19; 16: 7). Elsewhere he writes: "I hope in the Lord to send Timothy to you soon" (Phil. 2: 19 and 24), where "in the Lord" expresses the same acknowledgement of God's authority as "if the Lord wills". Heb. 6: 3 uses the phrase also.

Some have understood James's use of the word "say" to mean that these words must be audibly spoken, but this is to press the matter far too rigidly. The Rich Fool, in the parable, for instance, is described as "saying" certain things, but it is quite clear that they are really thoughts within his own mind (Luke 12: 17, 18). There are times when these words should be used in open speech, but very often, even when the words themselves are not used for others to hear, the attitude of mind which they represent is present in the speaker and it is the right attitude of mind that matters most. Calvin recognizes this: "No scruple ought to be entertained, as though it were some sin to omit them; for we read everywhere in the Scriptures that the holy servants of God spoke unconditionally of future things, when yet they had it as a principle fixed in their minds, that they could do nothing without the presence of God".

Indeed there is a danger that a facile and parrot-like use of the phrase "God-willing" or "D.V." may degenerate into a mere form of words, as Tasker reminds us: the phrase "may be used glibly and become a formality devoid of religious content".

At the same time a Christian's reluctance to use it at all in his speech *may* spring, not from a determination to avoid sham piety, but from a blameworthy timidity to bear testimony to his faith in God's controlling authority over his life. But whether the words are audibly spoken or not, it is important that our attitude to the future and our plans in it, should be made only with a humble awareness that all we intend is "under God".

The acknowledgement of our dependence on God should not, however, be made an excuse for inactivity. Plans both for human business and for God's work have to be carefully prepared in advance if they are later to be effectively carried out. We are to say: "IF THE LORD WILLS, WE SHALL LIVE AND DO THIS OR THAT".[1] To plan ahead is right, provided we approach it humbly before God. It is not wise forethought which is deprecated, but arrogant self-confidence towards God in our attitude to the future. It is this attitude which James rebukes in the words: AS IT IS YOU BOAST IN YOUR ARROGANCE.

**4: 16** This word "BOAST" (*kauchaomai*) is a common one in the epistles of the New Testament. Paul treats it as almost the fundamental human sin (cf. 1 Cor. 1: 31; 2 Cor. 10: 17; Gal. 6: 14). It is very near to what is meant by "pride" in the list of the Seven Deadly sins. It refers not so much to spoken words (as our English word "boast" suggests) as to an attitude of mind. It represents human self-confidence and self-congratulation. This may find expression in defiance of God, in disregard for God, and also in the service of God. It was the characteristic sin of the Pharisees, which turned their devotion to God into what our Lord called "hypocrisy". They claim to be serving God but fundamentally it was their own self-interest and self-importance they were seeking to further. It was not the humble endeavour to please and honour God which filled their thought, but

---

[1] Some ancient manuscripts punctuate this sentence: "If God wills and if we live, we shall do . . ." This is how it appears in the Latin Vulgate, and some early English translators (e.g. Tyndale) accepted it in this form. The A.V., however, and other English translations since have abandoned it in favour of the reading represented in the R.S.V., and supported by stronger manuscript evidence. The reading with the weaker manuscript evidence is also the one with the less satisfactory meaning, since it fails to emphasize that for life itself, as well as for what we do with it, we are utterly dependent on God.

the aim to establish themselves before God and men as religious people of outstanding achievement and merit. It was this that Paul chastised, in himself no less than in others, because it was the very thing which had long shut him out (when he was a Pharisee) from the free grace of God.

Here, however, the "boasting" which is deplored does not spring from a misdirected religious zeal, but from a complete disregard for God, as though human skill and cleverness were omni-competent.

The word "arrogance" (*alazonia*, translated by Ropes as "acts of presumption", and by Moffatt as "proud pretensions") is also used in 1 John 2: 16, where it is translated "the pride" of life. In association with "the lust of the flesh" and "the lust of the eyes" it represents the spirit of "the world" which is at enmity with God and with all God stands for. ALL SUCH BOASTING, with its accompanying "arrogance", writes James, IS EVIL.

**4: 17** This verse, like so many other verses in James, represents with striking accuracy one element in the teaching of Jesus. It emphasizes that sin consists not only in doing what is forbidden by God, but also in failing to do what is good, when the opportunity to do good is there. WHOEVER KNOWS WHAT IS RIGHT TO DO AND FAILS TO DO IT, FOR HIM IT IS SIN.

The R.S.V. uses the phrase "what is right", where we have preferred the words "what is good". The Greek word is '*kalon*' (not *dikaion*) meaning "good" rather than "right" and this appears to be the meaning James intended. N.E.B. translates: "He who knows *the good*. . . ."

Some commentators have made ingenious attempts to relate the meaning of this verse to the preceding section, but without much success. It might be argued that "the good thing" which has been neglected is the precaution of adding the proviso, "God willing", to any statement about future plans. But this is very far-fetched, and restricts the meaning of the verse to such an extent as to rob it of significance. Barclay explains the connection: "So James ends with a threat. If a man knows a thing is wrong and still continues to do it, that to him is sin". Ropes is less confident: "This is a maxim added merely to call attention to the preceding and with no obvious application". Mayor's explanation is a little more probable: "The verse sums up all that has been said before, going as far back as 1: 22; 2: 14; 3: 1, 13; 4: 11".

Moffatt, on the other hand, so completely despairs of establishing any link with the context that he suggests it has been misplaced, and in his translation actually transfers it to follow 2: 21. This is a desperate remedy without any manuscript authority. It does, however, underline the inescapable conclusion that this verse must be treated as an independent saying (and a very important one) which is slipped in at this point in the epistle, but without any pretence that it arises out of what has gone before. It would be better if it were printed to form a separate paragraph on its own.

The emphasis on one "who knows what is right and fails to do it" creates a superficial resemblance to the saying of Jesus in Luke 12: 47 where our Lord declares that a much more severe punishment will be administered to one who does wrong, knowing that it is wrong, than to one who commits the same offence, without realizing that he is doing wrong. But James here is not really making this particular point at all. Rather he seeks to say that to miss an opportunity of doing good is a sin, no less than actually to do an evil thing.

It is an insistence that "sins of omission" should not be treated as less serious than "sins of commission". The sins which we confess when we say, "We have left undone those things which we ought to have done", are just as much sin as those we mean when we say, "We have done those things which we ought not to have done". It is a common fault, however, to regard the former as insignificant. To miss a chance of doing good is not what most people regard as "sin". To rob a starving child of its food is ugly sin, but we are not so disturbed about the apathy that fails to relieve hunger, when it is in our power to do so. To lock an old person in a room and keep all her friends away is obvious sin, but we do not think of it as sin to leave an old person in continuing loneliness, when it may be in our power to relieve it.

"Sin is lawlessness" is the definition in 1 John 3: 4. This is easy to understand and not too difficult to apply. We can learn what kind of conduct is precisely prohibited, and with diligence we can perhaps avoid breaking these laws. But James's further definition sets up a standard of perfection which convicts our best endeavours of sin. We may be able to avoid committing forbidden evil; but who can ever seize positively every opportunity of doing good? Yet this emphasis is deeply true to the teaching of Jesus. Not only is positive cruelty wrong, but the absence of positive love is wrong. In the parable of the Good Samaritan, the priest and Levite do the injured man no positive wrong; they only fail to provide help in his need; yet for ever they stand branded as sinners by this failure. In the parable of Dives and Lazarus the rich man was not guilty of breaking any law by ill-treating Lazarus, only of neglecting a recurring opportunity to show mercy. The one-talent man is condemned, not for what he did, but for what he failed to do. In the moving parable of the Sheep and the Goats, those who stand condemned before Christ have done no conscious wrong to anyone at all; their only failure is the neglect to do good when they might have done it, because they regarded the needy people as not important enough to bother with.

Leading teachers of the Jewish law, even before the time of Jesus, had suggested that the whole tenor of the law could be summarized in the one sentence: "What is hateful to thyself *do not* to another". This sets a high standard of conduct, but one which is much less demanding than the positive re-phrasing of it which Jesus commended: "Whatever you wish that men should do to you, *do* so to them". This means not only the avoidance of what may hurt them, but the positive seeking of every opportunity to do them good. It is an interpretation of the second great command of Jesus: "You shall love your neighbour as yourself".

This positive commandment and the reflection of it in this description by James of what is meant by "sin" lays an obligation on man which he can never completely fulfil. He may at his best be able to avoid doing forbidden wrong, but who can ever seize *every* opportunity of doing good? It is this continuing obligation laid on us as Christians which makes the words of Jesus so pointedly true: "When you have done all that is commanded you, say, 'We are unworthy servants; we have only done what was our duty' " (Luke 17: 10).

This obligation of active love towards all, which longs not only to take, but also to make opportunities of doing good to others, man cannot ever altogether fulfil. If he recognizes this, he will always be humble before God. He will never become guilty of the sin of "boasting" or of "arrogance" before God—the sin rebuked in 4: 6–17.

These words of James are not to be regarded as in themselves a complete definition of sin. They are a kind of codicil to more elementary definitions, already accepted, and not needing to be repeated. This word of James emphasizes an oft-forgotten element in what God means by "sin". And "sin", we must remember, is that which is an offence against God, as well as against man.

# CHAPTER FIVE

*5: 1–6. Come now, you rich, weep and howl for the miseries that are coming upon you. 2. Your riches have rotted and your garments are moth-eaten. 3. Your gold and your silver have rusted, and their rust will be evidence against you and will eat your flesh like fire. You have laid up treasure for the last days. 4. Behold, the wages of the labourers who mowed your fields, which you kept back by fraud, cry out; and the cries of the harvesters have reached the ears of the Lord of hosts. 5. You have lived on the earth in luxury and pleasure; you have fattened your hearts in a day of slaughter. 6. You have condemned, you have killed the righteous man; he does not resist you.*

The rich, so often the object of other people's envy, are here the object of James's scorn and condemnation. This is because they are putting their arrogant trust in things that are doomed to decay and destruction. Moreover their greed for wealth, and their confidence in its power to solve every problem have led them into an attitude of cruel unconcern for the needs and rights of others poorer than themselves, and they accept as their due a manner of life which is self-indulgent, luxurious and demoralizing.

**5: 1** COME NOW, YOU RICH: as in 4: 13 attention is asked of a new group of people by the words: Come now. N.E.B. renders it: "Next a word to you who have great possessions". The denunciation which follows reads like a passage from one of the prophetic writings. The same highly-coloured, rhetorical phrases are called into use, as for example, "weep and howl", and "a day of slaughter".

The "rich" who are condemned are probably not members of the Christian community. There were some who were members who could be described as "rich", since they are referred to in 1: 9–11. Here, however, as at 2: 2–6, the rich are not those within the church, and the words addressed to them are not primarily intended for their good, but rather for the benefit of the Christians who read them. Their intention is not to awaken the rich to a sense of their imminent peril, but rather to dissuade hesitant Christians from falling into a foolish attitude of envy towards the powers and privileges which wealth seems to confer on those who possess it. In 2: 2–6 the Christians were rebuked for showing fussy and fawning deference to a newcomer, merely because he looked rich. Such false deference is very close to envy. James here tries to show that for those with eyes to see the truth their present state should awaken pity rather than envy.

The danger to spiritual values which lies in riches is strongly emphasized by our Lord. One of His "woes" is: "Woe to you that are rich, for you have received your consolation" (Luke 6: 24). He told the parable of the "Rich Fool" to teach that "a man's life does not consist in the abundance of his possessions" (Luke 12: 15). He insisted that it is "hard for those who have riches to enter the Kingdom of God", so hard in fact as to be virtually impossible, since it is "easier for a camel to go through the eye of a needle" (Luke 18: 24–5).

It may be true, as many continue to affirm, that the Bible does not condemn wealth as such but only the misuse of it, but this comforting palliative should not be allowed to blind us to the severity of the words of Jesus on this subject. Barclay comments: "There is no book which more strenuously insists (than the Bible) on the responsibility of wealth and on the perils which surround a man who is abundantly blessed with this world's goods". This is certainly not an overstatement.

Just as our Lord calls on those who "laugh now" to "mourn and weep", so James summons the rich so to realize the desperate peril in which they stand as to WEEP AND HOWL. To western ears this sounds somewhat over-dramatic, but in the east deep sorrow and distress do receive more open and vocal expression than is customary amongst us (cf. Mark 5: 38). The rich may appear now to be enjoying comfort and security, but these are illusory. MISERIES ARE COMING UPON YOU. The reference here is not merely to the uncertainty of riches, which can suddenly vanish leaving a man poor and friendless, but rather to the thought that God's time is near. His judgement is soon to be upon the earth. The coming of the Lord is near (see 5: 7, 8, 9), and with it the end of this present dispensation. The rich will have to endure the tribulations which precede His coming, and rejection from God when the judgement is pronounced.

**5: 2** Riches in the ancient world fell mainly into three groups: foodstuffs (cf. the Rich Fool, Luke 12: 18), costly garments (cf. apparel in Acts 20: 33), and precious metals. James has these three groups in mind. He does not specifically mention them, but the three different kinds of destruction which he mentions as overtaking gathered wealth apply to these categories. When he writes: "YOUR RICHES HAVE ROTTED" it is of foodstuffs that he is thinking. In storage they have become unfit for human consumption and are valueless. The precious GARMENTS ARE MOTH-EATEN. Moth grubs have eaten holes in them, and now nobody wants them. Even GOLD AND SILVER, usually unaffected by damp or vermin or age, HAVE RUSTED.

It is curious that these verbs are all in the past tense, as if they described something which had already taken place. Tasker takes them literally, and understands James to be describing a disaster which has already overtaken the rich. But this seems unlikely. Mayor must be right when he characterizes these tenses as "prophetic perfects". A prophet, speaking of some future event, whether good or ill, which he was quite certain was going to happen, could give expression to his certainty by speaking of the event as already having happened (as, for instance, at Isa. 44: 23; 53: 5–10). The complete reversal of fortune for the rich and the end of their present enjoyment of comfort and privilege is so certain that James speaks of it as if it had already taken place. It is possible to regard this disaster as involving the actual loss of their material wealth. More likely the disaster is described in physical terms, but it refers to the complete worthlessness of material wealth when man stands before the judgement of God.

**5: 3** It is strange to find James speaking of silver and gold as "rusting", because in fact these metals are not subject to rust. Some suggest that James, being himself a poor man, was not sufficiently acquainted with silver and gold to know this truth about them. Others think that he knew this perfectly well, but was indicating the magnitude of the disaster that lay ahead, by saying that even those things that normally keep their value in all circumstances would in this particular catastrophe become as valueless as old iron, corroded by rust. More probably the word "rust" is used metaphorically of that which ruins metals, and here simply expresses strongly that gold and silver, the source of their wealth, become worthless like the rest of their property.

THEIR RUST WILL BE EVIDENCE AGAINST YOU, that is, the fact that such permanently valuable materials as silver and gold become valueless in this emergency gives them proof "of the perishableness of all earthly things" (Mayor). If these cannot be trusted to keep their value, we see how insecure is trust placed in any kind of riches at all.

IT WILL EAT YOUR FLESH LIKE FIRE. The Greek word here translated "flesh" is in fact a plural form, and this could be signified by translating it as "your fleshly parts", but the singular "flesh" serves just as well. The sentence is another highly metaphorical way of saying that the failure of their wealth brings complete ruin on the rich, for they have nothing else in life to rely on. Some wish to press the metaphor a little further and see in it a reference to wealth holding a man in its grip as if it were an iron fetter, which in time expands with the process of rust until it eats into the flesh of the limbs which it surrounds. But this is to press the metaphor further than is necessary.

It acts LIKE FIRE, ruthlessly destroying all it touches. There may be an implied reference to the fire of Gehenna, consuming all that is corrupt and evil and unfit to survive. This is a common idea in the

New Testament (cf. Matt. 5: 22). God, when He comes in judgement, is a devouring fire (Deut. 4: 24), and His punishments are likened to fire (Isa. 10: 16; 30: 27, 30).

YOU HAVE LAID UP TREASURE FOR THE LAST DAYS: that is, you have been laying up treasure on the earth at a time when such an accumulation of material wealth is ludicrously inappropriate. Treasures on earth which moth and rust consume (Matt. 6: 19) are out of place "in an age that is near its close" (N.E.B.). There will never be time for the owners to enjoy it all, and, what is worse, it has distracted their thoughts from urgent issues of life and death, with which they should have been vitally concerned.

It is rather odd that R.S.V. translates the Greek phrase which means "in the last days" as "*for* the last days". This seems a quite unwarrantable change. Presumably the R.S.V. treated "in" as used in a kind of proleptic sense, "to be available in" the last days.

In striking contrast to this mistaken storing up of false treasure, Tobit 4: 7–11 commends those who, by practising almsgiving and charitable deeds, and generously sharing their plenty with those less fortunate, store up good treasure with the words: "So you will be laying up a good treasure for yourself against the day of necessity".

There is a divergence of opinion over the punctuation of verse 3. The two Greek words translated "like fire" may, in fact, be attached to the words which follow rather than (as in R.S.V.) to those which precede. In this case the translation would be (as in R.S.V. footnote) ". . . will eat your flesh, since you have stored up fire for the last days". This would mean that their short-sighted conduct has secured for them punishment by fire in the last judgement. Ropes favours this punctuation,[1] but most other commentators prefer the other.[2]

One element in the sin which rich men are prone to is that they store up wealth for their own future use, when about them are numbers of their fellow men actually perishing in bitter need of the food which this wealth could be used to provide for them *now*. They even continue to store it, when it is likely to go rotten, preferring to see it go bad on their own hands than shared out while still good for the benefit of others. In the end the rich lose it, and the poor remain hungry. Calvin in his commentary denounces this callously selfish misuse of the good gifts of God: "God has not appointed gold for rust, nor garments for moths; but on the contrary has designed them as helps and aids to

---

[1] Ropes's argument in favour of this punctuation is based mainly on the ground that the Greek verb *thesauro*, meaning "lay up treasure" or "store", requires a direct object. "Fire" can be treated as this object; if, however, it is associated with the preceding words, then the verb is left without an object. Other scholars do not feel this to be a serious difficulty, and some regard the phrase "store up fire" as strange. It is, however, found also in the LXX of Prov. 16: 27.

[2] Some late MSS introduce "wrath" as object of "store up", probably on the pattern of Rom. 2: 5.

human life. Therefore even spending without benefit is witness of inhumanity". If this is an inhuman treatment of wealth, the "human" way is commended in Ecclesiasticus: "Lose your silver for the sake of a brother or a friend, and do not let it rust under a stone and be lost. . . . Store up almsgiving in your treasury" (29: 8–13).

**5: 4** James has condemned the rich for their folly in putting their trust in material wealth, which is insecure even here on earth, and is worthless in the Day of Judgement. Implicit in his condemnation is also a rebuke to their indifference to the crying needs of others. Now he turns to other sins with which wealth is all too often associated. The first is a callous disregard for the rights of others, which Calvin describes as "the inevitable companion of avarice". Food is no problem for the rich. They have plenty for the present and also for the immediate future. They show no understanding of the needs of those who need each day's wage immediately in order to buy food for that day, even though these needs are recognized and protected by the law.

The great poverty of the day-labourer in Palestine in the first century is frequently reflected in the Bible. Both law-makers and prophets tried to safeguard his interests against callous employers. The law, for instance, required that "The wages of a hired servant shall not remain with you all night until morning" (Lev. 19: 13; see also Deut. 24: 15, Tobit 4: 14). In the parable of the Workers in the Vineyard (Matt. 20: 1ff.) all are paid at the end of the day. The primary purpose of this legislation was probably the extreme poverty of the worker. He needed the money for his family's immediate needs. There may have been a secondary purpose: a delay in payment made it easier for the employer to underpay the worker, since hours of work become more open to dispute the longer a calculation is postponed. Immediate payment therefore was to the advantage of the worker. "To oppress the hireling in his wages" was a fault frequently rebuked (Mal. 3: 5; Amos 8: 4; Prov. 3: 27–28; Hermas Vis. III, 9: 4–6). At a time when so many were unemployed and desperately poor, it was all too easy for the employer to defraud the worker, since the poor man feared that to demand justice might exclude him from future opportunity to earn.

So here James rebukes the rich for breaking this just law of God by failing to make daily payments, and by using the delay in payment to defraud the worker of his due.

The word translated "fields" would be better rendered by "estates" or "farms". The Greek word implies something more extensive than what we usually mean by "fields", and indicates the great wealth of the owners.

This offence of the rich against the poor is not just a contravention

of a human law; it is an offence against God Himself. Using a Biblical
turn of speech he says that wages, unfairly withheld, CRY OUT to
God, for the punishment of the wrong-doer and the vindication
of the wronged. So the blood of the murdered Abel "cried out
to God" (Gen. 4: 10). So in the actual law about the immediate
payment of labourers in Deut. 24: 15 (already cited) the unjust
employer is warned that the defrauded labourer may "cry against you
to the Lord, and it be sin in you". Our Lord also speaks of the very
stones *crying out* in protest (Luke 19: 40). THE HARVESTERS are named
as a particular type of labourer, the casual nature of whose work
exposes them even more than regular workers to fraud in the event of
any delay in the payment of wages.

"Their cries have reached the ears of THE LORD OF HOSTS". This
name for God has a special note of majesty about it. "Hosts" may have
originally meant "armies", but was commonly understood to mean
"the heavenly bodies". It is of interest that this name, indicative of
the might and transcendence of God, should be used here. James
is saying that it is the same God, who created the sun, moon, and
stars, and who orders their courses, who is also deeply concerned
about the just treatment of the poor and insignificant, ready to
defend them from injustice and punish the wrongdoers. As, in Ps.
147: 3–4, the One who heals the broken-hearted is the same mighty
God who "determines the number of the stars", so here (and also
at Isa. 5: 9) He who is Lord of Hosts is the protector of the oppressed
and ill-treated.

The Greek word here translated "hosts" is a transliteration into
Greek letters of the Hebrew word for "hosts" (*sabaoth*). In the older
English versions this form was retained (not translated) and the
"Lord of Sabaoth" is found both here and elsewhere (e.g. Isa. 1: 9;
Rom. 9: 29), and occurs also in the Te Deum.

**5: 5** A further sinful accompaniment of wealth is now rebuked—
a demoralizing self-indulgence in an extravagant and luxurious
standard of life. YOU HAVE LIVED ON THE EARTH IN LUXURY AND
PLEASURE. The word for "luxury" implies only extravagant comfort,
but the word for "pleasure" suggests dissoluteness as well. The
phrase "ON THE EARTH" appears to be used in contrast to the judgement
which proceeds from the God of heaven. So, in the parable of Jesus,
Father Abraham says to the rich man suffering punishment: "You
*in your lifetime* received your good things". Such self-indulgence and
sinful pleasure-seeking is a poor preparation for the Judgement of God.

This luxurious idleness is further condemned in the words: "YOU
HAVE FATTENED YOUR HEARTS (AS) IN A DAY OF SLAUGHTER". Some
MSS introduced "as" into the sentence. A.V. retained it, but R.V.
and R.S.V. omit it.

Various explanations have been offered for "A DAY OF SLAUGHTER" (some assuming the "as" as part of the text):

(1) Calvin suggests that the most sumptuous banquets were normally held in connection with a religious sacrifice when animals were slaughtered, and their flesh was available in abundance for the meal. So for these rich people every meal has become such a resplendent feast.

(2) Blackman writes: "The metaphor seems to be from the unrestrained feasting of the victors after a battle".

(3) Barclay interprets it figuratively, the slaughter being not that of beasts or vanquished enemies, but the destruction of the people themselves: "Selfishness always leads to the death of the soul".

(4) Others understand it to mean that by all this overeating the rich are treating themselves like bullocks being fattened for the slaughter-house (cf. Jer. 25: 34). The N.E.B. translation suggests this interpretation: "fattening yourselves like cattle". In this case "the day of slaughter" is a symbolic phrase for the Judgement of God soon to fall on them.

Instead of "laying aside every weight and the sin which clings so closely" (Heb. 12: 1), their conduct shows a gross unpreparedness for the time of testing just ahead of them.

The callousness of the rich to the needs and rights of others has been exposed, and also their luxurious self-indulgence. Now a third fault is impugned: they make use of their influence and standing in society to humiliate and destroy (even by perverting the course of justice) men of honour and conscience, whose very uprightness stands as a rebuke to their own dishonourable practices. These men of honour are described as "the righteous man", that is, "righteous men" as a class. Since, however, the singular is used some have seen in "the righteous man" a reference to James himself, who came to be known as James the Just; but this is unlikely, especially in view of the words: "You have killed the righteous man". Others interpret it as a reference to Jesus, who is precisely called the Righteous One in Acts (3: 14; 7: 52; 22: 14), and who at the time of His death on the Cross was acclaimed by the centurion as a "righteous man" (Luke 23: 47). Certainly Jesus was "the righteous man", who suffered at the hands of wicked men, and, in a sense, has become the type of all those "who suffer for righteousness' sake". But it is very doubtful whether the words here refer specifically to Jesus.

We take "the righteous man", therefore, to mean "those who are righteous". The phrase is used in this sense elsewhere, for example at Amos 2: 6 and 5: 12. Particularly, however, this usage is reminiscent of the book of Wisdom (2: 10, 12, 16, 18). Indeed the whole passage,

Wisdom 2: 6-24, has much in common with this paragraph in James. The phrase means what we might call "one of God's saints", one who humbly acknowledges God and lives in obedience to the will of God.

Such people become easy victims of unscrupulously evil men, since they do not retaliate with injury on those who have injured them. These hapless people have been defrauded of their rights before the law. The rich control the law courts. Magistrates, judges and lawyers are themselves members of their group or else eager for the favours and patronage of those who are. So the innocent who should receive vindication from the courts find themselves condemned. So it has ever been. Amos castigates the rich because they "turn justice to wormwood, and cast down righteousness to the earth" (5: 7; cf. 6: 12). The history of every land contains instances of laws enacted, administered, or perverted to benefit the rich at the expense of the poor.

**5: 6** The rich are accused: YOU HAVE CONDEMNED the innocent, that is, you have robbed him of justice. Moreover, YOU HAVE KILLED him. So in Wisdom 2: 20 they say: "Let us condemn him to a shameful death, for according to what he says, he will be protected". The reference in James, however, may be not so much to a violent death as to the less illegal, but equally injurious act of depriving him of means of earning a livelihood. So in Ecclus. 34: 22 we read: "To take away a neighbour's living is to murder him; to deprive an employee of his wages is to shed blood".

Ropes feels that the concluding sentence in this paragraph, "HE DOES NOT RESIST YOU", is "wholly unsuited to the context". "It makes a triumphant denunciation end in anticlimax." He seeks to remove the difficulty by understanding it as a question: "Does he not resist you?" and interpreting it to mean: "He will resist you". But this is very forced and unconvincing.

Others try to evade the difficulty by suggesting that the subject of "resist" is assumed to be God. Certainly in Jewish writings the name of "God" was avoided, where possible, out of a sense of reverence. This would give the translation: "Does not God resist you?" meaning that, however docile the righteous may be, God will range Himself against the wicked.

Not many commentators, however, find any serious difficulty in the sentence. Tasker indeed writes of it: "It brings the section to an end on a note of majestic pathos". The rich are represented, not as bold and fearless champions, defending a cause against dangerous enemies, but as brutal bullies, picking as the victim of their outrages those who either cannot or will not strike back. The Christian man who is the object of their violence is seeking to put into practice the words of Jesus: "Do not resist one who is evil" (Matt. 5: 39), agreeing with the guidance offered by the apostle Paul, "Never avenge yourselves, but leave it

to the wrath of God" (Rom. 12: 19; cf. 1 Pet. 2: 23; Isa. 53: 7).
Perhaps in English the significance of the sentence could best be
rendered in a concessive clause: " . . . although he makes no attempt to
defend himself".

> 5: 7-11. *Be patient, therefore, brethren, until the coming of the Lord.*
> *Behold, the farmer waits for the precious fruit of the earth, being patient*
> *over it until it receives the early and the late rain. 8. You also be patient.*
> *Establish your hearts, for the coming of the Lord is at hand. 9. Do not*
> *grumble, brethren, against one another, that you may not be judged;*
> *behold the Judge is standing at the doors. 10. As an example of*
> *suffering and patience, brethren, take the prophets who spoke in the*
> *name of the Lord. 11. Behold, we call those happy who were steadfast.*
> *You have heard of the steadfastness of Job, and you have seen the*
> *purpose of the Lord, how the Lord is compassionate and merciful.*

James turns now from the "rich" whose heartless conduct he has
condemned, and addresses himself to his Christian "brethren" who
are the victims of such ill-treatment. His words are intended to bring
them comfort and encouragement in the humiliations they are suffering and the exasperation and resentment which they cannot but
feel. He pleads with them to BE PATIENT UNTIL THE COMING OF THE
LORD.

**5: 7** New Testament Greek has two words, both of which may be
translated as "be patient". There is *makrothymeō*, used here, which is
most commonly applied to "being patient" with people whom we find
difficult and irritating. The other one is *hypomenō*, and this commonly
means "patience" in the sense of facing courageously discouraging
circumstances. It is this which is used in verse 11, where it is translated
"be steadfast". The two words, however, sometimes overlap in their
meaning, and in some cases appear to become almost synonyms. For
instance, *makrothymeō* occurs later in verse 7, not meaning patience
with other people, but indicating the "patience" of the farmer in his
attitude to the weather and the changing seasons. Sometimes the two
words are combined in the same sentence, as for instance Col. 1: 11,
where (in R.S.V.) the noun *hypomenē* is translated as "endurance" and
*makrothymia* as "patience". Patience, as opposed to endurance, should
mean that attitude which is the opposite of irritability, resentment and
retaliation.

Such "patience" is a characteristic of God Himself, in the face of all
the faults and unfaithfulness of men. In the orgy of wickedness which
marked the world of men in the days before the Flood, "God's patience
waited" (1 Pet. 3: 20). This unhurried patience is linked in Rom.

2: 4 with God's kindness and forbearance, and its purpose is "to lead man to repentance" (cf. Rom. 9: 22).

It is also frequently commended by Paul as one of the marks of the truly Christian character (Col. 3: 12; cf. Eph. 4: 2). It is included as one item in "the fruit of the Spirit" (Gal. 5: 22) and is named as characteristic of Christian love in its dealings with others (1 Cor. 13: 4).

Tasker suggests that here it means patience, not so much with our fellow men, but with God, in spite of His delay in punishing sinners. It seems, however, more natural to understand it as meaning patience in our attitude to unfair and insulting treatment which we receive from other people, and which by ordinary human standards would be met by open resentment and retaliation. "Vengeance", however, is God's prerogative, not ours (Rom. 12: 19). The Christian is summoned to show patience, meeting enmity and ill will (and overcoming it) with "good".

The thought of Paul in Romans 12 that punishment of wrongdoers is best left to God is present here also in James. The reason he gives for "patience" is that THE COMING OF THE LORD is very near. "The innocent sufferers," writes Calvin, "have this reason to be patient, because God would become their Judge." They must not think that God will continue to ignore the wrongdoing of wicked men. In His own good time He will summon them to Judgement. And that time is very near. Therefore, impatience, and the despair and vindictiveness which so often accompany undeserved suffering, are all out of place in the believing Christian.

THE COMING OF THE LORD is a common phrase in the New Testament for what today is frequently called the Second Coming of Christ. From Paul's writings we gather that among the early Christians it was expected to take place quite soon. Indeed he had to rebuke some believers at Thessalonica for giving up their daily work, because they thought its arrival was so near as to make the earning of money a purposeless waste of time. The grounds for this belief were attributed to words of Jesus (e.g. Matt. 24: 3, 27, 37, 39).

In the Old Testament writers there was a common expectation of "the Day of the Lord", when God would come in Judgement and Victory, and this "Day" was associated with the coming of His Messiah. The Christian believed that Jesus was that Messiah, but suffering and death had marked His coming to the earth. It is true that a note of triumph emerged at the end in His Resurrection, but even Christ Risen from the dead was not yet in fact the acknowledged ruler of all things. "We do not yet see everything in subjection to Him" (Heb. 2: 8). The promises of ultimate triumph in the Old Testament, therefore, led to a confident expectation that He would come again, and this time in glory and triumph, "to judge both the living and the dead" (Acts 10: 42), to bring judgement for sinners and vindication for His saints.

For some reason the early Christians came to believe that this Second Coming was not only certain, but also imminent. Why they made this mistake we cannot be sure. Probably it was due to a mistaken interpretation of some words of Jesus. He may have spoken of the future victory of His cause with such radiant certainty, that they mistook the certainty to mean immediacy. At any rate they came to expect it as an event in the very near future, even though there were, among the recorded words of Jesus, some sayings which warned against anyone presuming to know the time of its coming: "It is not for you to know times or seasons which the Father has fixed by his own authority" (Acts 1: 7). "Of that day or that hour no one knows, not even the angels in heaven, nor the Son, but only the Father" (Mark 13: 32), how much less any mere man.

The Greek word translated "Coming" is *parousia*. It literally means "presence", and could be used for an official visit of a king to some part of his kingdom. In Paul's writings in one place it once refers to a "coming" of Satan (2 Thess. 2: 9). But it soon came to be accepted as the regular term for the Second Coming of Jesus Christ on the earth (Matt. 24: 27; 1 Thess. 3: 13; 2 Pet. 3: 4; 1 John 2: 28). Like the Day of the Lord in the Old Testament, this was to be a time of disaster for all who were evil, and triumph for Christ's own people.

Some have argued that here in James "the Lord" means God, as in the Old Testament, but the "*parousia*", as used in Christian circles, was regularly associated with Christ as Lord. So "Lord" here must mean Christ, even though in verses 10 and 11 it means God.

BRETHREN: see 1: 2.

James proceeds to strengthen his plea for patience by citing examples of it in others. THE FARMER WAITS FOR THE PRECIOUS FRUIT (N.E.B. "crop") OF THE EARTH. He sows the seed; he may assist its growth by clearing away the weeds; when harvest comes he can gather the crop into barns. But the germination of the seed in the ground, and the mysterious process of growth from the first green shoot to the rich golden ears of corn are processes which he can only watch and wonder at: "The seed sprouts and grows, he knows not how. The earth produces of itself" (Mark 4: 28–9). Delays and disappointments there may be, but with dependable regularity seedtime and harvest form an invariable sequence, which he learns to trust, even though it takes time. He does not fret and worry because the seed does not sprout overnight, and the harvest come to fruition within the week. He learns to wait patiently for the germination of the seed and its imperceptible growth, he learns to wait for the changing seasons on which its growth and fruitfulness depend.

In particular, as in all hot countries, the seeds depend utterly on the timely rains. Without these nothing the farmer can do would be of any avail. In Palestine there were two customary periods of rain on which the success of the crops particularly depended, and among the pious Jews this rain was thought of as the direct gift of a kindly Creator. "Thou visitest the earth and waterest it", they sang in their services (Ps. 65: 9–11). The "EARLY RAIN" was expected at the end of October or soon after, and it was this which gave the farmer the opportunity to sow his seed in moistened soil which would be friendly to germination. The "LATE RAIN" usually fell in late April or early May, a little before the harvest, and provided the moisture needed to swell the grain in the ear, which made all the difference between a light or a heavy crop.

These two periods of rain, of such vital importance to the farmers, were characteristic of Palestine, but not of other parts of the Middle East. There are many references to them in the Old Testament (e.g. Deut. 11: 14; Jer. 5: 24; Joel 2: 23). Heavy rains during the winter were no adequate substitute for them.

In the Greek James does not actually use any word for "rain". The two adjectives "the early" and "the late" are used, and James leaves it to be understood that he means the two periods of rain. Since the word is not precisely mentioned, however, some suggest that instead of "rain" a word for "crop" should be understood. In this case the subject of the verb "receives" will be the farmer, not the earth, and the early and the late crops will be respectively the Barley and the Wheat Harvests. But the early and the late rains are such a common phrase in the Bible that it must be these which are intended.

**5: 8** The farmer exercises patience because he has learned to trust the providential care of God. So must Christians be patient, even when the triumph of God's cause seems slow to take effect. They must learn to ESTABLISH THEIR HEARTS, "to be stout-hearted" (N.E.B.). Ropes suggests the translation: "Make your courage and purpose firm". Their anxiety over what seems inexplicable delay must not lead them to self-pity and impatient complaining. The harvest, and the rains it depends on, can, in the good providence of God be relied on by the farmer. So the Christian can possess his soul in patience even under affliction because THE COMING OF THE LORD IS AT HAND.

In the parables of Jesus also, as they are presented in the gospels, the Second Coming of Christ is compared to the harvest (e.g. Matt. 13: 39).

This coming of the Lord IS AT HAND (ēngiken). This is the same word used by Mark when he summarizes the gist of the teaching of Jesus as: "The Kingdom of God *is at hand*" (Mark 1: 15), and it also occurs in 1 Pet. 4: 7: "The end of all things *is at hand*". James clearly believed, as others of his time did, that the Coming of Christ was imminent. Since, then, there was not long to wait, his plea for patience is greatly reinforced.

**5:9** Besides being asked to practise patience, they are urged: "DO NOT GRUMBLE AGAINST ONE ANOTHER". The Greek word *stenazō* literally means "groan", but a "groan" directed against another involves criticism, complaint and fault-finding, and so can be rendered as "grumble". Its meaning is similar to that in 4: 11: "Do not speak evil against one another".

This attitude of mutual recrimination easily develops in circumstances of special difficulty, when the outward stresses provoke people to quarrelsomeness and impatience. In wartime an unscrupulous enemy will deliberately foster this breakdown in morale in the prison camps. So the Evil One rejoices when Christians, facing unusual hardships and irritations, allow these things to provoke them into sharp criticism and censoriousness towards other Christians. Such a failure on the part of Christians signifies victory for Evil. "Do not blame your troubles on one another", translates the N.E.B. Christians who allow life's troubles and annoyances to provoke them into blaming others arc playing the Devil's game for him.

In a somewhat similar passage Paul also urges the Christians at Corinth to refrain from grumbling (1 Cor. 10: 10), reminding them of the terrible punishment which overtook the children of Israel in the wilderness, when they gave way to a mood of bitter discontent.

Recrimination and censoriousness involves "judging others", since it means naming their faults and blaming them for them. But "judging others" is explicitly forbidden by our Lord (Matt. 7: 1), and those who judge are warned that they in their turn will be judged. This word of Jesus is reflected here when James continues: "THAT YOU MAY NOT BE JUDGED". N.E.B. represents it as: "Or you will fall under judgement". The fact that this judgement has been pronounced to be very near should especially deter them from conduct which would bring them under God's condemnation, in that dread moment.

The nearness of this Judgement is vividly represented by James in words apparently borrowed directly from the words of Jesus: "THE JUDGE IS STANDING AT THE DOORS" (cf. Mark 13: 29: "He is near, at the very gates". Cf. Rev. 3: 20: "Behold I stand at the door").

In both Old and New Testaments God is spoken of as Judge (e.g. Gen. 18: 25; Heb. 12: 23), but in the New Testament judgement is particularly associated with the Coming of Christ (2 Tim. 4: 1; cf. also John 3: 19, Matt. 25: 31–2).

**5:10** James, in order to commend patience to Christian people, has already appealed to the example of the farmer, and also reminded them that they will not have long to put up with their present difficulties, because their awaited deliverance is very near. Now he uses a third plea: it is the example of the prophets of Israel, whose faithfulness to God had often to be maintained in the face of active opposition and hostility from others.

Their EXAMPLE is commended. The same word (*hypodeigma*) is used of the action of Jesus in washing His disciples' feet (John 13: 15), and of Enoch, who is cited as an "example of repentance" in Ecclus. 44: 16 (cf. also 2 Pet. 2: 6). A similar word is used at 1 Pet. 2: 21 of the "example" which Christ set of patient suffering.

Even where the word for "example" is not used, the same thought is often expressed in the New Testament in exhortations to "imitate" good examples. Eph. 5: 1 urges us to be "imitators" of God Himself, but more frequently it is Jesus we are advised to "imitate" (1 Thess. 1: 6; 1 Cor. 11: 1). Paul sometimes counsels his converts to imitate the standards of conduct which he himself follows (1 Thess. 1: 6; 2 Thess. 3: 7; 1 Cor. 4: 16; 11: 1). The churches in Judaea provide an example to be imitated by others (1 Thess. 2: 14). In Hebrews the readers are instructed to imitate the faith of their leaders (13: 7), and, looking back, to be "imitators of those who through faith and patience inherit the promises" (6: 12). Indeed the whole list of the great men and women of the faith in Hebrews 11 can be thought of as a roll-call of those most worthy of our imitation. Undoubtedly in the Christian life the good examples of those more advanced in the faith than ourselves can serve as a most valuable stimulus and guide to those who in times of perplexity and hesitation find themselves in danger of faltering.

The prophets are for us AN EXAMPLE OF SUFFERING AND PATIENCE. The meaning of this combination of words would best be rendered in English by joining them in a single phrase such as "patience in suffering", or, with N.E.B., "patience under ill-treatment".

God's spokesmen, the prophets, not only frequently failed to gain a hearing for their message (cf. Isa. 6: 9–10; Jer. 20: 8), but were also subjected to persecution. Jesus could refer to this as almost a proverbial truth: "So men persecuted the prophets who were before you" (Matt. 5: 12); "you are the sons of those who murdered the prophets" (Matt. 23: 31). So also Stephen demanded of his accusers: "Which of the prophets did your fathers not persecute?" Though all prophets were men who had suffered for righteousness' sake, Jeremiah especially tended to be known as the suffering prophet, typical of all others who suffer for doing God's will, and from his example God's faithful people in their sufferings took courage. Our Lord calls on those who suffer for God to "rejoice and be glad" to find themselves in such a grand succession. James is content to use their example more modestly as a call to patience. Calvin comments: "James has done well for us; for he has laid before our eyes a pattern, that we may learn to look at it whenever we are tempted to impatience or despair", and adds: "It is a real consolation to know that those things commonly deemed evils are aids and helps to our salvation".

The true prophets SPOKE IN THE NAME OF THE LORD, declaring not their own thoughts but what God gave them to speak. Faithfulness to God's commands so far from giving them immunity from suffering actually involved them in it.

**5: 11** Jesus said: "Happy (*makarioi*) are those who are persecuted for righteousness' sake", with the implication that their blessedness springs from their faithfulness under persecution. James gives expression to the same truth here when he writes: "WE CALL THEM HAPPY (*makarizomai*) WHO WERE STEADFAST".

The verb here translated "be steadfast" is *hypomenō*, which can sometimes be translated as "be patient" (see the note on verse 7). It means to show firm steadiness under stress and difficulty, whether these come from circumstances or from other people. The same verb is used in the saying of Jesus: "He who *endures* to the end shall be saved" (Matt. 10: 22; 24: 13). Similarly: "By your *endurance* you will gain your lives" (Luke 21: 19).

James has appealed to the example of the prophets as an argument for "patience". He is now seeking to commend "steadfast endurance", and for this he recalls the example of Job, who is often associated with the prophets (cf. Ezek. 14: 14, 20). YOU HAVE HEARD OF THE STEADFASTNESS OF JOB. K.J.V. translated "steadfastness" (*hypomenē*) as patience (not distinguishing it from *makrothymia*), and it is this old translation which has given rise to the proverbial phrase "the patience of Job". The book of Job itself does not portray him as an example of "patience" in the sense of bearing patiently with the foolish behaviour of other people, but it does represent him as an example of fortitude and courage in adversity.

When we read Job's impassioned outbursts against the shallow platitudes of his so-called "comforters" (e.g. 3: 3, 11; 16: 2, etc.) or his distressed protests to God Himself (7: 11–16; 10: 18; 23: 2; 30: 20–23) we should not characterize him as a model of "patience" in the ordinary sense of the word. But he does show brave endurance in that in spite of all his trials he remains true to God and his faith in God (see 1: 21; 2: 10; 16: 9–21; 19: 25–7).

The story of Job illustrates not only the "steadfastness" of Job, but also "THE PURPOSE OF THE LORD". K.J.V. and R.V. translate these words as "the end of the Lord". This is because the Greek word *telos* does basically mean "end", but may also mean "purpose". Indeed our English word "end" can sometimes mean purpose, as for instance in the catechism: What is the whole end of man? So commentators vary in their understanding of *telos* here as meaning "end" or "purpose", though since the same Greek word may have both meanings, it is possible that James meant both to be included. Often, indeed, the true purpose of a process only appears at the end. The end reveals the purpose. The purpose of Job's sufferings is seen only at the end in his vision of God in 42: 5–6, where his new awareness of the majesty and reality of God dwarfs into insignificance all the material comforts and blessings with which faith in God may sometimes be blessed. Others associate what is meant by the "end of the Lord" with the phrase in 42: 12: "God blessed the latter days of Job", and think of the peace and plenty with which in God's plan the closing days of his life were crowned.

Most commentators do in fact (as opposed to R.S.V.) prefer to treat *telos* as here meaning "end", rather than "purpose". Ropes understands it to mean "the conclusion wrought by the Lord to his troubles", and Mayor notes "how God makes all turn out for good". N.E.B. has: "how the Lord treated him in the end". Calvin comments: "Afflictions ought ever to be estimated by their end".

Augustine and Bede both interpreted "the end of the Lord" as the death of Christ. Many have felt it strange that James should speak so fully about "steadfastness under suffering" without the slightest reference to the example of our Lord, but it is not likely that James intended any reference to Christ here.

The end of Job's sufferings, whether seen in his restored happiness or his deeper experience of God, reveals not only the purpose of God (previously hidden from Job and his companions) but also the truth about the nature of God and His attitude to His creature man. Like the ultimate purpose of God this too may be hidden from us, when life's torments and tragedies are at their worst; but the basic truth about Him still remains that "HE IS COMPASSIONATE AND MERCIFUL". This is a free quotation of the words of Ps. 103: 8. Compassion is often ascribed to God in the Old Testament (Ps. 78: 38; 86: 15; 111: 4; 112: 4; 145: 8), and also to our Lord in the New Testament (Matt. 15: 32; 20: 34; Mark 5: 19; Luke 7: 13; etc.). The word for "merciful" is that used by our Lord, to describe what is true about God and what should be true about God's people (Luke 6: 36). In the actual process of events sometimes God's mercy may be hidden from us, but it stands revealed in the end.

5: 12. *But above all, my brethren, do not swear, either by heaven or by earth or with any other oath, but let your yes be yes and your no no, that you may not fall under condemnation.*

**5: 12** James returns to a subject on which he clearly feels very deeply—the evil which so easily finds its way into speech and conversation. He has already dealt with some aspects of this "restless evil", as he calls the tongue. In 1: 26 he insisted that an "unbridled" tongue is quite inconsistent with a genuine religious faith, whereas a proper control of this untamed member of the body is the mark of a "perfect" man (3: 2–5). The tongue in a community is as fraught with potential danger as a fire in a dry forest (3: 6–12). All too easily it leads a man into the sin of criticizing and condemning his fellow-Christians.

Here the fault in the tongue which James is most concerned to rebuke is the dishonesty of speech which has become so widespread that some special safeguard is needed to secure truthfulness. That safeguard was the oath. So low had ordinary standards of truthfulness sunk that a statement or a promise was felt to be valueless unless it was supported by a solemn oath. Moreover such an oath could itself be manipulated by tricks of phrasing so that though it sounded impressive and convincing, it was not regarded by the speaker as binding (Matt. 23: 16–22).

This firm prohibition of oath-taking is introduced by the words, "ABOVE ALL". Some interpret this as referring to the paragraph immediately preceding, where James has been warning his readers against a spirit of impatient discontent, which so readily expresses itself in the criticism of others. He is here to be understood as insisting that his warning against the use of oaths is even more important than this. Some have argued that the connection between these two paragraphs springs from the fact that discontent and a spirit of fault-finding may well lead to a hasty use of oaths to support rash and ill-considered statements.

Others think that the words "above all" must refer to all that has gone before in the letter as a whole. It is hard to believe that this is what James meant, because important though it may be to abstain from oaths, it is not easy to think that it can be thought of as more important than avoidance of murder and adultery, to which reference has earlier been made.

The words "above all", in fact, ought not to be pressed too literally. James uses them as a device to call attention to something he wishes his readers to take special notice of. Perhaps some bitter, recent experience has brought home to him how urgent this counsel is. It is as though he said: In present circumstances I want you *specially* to take heed of this warning.

It is quite probable that James originally spoke (or wrote) these words as a separate piece of advice, not precisely related either to what precedes or what follows. If so, we could think of these words, "above all", as meaning that in the particular situation in which he finds himself, among the Christians over whom he has pastoral care, this sin of dishonesty in speech is the one they most need to guard against.

It is not that it is worse than murder and adultery, but it is one that they, in their particular circumstances and stage of development, are most prone to fall into.

Others suggest that since this saying of James about oaths is substantially a quotation of words of Jesus, James wishes to indicate that as such it is worthy of far deeper reverence than any mere words of his own, however wise they may appear to be.

Certainly this verse is very closely similar to the words of Jesus as recorded in Matthew 5: 34–37. We quote the words in full printing in italics the words which James reproduces here:

> 34. I say unto you, *Do not swear* at all, *either by heaven*, for it is the throne of God, 35. *or by the earth*, for it is his footstool, or by Jerusalem, for it is the city of the great King. 36. And do not swear by your head, for you cannot make one hair white or black. 37. *Let what you say be simply "Yes" or "No"*; anything more than this comes from evil.

The words of Jesus would originally be spoken in Aramaic, and would be put into Greek differently by different people. One wonders whether the words translated "at all" in Matthew 5: 34 may conceivably represent what James intends by "above all". Similarly Matthew's "anything more than this comes from evil" may represent a rough translation of the same Aramaic, which James represents by "that you may not fall under condemnation". Quite clearly, at any rate, James is here reminding his readers of words that have come to him with the authority of Jesus.

James indeed represents what must certainly have been the original meaning of the words of Jesus more clearly than Matthew has done. The literal, and more natural, translation of Matthew 5: 37 is that found in the R.V.: "Let your speech be Yea, yea, Nay, nay", as though Jesus were insisting at the same time on two things: (1) simple truthfulness, and also (2) emphatic truthfulness (indicated by the repetition). As compared with this the wording found in James is much to be preferred. The R.S.V. departs from R.V. in translating Matt. 5: 37, giving it the same significance as this verse in James. This is a possible way of translating the Greek of Matt. 5: 37, but scholars may not have ventured to sponsor it, unless James here had pointed the way.

What Jesus is saying in Matthew (as James makes clear) is that whereas the Old Testament permitted the use of oaths, insisting only that a solemn oath must always be most solemnly fulfilled, and condemning most scathingly the careless breaking of an oath, for the Christian oaths are not permitted at all. For one who shares the life of the Kingdom of God every single word must be scrupulously true, and as binding upon the speaker as the most solemn oath. There must not be two standards of truthfulness—one not taken seriously, when we make a simple statement, the other binding, when we affirm it with an oath. For the Christian a simple "yes" or "no" must be as binding as the most solemn oath.

James is here re-affirming this teaching of Jesus. DO NOT SWEAR, he writes. This, of course, has nothing whatever to do with the use of bad language, though this is the usual meaning of "swearing" today. It means the use of God's name, or of some sacred object, to guarantee the truth of what we speak. The most binding of all oaths was that which called on God Himself to witness to the truth of what was said. It was believed that to call on God to witness to a lie was to incur in special measure the anger of God. Partly for this reason substitutes for the actual name of God were often used in oath-taking. People would swear BY HEAVEN, since it was God's dwelling place, OR BY EARTH the footstool of His feet. To a sincere man who used these words as reverent synonyms for "God" they would impose on his oath an obligation no less binding than the name of God Himself. Less sincere people, however, saw in this use of an alternative to the name of God a device for regarding the oath as less binding, since God Himself had not been called on to witness it. Something of this hypocrisy is reflected in the words of Jesus addressed to "hypocrites" in Matthew 23: 16-22. There Jesus rebukes the insincerity which regards an oath on the temple or the altar as not binding; only an oath on the gold of the temple or else on the gift on the altar need be treated seriously. By these duplicities (used in the name of religion) an uninstructed person could easily be deceived. Moreover the obligation to truthfulness in *all* speech was, by this practice, treated as if it did not exist.

In our present-day society we do not use oaths in our ordinary conversation, but that does not mean that these words of Jesus are not applicable to us. An oath was a special device for ensuring the truth of a statement. Jesus, and James his interpreter, insist that our simple words should be as binding just by themselves as when they are reinforced by an oath. The equivalent today of the oath is the signed agreement, perhaps with witnesses to attest it. The meaning of James, when translated into *our* social customs, is that our mere word should be as utterly trustworthy as a signed document, legally correct and complete.

The swearing of an oath to give added validity to a statement or a promise, though forbidden here, was authorized in the Old Testament. The only qualification was that in an oath it must be the name of Jehovah which is used, and not that of any strange god (Deut. 6: 13; Isa. 65: 16; Jer. 12: 16). "As the Lord lives" was often the form of words used. Once these words were used to guarantee a promise, it was deadly sin to break it. In the Decalogue it is stated: "The Lord will not hold him guiltless who takes His name in vain" (Deut. 5: 11).

In practice, however, it was found that the accepted use of oaths had three evil consequences: (1) It made untruthfulness seem unimportant, except when an oath was used. (2) It led to the introduction of a distinction between oaths that were binding and those which were not, so that the use of an oath might be a device for cheating the unwary, rather than a means of guaranteeing a statement. (3) It was responsible for an irreverent use of God's name, or words which were sacred through their association with God, since they came to be used merely as a means of ensuring honesty in commercial transactions.

For these reasons others, besides Jesus, registered objections to the current practice of oath-taking, though few did so from His very radical point of view. Protests against it are heard in Ecclus. 23: 9–11; 27: 14, and also in some of the Rabbis[1]. Josephus informs us that the Essenes[2] refrained from oaths: "Every statement of theirs is surer than an oath, and with them swearing is avoided, for they think it worse than perjury. For they say that he who is untrustworthy except when he appeals to God, is already under condemnation"[3] (BJ 2: 8). It is noteworthy that this reason for avoiding oaths is precisely that of Jesus and James. The very use of an oath acknowledges the prevalence of falsehood in ordinary speech.[4]

LET YOUR YES BE YES AND YOUR NO NO. There can be little doubt that James here represents the intended meaning of the words of Jesus reported in Matt. 5: 37 (though the translation of K.J.V. and R.V. make it appear different). Justin Martyr (Apol. 1: 16) and Clement of Alexandria (Strom. 5: 14) both quote the saying in this way. It is possible that James knew Matthew, and amended the phrasing of the quotation, as he borrowed it. He may, however, have been familiar with the teaching of Jesus independently of the written gospels, perhaps in the form of the earlier traditions, written and oral, out of which the gospels themselves were formed.[5]

Avoidance of oath-taking is demanded THAT YOU MAY NOT FALL

[1] "Accustom not thyself to vows, for sooner or later thou wilt swear false oaths" (*Nedarim*, 20 a).

[2] It is usually believed that the community of Qûmran were Essenes, and that the so-called "Zadokite Document" reflects their beliefs. In this document, however, there is a section on oaths (xv-xvi). Here the use of God's name is utterly forbidden, but other oaths are authorized. All are absolutely binding. Therefore either the statement of Josephus is inaccurate, or the people of Qûmran were not orthodox Essenes, or the Zadokite Document does not represent them.

[3] It is curious that James also uses these two words, "under condemnation", in this same connection.

[4] Ropes cites similar judgements from such writers as Philo and Epictetus.

[5] Ropes, without giving reasons, rejects this alternative explanation: "The theory that we have here in James the traces of an oral form of the sayings of Jesus preserved independently of Matthew's Greek Gospel is unlikely and unnecessary".

UNDER CONDEMNATION, that is, God's condemnation of those who
disobey His righteous will. The meaning is similar to the phrase at the
end of 5: 9, "that you may not be judged".

Erasmus and Tyndale in their translations represent the meaning
of this last clause in the verse as "lest ye fall into hypocrisy". This is
because the manuscripts they followed had a different reading from the
better ones available to us now (*eis hypokrisin* instead of *hypo krisin*).
Although it is not supported by the more reliable manuscripts, it does
in fact make good sense, since, as we have seen, Jesus condemns
misuse of oaths to deceive others as a form of hypocrisy (Matt. 23: 16–
22).

This explicit prohibition of oath-taking, both here and in the words
of Jesus, has led many devoted Christians to apply it quite literally to
the legal requirement that the words of a witness in court should be
spoken "under oath". Although in modern society this is almost the
only context in which a man may find himself expected to swear an
oath, it is a context which in fact neither our Lord nor James had in
mind. The oath taken in a court of law is a convenient means of
bringing all witnesses under the law against perjury. It is over this
single point, however, that most of the controversy about this verse has
raged. At the time of the Reformation on the continent the Anabaptists[1] caused consternation, even among the more moderate
reformers, by a refusal to take an oath even in court, and the Quakers
in Britain at a later date did the same. No doubt they could justify
their refusal by an appeal to the quite literal meaning of these words,
but it was to the misuse of the oath in ordinary speech not to its
specialized use in law, that these words were originally directed.

5: 13–18. *Is any one among you suffering? Let him pray. Is any cheer-*
*ful? Let him sing praise. 14. Is any among you sick? Let him call*
*for the elders of the church, and let them pray over him, anointing him*
*with oil in the name of the Lord; 15. and the prayer of faith will save*
*the sick man, and the Lord will raise him up; and if he has committed*
*sins, he will be forgiven. 16. Therefore confess your sins to one*
*another and pray for one another, that you may be healed. The prayer*
*of a righteous man has great power in its effects. 17. Elijah was a man*
*of like nature with ourselves and he prayed fervently that it might not*

---

[1] Calvin in his commentary, troubled by the intransigent attitude of the Anabaptists,
uses this passage as an opportunity to inveigh against their "ignorance": "James does
not speak of oaths in general", he writes, "but condemns the evasions which had been
devised", by which "men could swear with impunity provided they adopted some
circuitous expressions". Calvin, who is usually right in his comments on Scripture, is
surely wrong here. What he says applies to Matt. 23: 16ff. but not to James, who here
condemns not the misuse of oaths, but any use of oaths at all, since their use implies
the dishonesty of statements made without oaths.

*rain, and for three years and six months it did not rain on the earth.*
*18. Then he prayed again and the heaven gave rain, and the earth*
*brought forth its fruit.*

James now addresses himself to any Christians who are feeling
depressed and in low spirits, and even actually unwell, and recommends, as the means of their cure, the use of confident prayer and the
confession of sins.

**5: 13.** The English word "SUFFERING" has a stronger suggestion of
physical pain than the Greek word which it translates (*kakopathei*).
N.E.B. renders it by "is in trouble", and this is nearer to the meaning.
A similar Greek word is used also at 5: 10 and at 2 Tim. 2: 9 and 4: 5.
Such trouble, whether physical or mental, should not so overwhelm a
Christian as to reduce him to a state of petulance and self-pity. Rather
LET HIM PRAY. Such prayer can sometimes remove the distress.
If not, it will provide the courage we need in order to face it and win
through. The prayer of Jesus for His disciple Peter in Luke 22: 31–34,
for instance, does not even ask for him to be spared the ordeal that is
threatening, but rather that, in spite of it, "his faith may not fail". So
prayer if it does not bring relief from trouble can so sustain faith as to
give the power to endure and overcome (cf. Rom. 8: 37). "They that
wait upon the Lord shall renew their strength" (Isa. 40: 31).

Moods of depression may pass, and be succeeded by a period of
happy high spirits. Such times can easily come to be occasions of
carelessness and forgetfulness of God. Trouble is proverbially more
likely to turn a man's thoughts to God than success and prosperity (see
Ps. 107, especially verses 6, 13, 19, 28). If, however, God has granted
us a "season of refreshing" and we are CHEERFUL (N.E.B. "in good
heart"), that is the time to pause and remember Him who is the giver
of all life's good gifts, and to turn to Him in PRAISE and thanksgiving.

The word for "be cheerful" (*euthymeō*) occurs also in Acts 27: 25
where Paul and his companions are in imminent danger of shipwreck.
He calls to them: "Take heart" (*euthymeō*), "for I have faith in God".
The word, therefore, does not necessarily mean freedom from trouble.
It can also mean cheerful courage in spite of it. The proper response to
such cheerfulness of heart is to SING PRAISE. The word is "*psalletō*",
and our word "psalm" comes from the same root. K.J.V. translated it
here as "sing psalms", but this restricts the meaning too narrowly.
The same word occurs in Eph. 5: 19 and 1 Cor. 14: 15. It seems
natural to us to give expression to high spirits in singing, but it is
characteristic of Christians that their singing takes the form of praises
to God. This singing of praises from a glad heart may be found when
outward circumstances are far from congenial. Paul and Silas in the
darkness of a Philippian prison at midnight prayed and sang hymns

(Acts 16: 25), thus carrying into effect James's twofold counsel here for both those in distress and those in good heart.

**5: 14.** The use of the word "sick", which implies physical illness, confirms that the earlier word in verse 13, translated as "suffering", probably does refer to distress of mind rather than bodily ailments. The same word for physical illness occurs in Matt. 10: 8. It suggests a form of illness which incapacitates a man for work. In this case the advice of James is that we do not attempt to deal with the situation alone, but seek the help of Christian friends, especially those who by their position in the Church are known as men of spiritual understanding. They should add their prayers to those of the sick man, and as a further means of restoring health anoint him with oil.[1]

These Church leaders are called "ELDERS" (*presbyteroi*). In Greek as in English the word originally meant a person of advanced years. In the Christian Church, however, the word soon came to be used for certain leaders holding official position. It was apparently borrowed from the usage of the Jewish synagogue, where the "elders" were men of recognized authority (though, it seems, subordinate to the "rulers", cf. Luke 8: 41). Similarly in the Qûmran community a group of "elders" held high rank, exceeded only by that of the priests. It was almost to be expected, therefore, that the Church in Jerusalem would adopt the same term for its leaders, and this is confirmed in Acts (e.g. 11: 30; 15: 2, etc.). It was almost certainly on this same pattern that Paul and Barnabas appointed "elders" for the newly-formed churches in Asia Minor (14: 23), and "elders" are mentioned also at Ephesus (20: 17). Except in the Pastoral Epistles elders are not referred to by that name in the Pauline epistles, though 1 Pet. 5: 1–4 gives some precise instructions to them. The author of 2 John and 3 John refers to himself in the opening verses as an "elder". In Titus 1: 5–9 there is advice about the kind of man to be selected for this office, and the "elder" seems to be identified with the "bishop" in verse 7 (as also in Acts 20: 17 and 20: 28).

"Elders" is the title accorded to the leaders of the Christian communities for whom James writes (as in some Christian churches today). Their responsibility would be for pastoral oversight and spiritual direction. It is these who are to be invited to the sick man's home. Presumably, had he been well enough to leave home, his needs could have been met in the gatherings of the church, and prayers offered on his behalf there. Since this was not possible the "Church" in the persons of its accredited representatives goes to visit him.

The word here translated "CHURCH" is *ecclēsia*. By derivation it meant a group of people "called out" or "selected" from others. In secular Greek it was used for a consultative assembly. In the Septuagint

[1] A note on Spiritual Healing is added at p. 208.

it was used for the community of Israel (Deut. 4: 10, etc.). In consequence it was readily applied to the Church, since Christians thought of this as the New Israel. Usually in the New Testament it is applied to the local congregation of Christian people, but it came also to be used for the whole company of Christian people throughout the world (as for example in Eph. 1: 22). Here, however, it applies to a local group (as at 1 Cor. 4: 17, Acts 15: 41, etc.). In this context the N.E.B. translates it as "congregation".

The visitors are directed to PRAY OVER the sick person. We may imagine these devout people gathered round the bed, with hands clasped in prayer over the one they prayed for.

An over-spiritualized attitude may protest: Could not prayer have been offered just as effectively in the church gathering? Did they need to be physically present with the sick man? If our religion were a matter of theory, these questions would be justified. But we are dealing with men and women in need of help. Our Lord Himself did not decline to go to people in need, when invited, though He could heal from a distance with a word, when it was appropriate to do so. In fact, prayer offered in our presence and for our precise needs by Christian friends has a power and efficacy that may be lacking in prayers offered in our absence. We are creatures of flesh and blood, as well as spirit, and when love for us is proved by the readiness of Christian friends to give their time to come to our home in our need, we are more immediately aware of that love. Its effectiveness in prayer is increased by the fact that we have been made aware of it.

Along with the prayer there goes ANOINTING WITH OIL. The use of oil in the treatment of illness was very common in the ancient world. Mayor (p. 158) quotes evidence for this from such writers as Josephus, Philo, Pliny and Galen. Galen (Med. Temp. ii) calls oil "The best of all remedies for paralysis". There are also recorded instances of Jewish Rabbis visiting the sick and anointing them with oil, in order to cure such ailments as headache. Its medicinal use is mentioned in the O.T. at Isa. 1: 6 and in the N.T. at Luke 10: 34, where the Good Samaritan pours oil and wine on to the injured man's wounds.

It is understandable that massage with oil should benefit muscular complaints, and its application to an open sore have soothing and healing effects. How it would benefit internal ailments, when only applied externally, it is not easy to see. It may have been associated in people's minds with effective healing and so have awakened what today we should call "suggestibility" to the confident prayer for health. For whatever reason, Jesus, as well as James, authorized the use of oil for healing (Mark 6: 13).

Our Lord Himself was even willing to use saliva in some of His cures, in the one case to help a deaf man, in the other a blind one

(Mark 7: 33 and 8: 23). Saliva, like oil, was commonly regarded then as having healing properties, but we find it hard to believe that it had any essential part in the cure. Perhaps it was that, because of its common use in association with healing, its application helped to awaken expectancy and faith, and was therefore valuable in dealing with those who, through blindness or deafness, were in some measure cut off from normal contacts. For others the sound of the voice of Jesus and the look in His eyes were ready means of stimulating faith in His power and willingness to heal. When people in need lacked the faculty to be aware of these influences, He was ready to use subsidiary means of awakening faith, which was a prerequisite of healing (Mark 6: 5–6).

Similarly the use of oil, both by the disciples of Jesus (Mark 6: 13) and as recommended by James, was supplementary aid for awakening faith. The healing work is done by God's Spirit, offered freely to man's need and appropriated by faith, but material aids may sometimes prepare the way.

The prayer and the anointing are to be IN THE NAME OF THE LORD. This phrase occurs frequently in the N.T. The seventy disciples, returning from their mission, joyfully report to Jesus that demons are subject to them "in thy name" (Luke 10: 17). It was in the name of Jesus that Peter healed the lame man at the gate of the Temple (Acts 3: 6), and Paul the girl fortune-teller at Philippi (Acts 16: 18). Paul gives instructions "in the name of the Lord" (1 Cor. 5: 4, 2 Thess. 3: 6). The meaning in such instances is "with the authority of Jesus". It can be applied not only to special tasks, but everyday conduct: "Whatever you do, do everything in the name of the Lord Jesus" (Col. 3: 17).

In this context the phrase carries this meaning also, since in praying and anointing they will be obeying the command of Jesus (Mark 6: 7, 13), and acting with His authority. Some commentators, however, insist that in this instance the phrase means "by invoking the name of the Lord", the actual use of His name being regarded as effective for healing.[1]

A note on the use of verse 14 to support the Roman Catholic practice of extreme unction follows on page 209.

**5: 15.** THE PRAYER OF FAITH WILL SAVE THE SICK MAN.

James has already commended the "PRAYER OF FAITH" at 1: 6, where he advises, concerning a prayer for wisdom, "Let him ask in faith, nothing doubting". (See the notes on "faith" and "prayer" at 1: 6.)

All prayer implies some degree of faith, but it may be only a small

---

[1] So Dibelius (p. 232) insists that here the phrase means "appealing to the name of the Lord". As evidence in support of this he cites Heitmüller, *In Namen Jesu*, p. 86.

and uncertain measure, as in the prayer: "I believe, help my unbelief" (Mark 9: 24). The real prayer of faith, so welcome to Jesus, is that of the centurion: "Only say the word, and my servant will be healed" (Matt. 8: 8).

At 1: 5 the prayer is for a blessing we need for ourselves. Here it is prayer for another's need. Both must be uttered in faith. Undoubtedly faith can be effective for others as well as for ourselves. Jesus could use the faith of four friends to heal a paralysed man (Mark 2: 5), the faith of the centurion to cure his servant, and the mother's faith to cure her daughter (Mark 7: 29). So here, the prayer of Christian men for their needy brother must be offered in "the full assurance of faith" (Heb. 10: 22).

The word "SAVE" as used in the Pauline writings, is one of deep spiritual significance. In the gospels, however, it often appears to carry largely a physical meaning, and is used of bodily health more frequently than of the salvation of the soul (cf. for instance Mark 6: 56 where R.S.V. translates the word "were made well". So also at Matt. 9: 21–22). Perhaps, however, we do less than justice to the New Testament use of the word to make this kind of distinction. God's forgiveness can be a factor in the restoration of physical health (Mark 2: 5). This means that a right relationship to God and what we regard as physical health are sometimes very closely related to each other. Here too James links the spiritual blessing of forgiveness with the sick man's need for physical healing.

In this context, too, "save" clearly means primarily the restoration of physical health, but not that alone. It is the restoration of the man to total well-being, including his relationship with God.[1]

THE LORD WILL RAISE HIM UP.

The healing work is that of the Lord. It is idle, perhaps, to speculate whether here, or elsewhere, "the Lord" means the Lord God, the Creator, or the Lord Jesus Christ. For James, as for all Christians, God is the source of all Christian good which comes to men (see 1: 17), and Jesus Christ is God's special agent for bringing God's power and goodness to the very point of our human need.

---

[1] cf. John Baillie in the Gifford Lectures, 1962: *The Sense of the Presence of God*, pp. 196–7: "What exactly is meant by salvation? . . . Many will return the simple answer that it means going to heaven when we die. But that is certainly not what the Bible means by salvation. . . . Salvation means wholeness, health, well-being. It means well-being of the whole man, body, soul and spirit. The New Testament makes no such separation of body and soul as we have inherited from Greek philosophy, but thinks of a man, as we have recently learned again to do, as an essentially psychosomatic organism. . . . It is significant that the evangelists record Jesus as having on four different occasions spoken the same identical words—to a woman whose haemorrhage he had stanched (Mark 5: 34), to a blind man whose sight he had restored (Mark 10: 52), to a leper whom he had cured (Luke 17: 19), and to a woman of the streets whose only recorded disease was that of sin (Luke 7: 50); and the words were, 'Thy faith has healed (or saved, *sesōken*) thee'."

It is important to notice that it is explicitly stated that it is not the oil or the anointing by human hands or even the believing prayer which is the healing power. They are at best the means which God uses. It is God through Christ who is the Life-giver and Healer.

The word used here for "WILL RAISE HIM UP" (*egeirō*) is the word often used in connection with the resurrection. This, however, is not its significance here. It means rather: "raise him back to health", so that he can again stand up and walk about. In this sense also the word is used of the healing of Peter's mother-in-law (Mark 1: 31) and of the paralysed man in Mark 2: 9 and 12.

The connection between sickness and SIN is a problem which haunts the human mind. It appears again and again throughout the Bible, as men grope to discover an answer to it. In Old Testament times it was customary to assume that sickness was caused by sin, but Jesus emphatically denied that this was always the case (John 9: 3, Luke 13: 1-5). He did, however, make it plain that some sickness has its origin in sin, as in Mark 2: 5ff. Here James follows the teaching of Jesus. He does not take for granted that sin is necessarily the cause of sickness, but he recognizes that it may be. He writes: "IF (NOT 'SINCE'), HE HAS COMMITTED SINS. . . ". This is not meant to be a general statement, implying the possibility that a man may be entirely free from sin, but is related to the precise context and means: "if sin is the cause (or partial cause) of his illness. . . ."

Paul also believed that illness was sometimes a punishment for sin (1 Cor. 11: 30; cf. Deut. 28: 22, 27). So far from this being an out-moded superstition, it has found confirmation from modern psychological studies. A sense of guilt may lie at the back of many kinds of illness.

James has already made several discerning references to SIN (*hamartia*). The essence of sin is that it is an offence against God. If it is merely some misdemeanour, which runs counter to human conventions, it would not be "sin", because, however much it may offend man, God would not be offended by it.

We are inclined to associate sin with an improper indulgence of our human appetites, and this may be its basic meaning in 1: 15. James, however, has reminded us that "sin" is a much deeper and subtler thing than just this. What is an offence to God may even be what human friends would condone or even applaud. At 2: 9, for instance, the sin denounced is the very widespread attitude of treating a poor, ill-dressed man with less courtesy than we show to the rich man; and at 4: 17 sin does not consist of any act at all, but only of failing to seize an opportunity of doing good.

These sins of which James writes, are evil things in this human nature of ours which can sometimes become a cause of illness. That is why

God's healing act, in response to believing prayer, includes forgiveness of sins as well as the restoration of physical health. God deals with the cause of the illness, not just with its outward symptoms.

FORGIVENESS of sins is an essential part of the Christian Gospel. John the Baptist called men to repentance that thereby they might receive it (Mark 1: 4). Our Lord placed even greater emphasis upon it. Often on His lips we hear the words: "Your sins are forgiven" (e.g. Mark 2: 5, Luke 7: 48). "All sins can be forgiven," He declared, even though this was in the context of emphasizing the extreme seriousness of one particular sin (Matt. 12: 31). His parable of the Unforgiving Servant is told against the background of the astonishing generosity of God's forgiving mercy, when men cast themselves upon that mercy.

This readiness of Jesus to mediate the forgiveness of God to needy people stirred up bitter protests from the religious leaders of His time. They accused Him of usurping the prerogative of God (Mark 2: 7), but instead of withdrawing from His position, He offered forgiveness to an ailing man with even clearer emphasis. Their objection was also based on their fear that He was undermining morality by being far too indulgent towards sin and sinners (Luke 7: 39).

Our Lord knew that the health of man's life depended on his appropriation of God's forgiveness. He told us to pray for it continually. He included it within the Lord's Prayer, as though daily forgiveness were as necessary for our true welfare as daily food for our body. But while He offers it so freely, He recognized that man needed to appropriate it. Repentance was a necessary prelude to it, and a harsh attitude of an unforgiving spirit to a fellow man could shut us out from the blessing of God's forgiveness.

To be forgiven is to know that the barriers, which our sin has erected against God shutting Him out of our lives, have been removed—not by our own efforts, but by the generous mercy of God. It means that in spite of our sinning, when we come to Him, God accepts us as we are, and heals us by His grace.

**5: 16.** This verse also has to do with healing. Verse 15 recommended a formal visit of the elders of the congregation, to pray over the sick man. Here it is the less formal action of fellow-members of the same congregation availing themselves of each other's Christian friendship. Prayer is again stressed, this time intercessory prayer for one another, and also confession of sins. They are urged: "CONFESS YOUR SINS TO ONE ANOTHER AND PRAY FOR ONE ANOTHER THAT YOU MAY BE HEALED".

It is best to take this as a general instruction to all Christians. The pursuit of holiness and personal obedience to the will of God should be so sincere that we shall use every means to learn our sins and find strength to overcome them. To have the added strength which

Christian companionship gives in this battle against evil can be a major factor in gaining the victory. Some commentators, however, restrict the application of this verse, narrowing it down to the particular circumstances described in the previous verse. Blackman, for instance, thinks that it concerns primarily those who are actually ill, and for whom confession of sins may be a means of regaining health:"The thought is not confession in general (as urged in 1 John 1: 9), but of confessing sins which might be regarded as causing the sickness, or rather the confession by the sick of their sins".

On the other hand there are those who would make this verse apply more particularly to those who are aware that estrangement and ill-feeling exist between them, because of wrongs committed and suffered. In this case James is understood to be advising each party, instead of accusing the other, to be ready to admit his own faults, and by mutual apology to heal the breach. This interpretation would be in accord with the instruction of Jesus to seek reconciliation with a brother whom we have hurt before "offering our gift at the altar" (Matt. 5: 23–24). Mayor acknowledges that this may possibly be the meaning: "Let the sick man confess his trespasses to those against whom he has trespassed, and let them in turn confess any trespasses which they have committed against him", but after discussing it, rejects it in favour of the more general one. Calvin too notes that "many think that James points out here the way of brotherly reconciliation, that is, by mutual acknowledgement of sins, since hatred takes root and becomes irreconcilable because everyone pertinaciously defends his own cause".

Both Calvin and Mayor, however, and most other commentators, prefer to understand these words of James as directed to the general life of the Church, urging the Christian not to conduct a lonely struggle against his sins, but to seek guidance and strength through a shared relationship with others.

It is to be noted that this is shared CONFESSION (not just one-sided) in the confidence of a private conversation between two (or more) Christians. Perhaps a small group is visualized. In this case complete trustworthiness is required by all, since the slightest betrayal of a confidence would immediately destroy the atmosphere in which confession could take place. Some have attempted with legalistic precision to make this counsel of James into a rule to be imposed on all. Rather it is to be thought of, not as a rigid requirement, but as wise counsel to be followed wherever it is advisable and possible. Calvin insists on this: "Confession of this nature ought to be free so as not to be exacted of all, but only recommended to those who feel they have need of it".[1]

The practice of the confession of sin has played a considerable part

[1] *Institutes* III. 4.

in a number of Christian movements. John the Baptist required it of his converts (Mark 1: 5), probably because he recognized that a merely private and undeclared repentance was often short-lived, whereas the open confession of the sins repented of and renounced strengthened the convert in his determination to have done with those sins.

In the Didache counsel is given to early Christians which corresponds closely with what James recommends here: "In the congregation thou shalt confess thy transgressions, and thou shalt not betake thyself to prayer with an evil conscience" (Did. IV, 14). The same writer also insists on confession of sins before participation in the Eucharist, and also on the obligation to be reconciled to anyone from whom one is estranged (Did. XIV, 1–2).

Since the thirteenth century it has been obligatory upon Roman Catholics to make confession to a priest at least once a year, and in many monasteries there is a more rigorous requirement of confession.

Many Protestant revivals also have been associated with an emphasis on the value of confession, based mainly on this verse in James. Some of the Christian societies which sprang up in the early part of the eighteenth century in Great Britain and on the continent of Europe adopted it as a guiding principle for the conduct of their small fellowship groups. John Wesley, for instance, drew up rules for his "Bands", small companies of twelve people or so, who met regularly for the mutual furtherance of their Christian discipleship. At the head of these rules stands this verse from James, with the statement that "The design of our meeting is to obey this command of God". Each member was expected from time to time "to speak freely and plainly the true state of his soul, with the faults committed in thought, word or deed since the last meeting". And at every meeting each member was precisely asked (along with other enquiries) "What known sins have you committed since our last meeting?"[1] Such rigorous discipline can only be maintained where the spiritual fervour is very strong, and the practice has largely dropped out of use among the modern generation of Methodists.

Still more recently the so-called Oxford Group, now usually known as Moral Re-Armament, has made confession an integral part of its technique for winning people into the Christian life, and establishing them in it.

Confession of sins offers certain advantages for the sincere Christian, apart from being a very painful practice of humility:

(a) To one who has been worrying about some past sin, or some besetting sin which he struggles against in lonely battle, confession can bring a great sense of relief from strain, as one opens one's heart

[1] John Wesley's *Collected Works*, Vol. viii, pp. 272–3.

to a trusted and understanding friend. It brings into being a new hopefulness and energy.

(b) The fact that another now knows of our failure and our penitence and our determination to overcome it, gives strength to our resolution, since we do not want to let ourselves down in the eyes of our friend.

(c) Since the loneliness of the struggle is over, there is a sense of added strength through the Christian fellowship now enjoyed.

All this has to do with confession to one's fellow Christians. There is no dispute among Christians about the importance of confession to God as a regular part of our prayers. Some who shrink from confession to other Christians ask: "Is it not enough to confess to God?" We might answer: If confession to God produces in us the necessary hopefulness of victory, and courage in the fight against evil, and deliverance from the sense of fighting our battle alone, then confession to God alone is adequate for us. But often when our human need is deepest, part of that need is that God seems to be remote and His strength beyond our reach. Then it is that our fellow Christians can become God's servants in our need, representing God to us, and listening patiently to our confession and matching it with the promises of God and assurances of His forgiveness and delivering power.

Modern psychotherapy fully recognizes the great value, to patients suffering from various forms of mental or emotional strain, of being able to "open their hearts" to a sympathetic listener.[1] Experiments are also being carried out in "group therapy",[2] which has many features which are reminiscent of some of the evangelical groups associated with the early days of Methodism.

Roman Catholics quote this text in support of their practice of confessional, by which members of the Church are required to confess to a priest and from him receive absolution. To use this text in this way is, however, quite inappropriate. The text does of course advocate confession, but not confession to a priest. It recommends confession among Christian people. "Reciprocal confession is demanded here", comments Calvin. Indeed the only priests within the Church recognized within the New Testament are not a special group of Church members but the whole community of Christians (see Rev. 1: 6; 5: 10; 20: 6, and 1 Pet. 2: 5–9).

Confession is to be associated with PRAYER for one another. Human friends can mediate God's help by listening to our admissions of failure, but they must direct us to the very source of help, and this is done by supplementing confession with prayer.

[1] Cf. for instance Stafford Clark: *Psychiatry Today*, p. 170: "There must be ample time for the patient to describe his difficulties and the doctor must be disposed to listen to them with unwavering patience and attention".

[2] Id. p. 184.

The purpose of both confession and PRAYER is THAT YOU MAY BE HEALED. Since this mention of healing follows immediately on verse 15 with its reference to physical healing, it is natural to assume that physical healing is intended here also. Some, however, argue that it is spiritual healing which is here intended on the pattern of the use of the same word in 1 Pet. 2: 24: "By his wounds you have been healed". It is more than likely, however, that James did not sharply distinguish the two. If "salvation" may include the restoration of physical as well as spiritual health, so may the words "be healed".

The fourfold reference to prayer in the earlier verses of the paragraph (in verses 13, 14, 15, 16a) is followed by the general comment that THE PRAYER OF A RIGHTEOUS MAN HAS GREAT POWER IN ITS EFFECTS. As an illustration of this Elijah is named in the next verse, but many characters from the Old Testament could have been cited (e.g. Abraham and his plea for Sodom, Gen. 18: 22–32; Moses in Num. 11: 1–2; Hezekiah in 2 Kings 20: 2–5). The same conviction finds expression also in such contexts as Ps. 34: 17 and Prov. 15: 29.

The word (*deēsis*) translated here as "prayer" is not the same as the more general one so translated in the preceding verses (*euchē*). This word, *deēsis*, indicates more precisely that element in prayer which presents requests to God. Petition or supplication would perhaps be a more precise equivalent in English.

A "righteous" man is one who does right, who obeys the commands of God. "He who does right is righteous" (1 John 3: 7). In the Pauline writings a righteous man is one who is right with God and from that relationship seeks to do right towards his fellowmen. It may be that here in James the word carries this dual meaning, but one suspects that for James the moral rather than the spiritual content is uppermost. The word "righteous" itself has come to have a somewhat pompous sound about it, and the meaning of the original may be in modern usage better represented by the word "good" (so N.E.B.: "a good man's prayer").

The word translated as "in its effects" seems to add little to the preceding phrase "has great power". In the Greek it is a present participle (*energoumenē*) and can be interpreted in a variety of ways: (a) If it is treated as in the passive voice it would mean "when it is put into operation". (b) If it is a middle voice it would mean "when it became operative". (c) If it is merely adjectival, it could be translated as "fervent" (as in K.J.V.) or "effective" (as N.E.B.). Since, however, the meaning of the sentence is not seriously altered by any of these three possibilities, we do not need to make a decision between them.

**5: 17.** ELIJAH is selected as the outstanding instance of a righteous man whose prayers were granted by God. The character of Elijah figured very prominently among the Jews during the first century. On the basis of Mal. 4: 5 it was expected that his re-appearance would be a prelude to the advent of the Messiah. It was he that men thought of when John the Baptist came on the scene with his fiery message and ascetic way of life, and indeed our Lord spoke of John as a second Elijah (Matt. 11: 14; 17: 13; cf. Luke 1: 17). Later when the figure of Jesus overshadowed that of John, it was Jesus that was associated with Elijah in the popular mind (Mark 6: 15; 8: 28), and on the Mount of Transfiguration it was Elijah, along with Moses, whom the disciples saw sharing the glory of that moment with Jesus (Mark 9: 4). When from the cross Jesus called on God, "Eloi, Eloi" (Mark 15: 34) it was Elijah the bystanders thought He was addressing. Ecclus. 48: 1–14 is a kind of hymn in honour of Elijah, which reflects the contemporary estimate of his greatness. In it special reference is made to the tradition about his effectiveness in prayer: "Nothing was too hard for him" (verse 13).

The introduction of the name of Elijah in support of the effectiveness of believing prayer may have provoked the retort that ordinary mortals cannot expect from their prayers such striking results as those that followed his prayers, since they are not in the same category as he. James anticipates this possible objection by insisting that Elijah, for all his greatness, was still A MAN OF LIKE NATURE WITH OURSELVES. This is a better translation of the Greek word (*homoiopathēs*) than that of K.J.V., "subject to like passions as we are". The word "passions" is too strong for what is meant here. N.E.B. has "with human frailties like our own". The same word is used of Paul and Barnabas in Acts 14: 15. The word suggests that Elijah, no less than ourselves, was sometimes unduly influenced by his feelings. It recalls the mood of depression which overwhelmed him, soon after his spectacular triumph over the priests of Baal (1 Kings 19: 4), from which he had to be roused by God's sharp rebuke (1 Kings 19: 9, 15). In this we realize that he is one with us. Since his frailties link him with us, his achievements should serve us as an example that we may emulate.

James refers to two instances of Elijah's effective prayer, firstly when in response to his prayer rain ceased to fall, and drought and famine followed, and secondly, when in answer to a further prayer rain fell again to relieve the people's distress. If one wishes to be fastidiously correct it can be claimed that in the narrative of 1 Kings it is not precisely stated that Elijah prayed on either of these two occasions; nor indeed is it there stated that the drought lasted for three and a half years. But Biblical narratives come to be told in a conventional way, and elements of interpretation creep into the story. In 1 Kings we read that Elijah foretold the drought (17: 1–2) and that he later saw the tiny cloud which heralded the coming rain at the end of the drought

(18: 42ff.). As the story was commonly told, however, it was understood that at both these moments Elijah interceded with God, and the
events were God's answer to his prayer. In 1 Kings 18: 1 there is a
reference to the drought lasting on into the third year, and it was
probably this that led to the assumption that its duration was three and
a half years. That this period had become part of the accepted tradition is clear from the fact that our Lord makes mention of the same
length of time when He refers to the same incident (Luke 4: 25).

**5: 18.** When James writes that THE HEAVEN GAVE RAIN, it may
be that he is reverently using "heaven" as a synonym for "God",
but more likely it is just a picturesque phrase to mean that rain fell
from the clouds in the sky (cf. Gen. 7: 11: "The windows of heaven
were opened"), though clearly this was understood to be at God's
bidding.

The rain meant the end of the drought, and with it the end of the
famine. In the moistened earth the seeds would be able to germinate,
grow and become fruitful. THE EARTH BROUGHT FORTH FRUIT.

The implied argument is: If confident prayer from a righteous man
can become with God a means of controlling the forces of nature, how
much more will the prayer of faith be used by Him to restore health
of both body and spirit to a fellow Christian.

The paragraph raises two issues of practical importance:   (1)
Spiritual Healing. (2) The use of verse 14 by the Roman Catholic
Church to authorize their practice of Extreme Unction.

Note on SPIRITUAL HEALING.

There is no doubt that healing by spiritual means was practised in
the early Church. It was a prominent feature of our Lord's ministry,
and both Peter and Paul are represented in the narrative of Acts as
healing many people in a similar way. Paul (in 1 Cor. 12: 9) lists
"gifts of healing" among special graces with which God endows certain
individual members of His Church. These verses in James also provide
clear evidence that this practice of spiritual healing was familiar in the
churches for which James wrote. There is also evidence in the writings
of the early Fathers that it continued for some time longer in the life
of the early Church.

In time, however, it ceased. Was this as God intended? Was it
meant only for a brief period in the Church's life? Did increase in
medical skill make it unnecessary? Or did it cease to be, not because
this was God's intention, but because men's faith and their spiritual
apprehension grew dim.

Calvin, and others, believed that this gift of healing was granted for
only a short, special period, and was not intended to be permanent
in the Church. "As the reality of the sign continued only for a time in

the Church, the symbol (of anointing) must have been only for a time." In the Institutes he writes: "God does not exert these manifest powers, nor dispense miracles by the hands of the apostles because that gift was temporary".[1] John Wesley, on the other hand, and many modern Christians with him, was convinced that spiritual healing "had been designed to remain always in the Church", but the gift had been "lost through unbelief".

The same debate continues today. Some argue that, in God's good providence, scientific healing has now superseded non-scientific healing. They claim that the outstanding advances in medical and surgical skill, which have already conquered some illnesses and greatly prolonged the average expectation of life in Western societies, are no less the gift of God to His people than the more spasmodic ability to heal by spiritual means, characteristic of the early Church and of some movements within the Church today. Others take sides rather with John Wesley in asserting that if the Church had remained fully alive to her privileges and potentialities she would still today be able to exercise her ministry of spiritual healing, not instead of the cures made possible by medical science but in addition to them.

Recent years have witnessed a great revival of interest in this subject among Christians. Some movements make it one of the central themes of their interpretation of the Gospel, and many within the established churches long for a recovery of that early faith which made a healing ministry within the Church effective. This longing has been strengthened by the deeper knowledge of the human mind which psychological studies have produced, proving that much which was once regarded as entirely physical illness can have, either entirely or in part, a psychological cause, and therefore may be amenable to other than physical remedies.

Wherever this concern for a rediscovery of the powers of spiritual healing is awakened, there this verse in James will spring into prominence and begin again to exert its influence.

Note on EXTREME UNCTION.

We have already noted the use made by the Roman Catholic Church of the verse which advises, "Confess your sins to one another". Undoubtedly it is fair to appeal to this verse to support the value of confessing one's sins. It does not, however, support the manner in which confession is practised in that church. James says nothing about confessing to a priest, nor does his way of recommending confession suggest that he intended it to become a binding obligation on members.

It is even more difficult to understand the way in which verse 5: 14 has been claimed as not only justifying but requiring the practice of

---

[1] *Institutes* IV. xix. 19.

Extreme Unction as a sacrament. This sacrament is administered to one who is thought to be dying. The priest anoints various parts of his body with consecrated oil. By this means it is believed that forgiveness is bestowed on those who are no longer physically able to make conscious confession of sin in the confessional, and there receive priestly absolution.

The Douai version of the Bible, in a footnote attached to this verse, claims that it provides a "plain warrant for the Sacrament of Extreme Unction", and misleadingly translates the Latin word "presbyteros" in the Vulgate, not as "elder" but as "priest". Monseignor Knox, however, in his modern translation which is authorized for use by Roman Catholics, reverts to the correct translation "elder". The Council of Trent officially named Extreme Unction as one of the seven sacraments recognized by the Roman Catholic Church, and described it as "commanded to the faithful by James the Apostle and Brother of the Lord".

It is clear, however, that James was not thinking at all in this verse of people expected to die. His whole concern is to suggest means by which their recovery may be assured. There is no mention of a priest, but only of elders, and they are named in the plural.

*5: 19–20. My brethren, if any one among you wanders from the truth, and some one brings him back, 20. let him know that whoever brings back a sinner from the error of his way will save his soul from death and will cover a multitude of sins.*

James's final plea begins as so many of his earlier ones with "My brethren". He has had some hard words to say to his readers, words of rebuke and correction. The tasks to which he has directed them are tasks which they will find uncongenial, and their human nature will shrink from them or rebel against them. But he reminds them that he speaks to them within the brotherhood of Christian love. He is making known to them the will of their Father whom they all acknowledge, and obedience to that is not only pleasing to Him, but for their own true good also, and certainly for the good of the Christian community to which they belong.

**5: 19.** His appeal here is not to all brethren in general, but to each one in particular, the "some one" who happens to be at hand when the opportunity to help arises. It is not only the leaders of the community who are involved in this instruction, but each individual member of the Church. Each one is expected to feel a constant and immediate sense of responsibility for the Christian good of his brother. To see a fellow Christian slipping away from his loyalty to Christ and growing careless in his commitment to Him should mean becoming aware of an inescapable obligation to do all in our power to win him back, till he is restored in his communion with God and loyalty to God's cause. "If *anyone* wanders . . . and *someone* brings him back" emphasizes our mutual responsibility for one another, a responsibility from which no Christian should seek exemption, from which no one can feel himself free.

In verses 15 and 16 James has referred to the evil consequences which follow upon sin. There is not only the obvious consequence of loss of fellowship with God, but even sometimes loss of physical health also. As proved remedies he has urged the practice of mutual confession of sin and corporate prayer for each other. Now James returns to this same subject to emphasize that in order to win back someone who has slipped out of Christian discipline persuasion must be used as well as prayer. Prayer in his absence is good, but it is no substitute for the concern which leads someone to seek him out and prove in action the continuing love his fellow Christians feel for him.

The word "WANDER" in the R.S.V. translation may suggest something almost accidental and unpremeditated. The Greek word (*planaomai*), however, means simply to "fall into error". R.S.V. translates the same word elsewhere as "go astray" (2 Pet. 2: 15) or be "wayward" (Heb. 5: 2). It stands here actually in a passive form, and could be rendered "is deceived" (as at Rev. 18: 23) but more probably it is best rendered by an intransitive verb, such as "goes astray" (Moffatt). Not only this word but the whole sentence is strikingly similar to Wisdom 5: 6: "We wandered from the way of the truth".

TRUTH is one of the big words of the New Testament. Its meaning here, however, is different from that in secular Greek, where its connotation is primarily intellectual. In the Bible, however, it is predominantly moral. William Barclay writes: "Christian truth is always moral truth: it is always truth which issues in action; it is a way of Life". This is shown by the striking phrase in 1 John 1: 6, where Christians are bidden to "*do* the truth". This is a Biblical emphasis which would have been hardly intelligible to the Greek reader who was not a Christian. For the Christian, however, truth is not only something to apprehend or believe, but also to *do*. Ropes understands it as meaning "the whole code of religious knowledge and moral precept accessible to the members of the Christian Church. . . . It is God's revealed will, to which the loyalty of the heart must be given".

This thought of truth is found not only in John, but also in Paul. In Gal. 5: 7, for instance, he writes of those who have been hindered "from *obeying* the truth". James too has already at 3: 14 pronounced selfish ambition and bitter jealousy to be evidence of a life which is "false to the truth".

IF SOMEONE BRINGS HIM BACK: the older versions here used the word "convert" for "bring back". The modern versions usually abandon this word, perhaps because the word "convert" in its modern usage has come to have a more precise meaning than the Greek word (*epistrephō*) had. It is used in the Bible for winning men from wickedness to uprightness, from the worship of idols or from unbelief to the living God. It occurs in Mal. 2: 6 (LXX), Luke 1: 16, Acts 3: 19; 14: 15. In some cases it means what we usually mean by "conversion", the first winning of a man for God, though elsewhere, as here, it applies to the winning back of one who has already been a Christian but fallen away. It is this sense which is also found in Luke 22: 32, when Jesus says to Peter, referring to his coming denial of his Lord, "when you have turned again . . ."

**5: 20.** LET HIM KNOW (*ginōsketō*) is found in manuscripts ℵ, A, etc. and is on the whole to be preferred to the alternative reading *ginōskete* (know ye, R.V.<sup>mg</sup>), although this is found in B. Since, however, the meaning is much the same in either case, it matters little which reading is accepted.

THE ERROR OF HIS WAY: the Greek word for "error" here (*planē*) is from the same verbal root as "wander" in the previous verse. Error and truth are similarly contrasted in 1 John 4: 6. In 1 John 4: 2–3 the Spirit of Truth is the Holy Spirit of God, and the spirit of error is the same as the spirit of evil or of anti-Christ.

WHOEVER BRINGS BACK A SINNER FROM THE ERROR OF HIS WAY WILL SAVE HIS SOUL FROM DEATH. The one who "wanders from the truth" is here referred to as the "sinner". To "save a soul from death" is apparently regarded as the same as "to bring a sinner back from his error". If it were a non-Christian who is involved here, to turn him back from error may mean no more than a moral improvement in conduct. But James is here thinking of one who has been a believing Christian, and whose lapse in moral conduct coincides with abandoning his faith in God. Indeed the outward moral lapse is the symptom of the inward spiritual failure. To win such a man back to his Christian way of life assumes that it implies also the restoration of his right relationship with God through forgiveness and reconciliation. So he will be not only a morally improved man but also a "saved" man.

We noted in the comment on 5: 15 that "SALVATION" in the New Testament means the restoration of the whole man, body, soul and spirit, and in that earlier context its effect in restored health and inward happiness was stressed. Here, however, the emphasis is primarily on the spiritual elements in salvation. DEATH (from which the sinner is to be saved) in the New Testament is in its essence separation from God. It is the ultimate consequence of sin (1: 15). In this James and Paul are in full agreement, as a study of Romans 5–6 makes clear (see especially 5: 17 and 21; 6: 23, "The wages of sin is death"). Men may find themselves engulfed in this "living death" even while physically they still continue to live. Living men may, in Paul's thinking, be "dead in trespasses and sins" (Col. 2: 13). But its dread climax lies beyond this earthly life when the soul in a kind of "second death" is made to realize the misery of its alienation from God.

James speaks of a man as "saving a soul". Is it not, however, only God who can bring salvation to men? James is being perhaps a little less than precise. What he means is that man may become God's agent in the life of another to bring to him God's great gift of salvation. It is not only James who speaks in this way of man bringing salvation to his fellowmen. Paul writes similarly in Rom. 11: 14, 1 Cor. 7: 16, 1 Tim. 4: 16.

This act of bringing a man back into the way of salvation WILL COVER A MULTITUDE OF SINS. "Cover" here is used in a way familiar in the Old Testament to mean "cause to be forgotten" and so to "secure forgiveness". "Blessed is the man whose transgression is forgiven, whose sin is *covered*" (Ps. 32: 1). So important is this salvation which he has found that it can be said to make up for many sins in the past. We shall later discuss whether the sins to be covered are those of the recovered sinner or of the one who brings him back.

The phrase about "covering a multitude of sins" appears to have become a kind of proverbial saying among Christians. In I Pet. 4: 8 we read that "love covers a multitude of sins" (a free translation of the Greek of Prov. 10: 12), and the phrase also occurs in the Apostolic Fathers (e.g. Clem. Rom. 49: 2; 2 Clem. 16).

Though the meaning of the individual clauses in verse 20 is not difficult to determine, there is great difference of opinion about the identity of the one to whom they refer. Opinions fall into three groups:

(i) Those who insist that the soul which will be saved and the sins which will be covered are those of the sinner who has been restored.

(ii) Those who argue that both these clauses refer not to the recovered sinner but to the Christian who has been the means of restoring the sinner. It is his soul which, as a result of his action, will be saved, and his sins that will be forgiven.

(iii) Still a third group prefers to separate these two clauses, and maintains that the first, "he will save his soul from death" refers to the recovered sinner, but the final clause "will cover a multitude of sins" refers to the sins of the Christian who has been the means of his recovery.

The Greek of the sentence does not make the issue clear, and commentators have to argue mainly from what meaning they think is most appropriate in the context.

Of these three possibilities, the first, (i), is accepted by Mayor, though with a measure of hesitation because he feels that (ii) does in fact seem to fit the form of the Greek better. He finally rejects (ii), however, because in his judgement it represents something less than a fully Christian point of view. It is equivalent, he thinks, to James arguing: "You have done much evil in the past, try and make up for it by the good you do in the future". This, however, he takes to be salvation by works and not in accordance with Christian truth. We have no grounds for saying, he insists, "If you make a convert, your own sins will be forgiven". So the interpretation he recommends is: "However many sins the wanderer has been guilty of, still if he turns, he will be saved from the death he has deserved, and all his sins will be forgiven" (though Dibelius points out that James says "many", not "all" his sins will be forgiven).

This is the view accepted by Calvin, who does not pause to take into account any other. He writes: "We must therefore take heed lest souls perish through our sloth, whose salvation God puts in a manner in our hands. Not that we can bestow salvation upon them: but that God by our ministry delivers and saves them who seem otherwise to be near to destruction."

Tasker not only confidently chooses (i) as the right interpretation, but rejects the mere possibility of (ii), on the grounds that it is a travesty of evangelical truth, which cannot conceivably have any place in the New Testament. To suggest, as (ii) does, that anything we ourselves do may atone for our sins "is wholly alien to New Testament Christianity and to what James has said in 1: 21". He adds: "It is very strange that Christian commentators should even have thought that James is advocating the recall of backsliders on the grounds of the benefits it confers on him who is responsible for it."

This interpretation (i), therefore, may be regarded as the orthodox exposition of the verse. It affirms that one who rescues a fallen Christian from his sinful regression will be the means under God of recovering also for him his share in God's salvation, no matter how many or how serious may be the sins which the backslider has committed.

We must, however, give attention to the arguments of those who believe that (ii) is the right interpretation. Those who advocate this usually regard James as the conventional Jewish Christian who still feels a deep attachment to the Old Testament truths on which he has been brought up, and regards the words of the Old Testament as still offering valid truth. There is no doubt that in Judaism it was recognized that persistence in righteousness can to some extent atone for past sins. In Ecclus. 3: 30 we read: "Almsgiving atones for sin", and in Tob. 12: 9: "Almsgiving delivers from death and it will purge away every sin". It is true that this emphasis is not repeated in the New Testament, but it does reappear in the Apostolic Fathers, the Christian leaders whose writings stand nearest in time to the New Testament. In 2 Clem. 16 we find: "Almsgiving is therefore good even as penitence for sin; fasting is better than prayer, but the giving of alms is better than both and 'love covers a multitude of sins'". He adds, "Almsgiving lightens sins". 1 Clement also affirms that "we are saved by works and not by words". Hermas writes: "If thou doest any good over and above the commandment of God, thou shalt obtain greater glory for thyself". Barnabas urges his readers to "strive to save souls by the word, and work with thine hands for the ransom of thy sins" (19: 10). And in the Didache (4: 6) we read: "Of whatsoever thou hast gained by thy hands, thou shalt give a ransom for thy sins". All these quotations show that among Christians in the period immediately following that of the New Testament, the idea was familiar that good deeds could be regarded as cancelling out past sins.

Origen, writing from the third century, shows this belief in fuller form. In Hom. in Lev. ii. 4 he lists those things which may be regarded as conferring forgiveness of sin. They are: Baptism, Martyrdom, Almsgiving, Forgiveness of others, Converting a sinner, and Love. In support of the sixth of these he cites 1 Pet. 4: 8 and claims validity for the fifth by reference to James 5: 20. Apparently, therefore, Origen understood this verse in this particular way.

It is true that all this represents something less than the clear truth of the Gospel, in which our forgiveness and salvation is always the free gift of God to our human need through Christ. It is clear, however, that a less lofty way of thinking on these matters did continue within the Church, and it may be argued that this element may occasionally make itself felt even within the New Testament. For instance, when 1 Pet. 4: 8 declares that "love covers a multitude of sins", in the sense that love makes up for sins, atones for them, it is approximating to this point of view, and the supreme example of love for others is to seek to win them from sin back to God (which is what James is speaking of here). Certainly to give oneself to the task of bringing a fellowman to the point of conversion is a much greater demonstration of love than the almsgiving which the Apostolic Fathers so greatly applauded.

It is on such grounds as these that Ropes (and others) confidently accepts (ii) as the meaning which James intended us to find in this concluding verse of his epistle. It is the "sins of the converter" which are to be covered. He adds: "To refer it to the sins of the converted person, as many do, makes a bad anticlimax". Mayor, also, though finally deciding in favour of (i) admits that the form of the sentences and their place in the whole verse does in fact favour (ii), and he feels "something of incongruity" about (i) even while he decides finally in its favour.

(iii) The third method of interpretation combines the advantages (and difficulties) of both the other two. It understands the first clause, "he will save his soul from death", as referring to the soul of the converted sinner. It is his soul which is to be saved. The second clause, however, is referred to the Christian who wins back another into the faith; it is his sins which are "covered" by his endeavour and his success.

Moffatt expounded this third mode of exposition and has been followed by Blackman, who, however, feels he must apologize for accepting interpretation (ii) even in this modified form. He writes: "James did not aspire to precise theological statement. He is content with the more naïve conceptions of atonement which are typical of Judaism and Jewish Christians of his time." W. Barclay also follows this third interpretation, saying of the second part that "The highest honour God can give is given to him who leads another to God".

Undoubtedly it is (i) which is the most explicitly evangelical interpretation of the three. It is very doubtful if (ii) can be accepted in its entirety. There is a similarity between the words of James here and those of Ezek. 18: 27: "When a wicked man turns away from his wickedness . . . he shall save his life" (R.V. has "shall save his soul alive"). The similarity suggests that James too would mean that it was the one who turned from wickedness who would find his soul saved from death. It is, however, possible that (iii) is the right interpretation. Certainly we should need to take the phrase "cover a multitude of sins" as used somewhat loosely to describe an action over which God delights in a special way, rather than as a precise statement of a doctrine of atonement. After all, James is not here aiming at making a comment on the way of atonement. He is simply wishing to underline the unequalled privilege accorded to a Christian when he is used by God to win another into the Christian faith. This should be the aim and aspiration of all Christians (see Gal. 6: 1). "Every Christian a soul-winner" is a motto which James here approves. To be used by God in this way, though a deeply humbling experience, is one of the greatest of all spiritual tonics. By it our own sense of God's power in human life is vividly renewed, our own assurance of our place within God's family is strongly reinforced, and a new sense of victory over sin is communicated to us.

Whichever way of interpretation we adopt, it is at any rate exhilarating to find James ending his epistle on this note of evangelical urgency, as he summons every single Christian to feel it to be his own responsibility to seek by every means in his power to win back into the faith any who may have lapsed from it. It is a good thing to be a devout and obedient Christian, but it is an even better thing to be devout and obedient ourselves and at the same time the means that God can use to bring others into (or back into) that devotion and obedience which to us is the greatest privilege that life can afford.

It is good to find James ending his letter on this combined note of evangelical urgency and pastoral concern.

# APPENDIX

## The History of the Epistle

In King James's Version the title of this epistle is given as "The General Epistle of James". Traditionally this epistle has been included along with 1 and 2 Peter, 1, 2 and 3 John, and Jude in the group of New Testament writings known as "The General (or Catholic) Epistles". It has proved to be a useful way of referring to this group of seven letters. Eusebius, the Church historian (c. A.D. 300), appears to have been the first to use this name, and the convenience of having such a name has led to its being retained. The name indicates that the letters are not addressed to one particular congregation or person, as most of Paul's letters are, but to Christians in general, or at any rate to a large and representative group of Christians. It is true that this description does not in fact apply to 2 and 3 John, but it does apply to 1 John (as well as 1 Peter, Jude and James), and these two smaller letters by John clearly could not be separated from 1 John, even if they are not precisely "general" letters.

James is addressed to "the twelve tribes in the dispersion". The meaning of this is discussed in the commentary, but clearly it comprises a much more extensive company than one localized group of Christians.

Among these "General Epistles" James stands first. It is strange that it precedes those ascribed to Peter and John, who were among the first apostles of Jesus, and its position of priority can only be explained on the assumption that its author was regarded as the brother of the Lord, who later became the very influential head of the church at Jerusalem. When Paul has occasion to mention these three Christian leaders together, he too places James first. He speaks of them as the three "pillars of the church", and names them, in this order, as "James and Cephas and John" (Gal. 2: 9).

In the early life of the church there is no precise reference to the Epistle of James until as late as the end of the second century. There is no mention of it in the Muratorian Canon. This is the earliest formal list we have of books felt worthy of a place in the New Testament Canon. Its date is about A.D. 180, and it is believed to represent the considered judgement of the church in Rome at that time. It is also absent from the so-called "Cheltenham List", a list of New Testament books copied into an ancient manuscript and thought to represent the judgement of the church in Africa, perhaps as late as A.D. 360.

Some scholars have argued that they can detect similarity of words and thought between this epistle and I Clement and the Shepherd of Hermas, but the evidence is too slight and inconclusive to prove that these writers knew the Epistle of James.

There is nothing in the writings of Irenaeus (c. 185), Tertullian (c. 200) or Cyprian (c. 250) to indicate that they had any knowledge of this epistle. In fact in the West the earliest writer to make unmistakable reference to it is Augustine (c. 420). It was Jerome who at last gave it an assured position in the Western church by including it in the Vulgate, the official Latin version of the New Testament, which he had been authorized to produce. Even he, however, when he refers to it individually, speaks with some misgiving, as though he was not fully assured of its apostolic authorship, which was by that time regarded as an essential qualification for a place in the canon.

In the area of the church of which Alexandria was the centre this epistle was known much earlier. Even here, however, there is no explicit mention of the letter until as late as the time of Origen (c. 230), though it is probable that his predecessor Clement was acquainted with it. Origen, however, leaves the matter in no doubt, because he precisely quotes James 2: 20, and at the same time refers it to "James's Epistle", and explains that James is usually understood to be "the Lord's brother". His acceptance of it as a "canonical" book, however, has a note of uncertainty about it. He himself appears to have been favourable towards it, but he is compelled to acknowledge that in some parts of the Church it is not fully accepted. He is not able to include it in his list of "accepted" books, but places it, along with 2 and 3 John, 2 Peter, Jude, Barnabas and Hermas, in the list of what he calls "disputed" books. Indeed Eusebius also, as late as c. 300, still placed it with the "disputed" books, since it was "held by some to be spurious", and "not many ancient writers have mentioned it". The matter was finally settled for the area of Alexandria by the Easter Letter of Athanasius in 367, which listed the books of the canon of the New Testament as precisely that list which gained ultimate acceptance throughout the Church, and in this list James was given its place.

Further East, however, in Syria, it was even slower to gain full recognition. There is no record of its being translated into Syriac until the authorized Syriac "Vulgate", known as the Peshitta, in 412. This same delay in acceptance, however, similarly affected both 1 Peter and 1 John.

The Epistle of James was, therefore, one of the latest books in the New Testament to gain universal recognition as an integral part of the canon. It was only as it came to be generally regarded as the work of that James who was the brother of the Lord and head of the Jerusalem church (and therefore of apostolic rank) that misgivings were removed.

In the intellectual and spiritual awakening which heralded the Reformation a new interest began to be taken in the New Testament and its contents. Traditional attitudes were discarded and the various books were studied with fresh eyes, and searching questions were asked by minds no longer inhibited by oppressive authority. In this surge of enquiry, the Epistle of James was exposed to new investigation, and some of the early misgivings about it, already voiced by Origen, Eusebius and Jerome, began again to be heard. Doubt was expressed about its apostolic authorship, and also about the spiritual value and reliability of its contents. Erasmus, for instance, found himself unable to accept the traditional view of its authorship, on the ground that the Greek in which it is written reads like the Greek of one to whom Greek was his native language; and also because there is little sign of its being affected by Hebrew, as one would expect if the letter were written by the first bishop of Jerusalem. Erasmus did not, however, query the value of the epistle or its right to a place in the canon.

Luther was more radical than Erasmus. He divided the books of the New Testament into three grades. First were those which declared the truth of Christ in its fullness; secondly those which declared it in a somewhat less complete form; and thirdly those which were noticeably of an inferior quality. In this third group he included James, along with Hebrews, Jude and Revelation. He separated these four from the others, and placed them quite deliberately, apart from the others, at the very end of the New Testament. His characterization of James as "an epistle of straw" is well-known, though it should be noted that he makes this slighting reference only in comparison with the pure gold of the gospel as it is found in John, Romans, Galatians and 1 Peter, "books which show thee Christ and teach all that is needful and blessed for thee to know". At a somewhat lower level, however, he recognizes that James has its own real value: there are "many good sayings in it", he writes, and "I admire it for it presses home the law of God". He regrets, however, the apparent contradiction in James of Paul's forthright rejection of "works" as a means of Justification, and the absence of all reference to the Passion, Resurrection and Spirit of Christ. Perhaps Luther's harsh treatment of James is in part explained by the fact that the Roman Church appealed to James as their scriptural authority for denying the Reformation doctrine of salvation by faith alone, and also for such practices in their church as the confessional and the sacrament of extreme unction.

Tyndale, in his translation of the New Testament, followed Luther's arrangement and put James at the end, complaining that "it does not lay the foundation of the faith of Christ". He adds, however, more appreciatively, "yet it calls men to keep the law of God and makes

love the fulfilling of the law. . . . It has nothing which is not agreeable
to the rest of the Scriptures".

Calvin's judgement is more balanced. He concedes that "James
seems somewhat sparing in proclaiming the grace of Christ", but
pertinently remarks: "It is not surely required of all to handle the same
arguments . . . It contains nothing unworthy of an apostle of Christ".
He is not willing to hold it against James that he implicitly assumes
some of the great doctrines of the faith without feeling it necessary
explicitly to state them; nor does he question the value of the epistle
or its full right to an equal place with the rest in the body of the New
Testament.

After Tyndale the English versions of the Bible returned to the
customary order of the contents of the New Testament, and James
was printed between Hebrews and 1 Peter. Since then there has been
no serious attempt to deny to James its rightful place in the canon,
though it continues to be one of the lesser known of the New Testament
books.

*Authorship*

The epistle claims to be written by "James, a servant of God and of
the Lord Jesus Christ" (1: 1). No words are added to help us to
identify the writer. The later tradition of the Church came to identify
him with James the brother of the Lord. If, however, we had nothing
to guide us but what we read in the epistle itself, we should have to
choose between four possible options:

(i). He could be James, the brother of Jesus, who after the Resurrection became head of the church in Jerusalem. This came to be the
accepted belief in the Church, and it was this which finally overcame
the misgivings which some had earlier felt about the authenticity of
the book and its suitability for a place in the canon. Tasker feels
no doubt that this traditional ascription of authorship is the correct
one: "It ought undoubtedly to be accepted as true" (p. 21).

(ii). Prominent among the original twelve disciples of Jesus was
James the son of Zebedee and brother of John. He might seem
a suitable person to identify with the James who wrote this epistle,
especially as it contains so many echoes of the teaching of Jesus.
Indeed some Roman Catholics do ascribe the letter to him, especially
some in Spain where this James is honoured as their patron saint.
Not many Protestants have favoured this identification, however,
mainly because in Acts 12: 2 it is recorded that this James was
martyred by Herod Agrippa I. This makes the date of his death
A.D. 44, and few would feel able to argue for a date for the epistle
as early as that.

(iii). Among the twelve apostles there was a second one bearing the name of James. In Mark 3: 18 he is described as "James the son of Alphaeus". This may be the same person referred to in Mark 15: 40 as "James the younger", the son of Mary. Calvin seemed to favour him as a possible author of the epistle, but this particular identification was never made before Calvin, and has not received much support since.

(iv). A fourth possibility is that the James who writes the letter is not to be identified with any of those called by this name in the New Testament. The name is not an uncommon one. It was the Greek form of the Hebrew "Jacob". There must have been many Jameses besides these three. There may have been some prominent leader, well-known in his own area, but not famous outside it, who could have written such a letter as this, and called himself "James" knowing that all his immediate readers would know who he was, but after his death, in areas where he was not known, his identity was completely forgotten. So it would gradually happen that James of Jerusalem was credited with the authorship of it. As we have seen, Erasmus and Luther felt doubts about the traditional view, and were inclined to accept this as an alternative, and many modern writers, among them Dibelius, adopt it as well. The chief difficulty is to explain why such a relatively unknown figure should feel justified in addressing his "epistle" to so wide a constituency as "the twelve tribes in the dispersion".

It seems probable that variants (ii) and (iii) can be ignored, so that our choice must be between (i) and (iv). If a member of the original Twelve had been the writer, it is most unlikely that this would ever have been forgotten. It is not even likely that his name would have been superseded by that of James of Jerusalem. Moreover, had there been no knowledge whatever of the original writer, and yet at the same time a great desire had arisen to identify him with some James of importance in the early Church, it is probable that one of the two bearing that name, who was a member of the inner circle of the disciples of Jesus, would have been chosen. The fact that both of these were passed over and that the epistle was ascribed to the brother of the Lord suggests that this identification must have had some support in fact and not merely be the outcome of a pious wish to add prestige to the epistle by ascribing it to a person of importance.

*James of Jerusalem*

Before examining the arguments which have been used for and against the traditional view of the authorship, it will be useful to summarize what we know of James the brother of the Lord, and later head of the church in Jerusalem.

In Mark 6: 3 (=Matt. 13: 55) Jesus is referred to as "the carpenter, the son of Mary and brother of James and Joses and Judas and Simon". The evidence suggests that he was not sympathetic towards the ministry of Jesus at the time. In Mark 3: 21 it is reported that "the friends" of Jesus were distressed and bewildered by the reports about him that were brought to them. The Greek phrase so translated almost certainly means "relatives" (N.E.B. has "his family"), and therefore refers to the same group described later in Mark 3: 31 as "his mother and brothers". They had come to take Him back home where He could be restrained and cared for. It was at this point that our Lord had to assert His independence of them, and declare that from that time those whom He regarded as His mother and His brothers were His own disciples (Mark 3: 34-35). His family at this time were not among those upon whose support He could count. Very poignantly He says, a little later: "A prophet is not without honour, except in his own country, and *among his own kin,* and *in his own house*" (Mark 6: 4). What the great prophets had found, Jesus too was experiencing.

We do not know when the family of Jesus changed their attitude to Him, and threw in their lot with the followers of Jesus. Both in Acts 1: 14, which appears to refer to the days very soon after the Resurrection, and certainly before the coming of the Holy Spirit at Pentecost six weeks later, we read that, praying with the eleven disciples, were Mary, the mother of Jesus, and His brothers.

It is Paul who suggests the clue to this transformation in James. In 1 Cor. 15 he names carefully those to whom the Risen Christ had first appeared: "He appeared to Cephas, then to the twelve. Then he appeared to more than five hundred brethren at one time, most of whom are still alive, though some have fallen asleep. Then he appeared to James, then to all the apostles" (1 Cor. 15: 5-7). Here to James, as to Cephas, is granted a personal awareness of the Risen Lord. It might be argued that the James intended is one of the two of that name among the original twelve, who had been present when He appeared to the twelve, and then had a special revelation for himself alone. Usually, however, this passage has been understood to mean that the James mentioned is someone other than the twelve, to whom Christ had already appeared in His risen presence, and He is normally identified with James of Jerusalem. It is more than probable that it is this personal experience of Christ after the Resurrection which provides the key which accounts for the complete change which came over this brother of the Lord. Certainly the experience would qualify him to be accorded the status of an "apostle", since an apostle was one who was expected to be able to bear witness to the truth of the Resurrection.

The successor to Judas in the number of the Twelve, for instance, had to be one who was "a witness of the Resurrection" (Acts 1: 22), and Paul bases some of his claims to be an apostle on his own qualification to be such a witness (1 Cor. 9: 1).

Whether this was the moment of his conversion or not, at any rate we know that James did become a believer, and even more than that, he was quickly recognized as the leader of the church in Jerusalem. This does not necessarily mean that he took precedence over Peter and John. It is possible that they required freedom from local responsibility to travel wherever the needs of the Gospel required it, whereas James was permanently resident in Jerusalem. The process by which James reached this position of supreme authority in Jerusalem is not described in the New Testament. All we can say is that by the time James is first mentioned by name in Acts 12: 17 he is important enough for Peter, just escaped from prison, to instruct his friends: "Tell this to James and to the brethren". James is already in a position which not only associates him with the other Christian apostles, but suggests he is even regarded as leader among them.

Later in Acts 15 in the critical discussion about circumcision and the Gentile converts to the Faith, James holds a decisive role. It is almost as though he is presiding while those who wish to insist on circumcision present their case, and Peter and Paul and Barnabas plead for its abandonment in the case of Gentile converts. It is he that sums up the discussion and gives the ruling which is accepted. "Brethren, listen to me," he begins, and the words themselves suggest the authority he exercises. Later, at Acts 21:18, it is to James that Paul makes his report about his further work among the Gentiles. Having earlier ruled in favour of Paul, he now asks Paul to make a concession in the interests of conciliating the Jewish party among the Christians, and to pay the expenses of a man carrying through a vow (Acts 21: 23–26).

This position of pre-eminent authority at Jerusalem which in Acts is accorded to James is further vouched for by some casual references to him in Paul's letters. In Gal. 1: 19, as Paul recalls his first visit to Jerusalem after his conversion, he writes: "I saw none of the other apostles (apart from Cephas) except James, the Lord's brother". In Gal. 2: 9 he speaks of James and Cephas and John as "reputed to be pillars" among the Christians in Jerusalem; and in Gal. 2: 12 he speaks of him as the chief representative of the Christians in Jerusalem, who exercised what Paul regarded as an unfortunate influence on Peter's judgement and conduct. A further reference to the brothers of the Lord (1 Cor. 9:5), who have the right to expect financial support from the Church, both for themselves and for their wives, may or may not include James.

From this we can form some estimate of James. He was a strong

H

man, on whose strength others could rely. His fairness was trusted, and his judgement respected. Temperamentally he was cautious and conservative, and reluctant to jeopardize proved values by taking unjustified risks. But once he could see the wisdom of a radical change in policy, he could take it firmly and resolutely. Even then he felt it his duty to carry all sides in the dispute along with him, and in the interests of peace and harmony asked concessions from both sides. He was able to see that ritual practices from the past were not of the very essence of obedience to God, and to relax the observance of them; but where it was a matter of moral obedience to the will of God, he was adamant. Eusebius (H.E. ii. 23) records that he came to be known as James the Just (or the Upright). This entirely supports the picture of him derived from the New Testament. It is also exactly what we should have expected to be true of the writer of this epistle, if we try to assess his character from the words he wrote.

The New Testament does not record his death, but there is no reason to doubt the report which Josephus included in his history (Antiquities XX. 9: 1) that the high-priest Ananus, after the death of Festus in 61, and before the arrival of his successor, had James stoned to death.

At a later time many legends were told of him, most of them pious fictions, though there may be truth in the tradition which Eusebius preserved that "his knees had grown hard like a camel's" from his long and persistent kneeling in prayer.

### The Brothers of the Lord

There has been a sharp controversy over the brothers of Jesus. In what sense were they His brothers? The most natural interpretation is that they were the younger brothers of Jesus, sons of Mary and Joseph. In Luke 2: 7 we are told that Mary "gave birth to her *first-born* son." The very word "first-born" appears to suggest that she had other children later. Had Jesus been her only child, Luke could have (and would have) referred to Jesus as her *"only"* (*monogenes*) child, just as later he speaks of the *only* son of the widow of Nain and the *only* daughter of Jairus (Luke 7: 12 and 8: 42).

In the early days of the Church it was understood in this way. Tertullian, for instance, assumed that this was the interpretation. Later, however, as more and more reverence was accorded to Mary, the Church's estimate of her was felt to require her perpetual virginity, so that she was represented not only as a virgin at the time of the birth of Jesus, but to the end of her days. Some other explanation of the brothers of Jesus was therefore necessary. Two were suggested: one argued that they were half-brothers, sons of Joseph by an earlier marriage. Others, less convincingly, suggested that the word "brother" included also what we mean by "cousin" (although the Greek language has, in fact, a quite different word for "cousin"). Both these explanations arose at a late date, and seem to have sprung out of the need to support a growing dogma, rather than to represent any genuine historical tradition.

We understand James, therefore, to be a younger brother of Jesus, the son of Mary and Joseph, and probably the next oldest in the family after Jesus, since he is mentioned first by Mark when four brothers are named (Mark 6: 3).

*Difficulties in the Traditional View of Authorship*

Those who have hesitated to accept the traditional view have done so mainly on two grounds:

(i). If James of Jerusalem were the author, is it likely that the epistle would have been apparently unknown in the Church until the time of Origen, later than A.D. 200? And after it came into general circulation would there have been such prolonged reluctance to give it an assured place in the Canon? Would this reluctance have been found not only in the West, furthest from Jerusalem, but in Syria, quite near to Jerusalem?

(ii). The second reason is the excellent quality of the Greek found in the epistle, some of the best in the New Testament. It is argued that such fine Greek is not at all what one would expect to find from the pen of a Galilean. Mayor claimed that the Greek of this letter approached "more nearly to the standard of classical purity than that of any other book of the New Testament, with the exception perhaps of the Epistle to the Hebrews" (p. clxxxix). Not all would rate it quite so high, but certainly it is the kind of Greek that a man would use for whom Greek was his native tongue, rather than a language he had acquired late in life.

These are real difficulties, and explanations do not wholly remove them. It will be best here to give the gist of Tasker's answers to them, since he is confident that they are not at all insuperable obstacles.

(i). With regard to the first difficulty, he points out that the early Church was pre-eminently a missionary Church. Writings which came from the missionary apostles, with a special emphasis on the evangelical doctrines of the Faith, would be more readily valued than an epistle from one whose task in the Church was not primarily evangelical or missionary. Moreover a letter addressed to a precise community would be more likely to be read and preserved and copied than a "general" letter which was the responsibility of no one group in particular. "Its author might indeed speak with authority and be addressing a wide audience on important matters, but that authority could never be quite the same as that of apostles who had first spoken to them the gospel of God" (Tasker, p. 19). So James would have only a limited appeal. When later it was brought to the wider notice of the Church at large, it carried little weight until it was established as the work of James, the brother of the Lord.

(ii). In answer to the criticism that the quality of the Greek in the epistle is too good for a Galilean to have written, Tasker contends: "There would seem to be no real ground for supposing that an intelligent artisan living in Galilee in the first half of the first century could not have acquired skill in the use of the Greek language". He complains that the excellence of the Greek has been overstressed, and quotes experts to support his view that "the author of Hebrews, Luke and Paul far surpass James in formal rhetoric". Moreover it should not be forgotten that, as far as we know, after the Resurrection of Jesus, James resided continuously at Jerusalem until his martyrdom thirty years later. During this time, as leader of the church in Jerusalem, he would have frequent contact with Jews and Christians from all parts of the world. He would probably not only speak in conversation in Greek, but need to speak publicly and even debate publicly in the Greek language. This experience would have enabled him to develop an easy skill in the use of the language. Add to all this that James must have been a man of quite extraordinary intelligence and ability to have risen so quickly to the position he achieved. What might have been improbable for a more ordinary person is not so improbable for one of his unusual calibre.

Since only students of Greek can appreciate fully this argument from the original language of the epistle, those who wish to pursue the matter further are advised to consult such commentaries as those by Ropes and Mayor.

*Pseudonymity*

If James of Jerusalem, to whom tradition confidently ascribes this epistle, is not to be regarded as the author, what is the alternative? It must be the work of some otherwise unknown person, bearing the name of "James", who later came to be identified with James of Jerusalem. We cannot think of the epistle as being originally written in order to be passed off as the work of the brother of the Lord. Had this been so, the actual writer would have been at much greater pains to ensure that every reader would know which James was intended. Some further details of identification would certainly have been added. It must, therefore, have been written by a completely unknown James, for a constituency where he was known and respected. Outside this constituency, however, he was not known, and what he had written carried little weight, until a tradition sprang up that it was indeed James of Jerusalem who was this hitherto unknown James.

This is a possible explanation. Indeed it was such an explanation which Erasmus and Luther accepted, and many modern commentators, including for instance Dibelius, take this same line.

The defence of the traditional view consists partly of pointing out the weaknesses of this alternative, and partly of showing how well the traditional view fits the evidence.


*Support for the Traditional View of Authorship*

(i). In answer to those who favour pseudonymity, there is the argument, already noted, that a document written by an unknown James would not have been ascribed to James of Jerusalem without good reason. Had an impressive personality been felt to be necessary to ensure the book's acceptance in the Church, either of the two Jameses in the number of the twelve apostles would have seemed much more attractive. On the other hand, if it had been one of these who had been the actual author, it is most improbable that it would have been thought necessary to invent someone else. Those who favour the pseudonymous explanation must be able to provide an explanation why James of Jerusalem seemed a better choice than either of the two original apostles of that name. The assignment of the book to James appears to have some basis in fact rather than just a general desire to enlist the help of a great name. Moreover its address "to the twelve tribes in the dispersion", though appropriate to James of Jerusalem, is not appropriate to an unknown James of only local importance.

(ii). The character of the letter itself is consistent with what we know of James of Jerusalem. On pp. 225–6 we indicated some aspects of his character as he appears in Acts, the Pauline letters and early tradition. We see him as a stern, self-disciplined man, upright and honourable in all his dealings, deeply concerned that the Christian community should observe only the highest standards of conduct, though ready to relax ritual observances in special cases provided always that moral standards were not lowered. We see him also as a man strongly determined to keep harmony and peace within the community, in spite of the presence of sharp differences of opinion on vital issues.

What we read in the epistle accords well with the character of such a man: his many strictures on the careless indiscretions of the tongue, his insistence on equal courtesy being shown to the poor as to the rich, the exhortation to steadfastness in trials, his urgent reminder that for a Christian his daily life should be marked by invariable honesty, patience and purity, and by that love which, as a true concern for the other's welfare, is the best guide a Christian can have for right conduct. We find in the epistle also a deep sense of the over-ruling power and majesty of God, and also of the love and mercy of God, as He stands ready to bring healing and salvation to all who call upon Him in faith. Faith, however, must be "whole" faith, not just nice feelings or fine words, but a relationship to God which includes obedience to His will in practical acts of justice and mercy and love, which alone are capable of demonstrating the reality of faith.

All this that we find in the epistle fits well with the portrait of James of Jerusalem as we know of him from other sources. His reputation as James the Just fits equally appropriately what we know of the first bishop of Jerusalem and what we can learn of this author from his epistle.

(iii). There is an unmistakable note of authority in the epistle which suits well the position of James of Jerusalem, but is not so appropriate to an unknown James, of so little importance that his identity was soon totally forgotten. The author writes not as an equal, making wise suggestions to his fellows for their consideration, but as one who knows that his standing in the community gives weight to all he says. It is true that he addresses his readers as "brethren", but this is the customary mode of address among Christians, and does not disguise the impressive status of the writer. An instance of his sense of authority appears in his somewhat peremptory: "Listen, my beloved brethren" (2: 5).

This assumption of unquestioned authority accords with the position of James of Jerusalem more readily than with an unknown James no longer identifiable.

(iv). Moreover there are some curious correspondences in words and style between this epistle and words credited to James in the Acts of the Apostles. For instance, the sharp call for attention, just noted, in 2: 5 occurs also in Acts 15: 13, where James of Jerusalem, presiding over the important conference on circumcision and the Gentile Mission, finally sums up the proceedings and gives, as it were, the "sense of the meeting" in his ruling: "Brethren, listen to us."

Also in James 2: 7 we read of "that honourable name by which you are called", and note a similar phrase on the lips of James in Acts 15: 7, when he speaks of "the Gentiles who are called by my name". Interestingly enough a word for "visit" which occurs only rarely in the New Testament (*episkeptomai*) is used both in James 1: 27 and Acts 15: 14; and the word for "greeting" used in each context is in the same peculiar form, an infinitive being preferred to the usual imperative (Jas 1: 1; Acts 15: 23).

These correspondences are not sufficient in themselves to prove the identity of the two speakers, but have a certain force when added to the other favourable arguments.

The two arguments against the traditional view of authorship are serious ones and not easy to dispose of. But they are not insuperable, and the arguments in favour of the traditional view have considerable weight. We have, therefore, felt justified in expounding the epistle on the basis of the traditional view.

If, in spite of the real difficulties, the traditional authorship of the epistle be adopted as offering as good a solution as any alternative which has been suggested to the various problems involved, is it possible to suggest any occasion in the life and ministry of James which will fit the peculiarities of this epistle? Something is needed which will account for its predominantly ethical emphasis, for the fact that it appears to consist of brief affirmations and exhortations which are relatively unconnected to each other, for the curious delay in the letter becoming known and accepted in the Church at large, and for its somewhat odd address to "the twelve tribes in the dispersion".

One can imagine just such an occasion: James as the head of the church in Jerusalem, permanently resident there, whereas the other apostles were absent often on missionary enterprises, would become a very important figure to all Jewish Christians. When the Jewish festivals came round, and Jews from all over the world made their pilgrimage to the Holy City, increasingly among them would be those recently converted to the Christian Faith. During their stay in Jerusalem they would eagerly seek to make contact with the Christian community there, and with its leader. They would be deeply impressed by his sound Christian sense and practical devotion, and his frank and searching insistence on the quality of life to be expected of those who had become Christians. They would come to know him, and he would come to know them and through them their home churches, their problems and doubts and shortcomings.

It would not be surprising if, as they prepared to make the return journey home again, they wished to have some written record of some of the striking words they had heard James utter. This epistle may, therefore, be a selection from his teaching which came to be made available to them, so that they could take it back for the guidance of all other Jewish Christians, wherever they were, who would respect the spiritual direction of the Christian whose wisdom and strength shaped the life and character of the Christian group in Jerusalem.

Such a suggestion would explain the somewhat artificial epistolary form of the writing, and, at the same time, the character of its contents as a loosely integrated collection of didactic material. It would also explain the comparative absence of Christian theological affirmations, because those who wanted this collection of James's words were already familiar with the basic doctrines of the faith, but felt the need of these down-to-earth rules of Christian conduct. It might also explain the delay in the letter's publication throughout the Church, because it would not be the special treasure of any one great Christian centre, but would remain the property of individuals who had visited Jerusalem, and acquired a copy for their own use or for other Jewish Christians of their acquaintance. It would explain the address of the epistle, since James might well have authorized its distribution among "all Jewish Christians whom it might concern, wherever they might be" (that is, "the twelves tribes in the dispersion"). It would also explain the simple description of the writer as "James", because to these Jewish Christians who had made the pilgrimage to Jerusalem, there would be only one "James".

### Date

Any conclusion which has been reached concerning authorship clearly has a very close bearing on the date to be assigned to the epistle. If we are satisfied that the traditional view of authorship can be accepted as correct, then the latest date which can be allowed for the epistle is A.D. 61, since, according to Josephus, it was in that year that James of Jerusalem met his death at the hands of Ananus, the high priest, who seized his opportunity in the interval between the death of one Roman Governor, Festus, and the arrival of his successor.

There are certain features of the letter which favour this early date. For instance, the meeting place of the Christian congregation is called a "synagogue" (2: 2). This was the normal name for a Jewish place of worship, and though the Christians may well have taken it over for a time, the custom is not thought to have been maintained for very long. Moreover the church order reflected in the letter is very primitive. Although the subject matter lends itself to some indication of how the community was organized, no officials are mentioned except the "elders" (5: 14), a somewhat informal word which may even mean only "older men". Further, there is no hint in the letter that the catastrophe which overtook the Jewish people, when Jerusalem was destroyed in A.D. 70, has yet happened. These considerations have been sufficient to persuade even such a radical critic as A. T. Cadoux that the date of the epistle is very early.

On the other hand some of the contents of the letter do not suggest a Christian congregation of the first generation. The faults which are rebuked appear to reflect a community in which the first evangelical fervour has waned, and a spirit of worldliness has begun to assert itself. Ropes, however, even though he himself finally chooses for the epistle a date later than the death of James of Jerusalem, insists that these faults do not compel us to accept a late date, since they are not any worse than those which Paul had to deal with at Corinth and Thessalonica, churches which were both in their very early days.[1] Sanday, however, though favouring an early date, notes that the condition of things is apparently settled; there is an absence in the letter of any concern about laying the foundations of the faith; the distinctive doctrines of the faith are assumed rather than proclaimed; rich people are present in the services. These factors tell against a *very* early date. The skilful use of the Greek language is felt to favour a later date, and also the fact that the author appears to use the Greek LXX rather than the Hebrew Bible. The absence of any reference to Jewish-Gentile controversy within the Church is said to indicate a period when it had ceased to be a current issue.

There is also the question of the relationship of James 2: 14ff. to the corresponding passages in Paul's letters to the Galatians and Romans. If James reflects an actual acquaintance with these letters, and is deliberately seeking to correct an emphasis in them he dislikes, that would point to a later date, since it is doubtful if Paul's letters were known beyond the churches to which they were sent as early as A.D. 61.[2] It is more probable, however, that James is answering not Paul himself, but a perversion of Paul's teaching as it had been represented in the area where James lived. This interpretation of the words in James would allow a date prior to A.D. 61.

These considerations which make a very early date improbable have the effect of causing those who accept the traditional view of authorship to insist that the letter must have been written at the end of James's life. Sanday says it must be put "as late as it can be in the life of James". Hort thinks that "60 or a little after seems not far wrong," and Tasker concurs in this opinion.

Those who on other grounds reject the traditional view of

---

[1] Ropes, p. 41: "We have no right to infer from the faults of James's readers a relatively late stage in their Christian history".
[2] C. L. Mitton: *The Formation of the Pauline Corpus of Letters.*

authorship lay greater emphasis on those features which require a later rather than an earlier date. If James of Jerusalem is not the author, then, so far as external evidence is concerned the letter can be placed as late as the end of the second century, for Origen is the first to make specific reference to it. Since, however, he accepts it as the work of James of Jerusalem, a sufficient period of time must be allowed between its first appearance and Origen's acquaintance with it, to allow for this tradition to be established. At the latest a date of A.D. 150 might be allowed, though not many scholars urge one later than A.D. 100 or soon after.

Those who decide in favour of a date later than A.D. 61 find difficulty in accounting for the primitive features of the letter which favour an earlier date. The use of the word "synagogue" for a Christian place of worship, and the absence of any developed church organisation are explained by Ropes as due to the fact that this epistle took shape in a Christian community "of extraordinary intellectual isolation".

*Language and Style*

This subject can be more adequately discussed in a commentary based on the Greek text, but some features of style are recognizable in a translation, and these may be mentioned.

There has already been occasion to indicate the good quality of the Greek in which the epistle is written. It is fluent, even elegant Greek. For this reason it is impossible to regard it as a translation into Greek of an Aramaic original. Some scholars have found it difficult to believe that someone other than a native Greek could have produced it. But many people have become so skilled in a foreign tongue as to be able to write it expertly.

Scholars vary in their estimate of the excellence of the Greek style. Mayor ranked it with Hebrews as the nearest of all New Testament writers to the classical style (clxxxix). Others, however, while allowing that it is written in good Greek, would not grade it any higher than 1 Peter or even Paul. Ropes even claims to sense in it what he calls a "Biblical tinge".

Certainly the author was very familiar with the Septuagint. Indeed his knowledge of the Old Testament, so far as it is reflected in the epistle, is derived from the Greek Septuagint rather than the Hebrew Bible. There are 73 words in James (out of a total of about 570) which are not found elsewhere in the New Testament. Of these, however, about 50 do occur in the Septuagint. Two quotations in the epistle from the Old Testament clearly come from the Septuagint rather than the Hebrew original. They are 1:10f. (from Isa. 40:6f.) and 2:21 (from Gen. 22:2, 9).

The author has a sensitive appreciation of the well-chosen and expressive word, and shows a taste for alliteration and plays on words. Sometimes his words are used impressively and even trenchantly, as in the style of an Amos; sometimes they are moulded and arranged with a touch of almost self-conscious cleverness, like that of a cultured scholar of the Wisdom school.

Throughout the style is largely hortatory. There are about 60 imperatives in only 108 verses. Sometimes, with a touch of rhetoric, he apostrophizes groups of individuals, "adulterers", "sinners", "you rich", etc. (cf. 4: 13–5: 6). Sometimes he avails himself of the popular device of the diatribe, and conducts, as it were, a dialogue with an imaginary disputant (e.g., 2: 14–20). He has a taste for similes and comparisons, and uses the figures of the rudder, the bridle, and the forest fire with good effect (3: 3–6). He has skill in introducing illustrations from the lives of well-known people, like Abraham, Rahab, Job, Elijah. He can use the vinegar of irony (as in 2: 14–19, and 5: 1–11), and command flagging attention with an arresting paradox (1: 2, 10; 2: 5).

## *The Plan of the Epistle*

There is in fact no discernible plan in the epistle. As we have already suggested it is a collection of separate units, and not an ordered essay or sermon developed according to a pre-arranged plan, and moving towards a pre-determined goal. The fact that those who try to find some pattern of arrangement in its material reach different conclusions shows that no clear plan is evident.

The most we can say is that a few main themes keep recurring. Among these may be listed: Steadfastness under trial (1: 2–4; 12–15; 5: 7), True Wisdom (1: 5–8; 3: 13–18), Rich and Poor (1: 9–11; 2: 1–13; 5: 1–6), the Danger of an ill-controlled tongue (1: 19–21; 1: 26–27; 3: 1–12; 4: 11–12; 5: 12), Practice more important than theory (1: 22–25; 2: 14–26), Peace and Strife (4: 1–4,) Prayer (5: 13–18), Humility before God (1: 16–18; 4: 4–10; 4: 13–17).

These, however, are only the main headings. Included with them is a variety of other material which does not fall wholly under any of these themes.

## *Provenance and Destination*

These questions, as with that of the date of the epistle, are closely related to that of authorship. If James of Jerusalem is accepted as the writer, then the letter must have been written from Palestine. This, however, is not the only reason for locating it in Palestine. Ropes, even while he rejects the traditional view of authorship, gives it as his opinion that the epistle "reflects conditions of Jewish life in Palestine, and almost all the ideas have their roots in Jewish thought" (p. 41). The references in the letter to the "synagogue" (2: 2) and the "elders" (5: 14) bear this out, and also the illustration from the "early and late rain" (5: 7). This is a climatic peculiarity, familiar to dwellers in Palestine, but not characteristic of areas further to the West. Also the "scorching heat" (what some would translate as the "sirocco", Greek *kausōn*) which withers the grass is also a regular feature in Palestine.

This is the prevailing view, and should probably be accepted with assurance. There are, however, divergent opinions. Elliott-Binns (in *Galilean Christianity*, pp. 45–52) argues for a Galilean origin rather than a Judean one. S. G. F. Brandon,[1] following the lead of some earlier German scholars, argues in favour of Alexandria. T. Henshaw[2] follows Streeter in advocating Rome as the place of origin, arguing that the thought of the epistle is based in Hellenistic rather than Palestinian Judaism, and attaching more significance than most scholars do to the supposed influence of James upon Hermas. The very diversity of alternative views, however, seems to confirm Palestine, probably Judean Palestine, as the provenance of the epistle.

E. F. Scott,[3] while not suggesting any country of origin, wonders if the cultured Greek of James could have been written in Palestine. He speaks of its "occasionally ornate language" and thinks it suggests one for whom Greek was his native language. But Greek culture, with its language and its ideas, was more commonly used in Palestine in the first century than used to be thought.

The destination of the letter is precisely named in the opening verse as "the twelve tribes in the dispersion". The meaning of this phrase is discussed in the commentary (p. 16). Here it is sufficient to say that it is probably a picturesque way of indicating that the letter is meant for all Christians, especially Jewish Christians, who care to read it. The "twelve tribes" of Israel was a customary phrase to indicate the whole of Israel. The Christian Church regarded itself as the New Israel, God's new instrument for the fulfilment of His purposes. The letter is, therefore, directed to all who feel themselves to be members of this New Israel, perhaps specially to those who had belonged to the Old Israel before becoming Christians.

This "epistle" is hardly a letter in the ordinary sense of the word. It is rather a collection of units of Christian instruction. James as leader of the Church in Jerusalem, and so in a sense probably regarded as the leader of Jewish Christians everywhere, would come to know Jewish Christians from all over the world. As they continued to come to Jerusalem for the great national occasions, they would make contact

---

[1] *The Fall of Jerusalem and the Christian Church*, p. 238.
[2] *New Testament Literature*, p. 357.
[3] *Literature of the New Testament* p. 211.

with the *mother church* of the Christians which was there. So he would come to know them and their problems, their virtues and their short-comings, and they would come to know him, with his sound Christian sense and practical devotion. It would not be surprising if, as they set off back to their distant homes and churches, they asked to have some written record of the things they had heard from his lips. This letter may be such a selection from his teaching as was made available for them to take to Jewish Christians, and indeed to all Christians, throughout the world.[1]

If the epistle is not to be ascribed to James of Jerusalem, it is difficult to find any suitable meaning for these words indicating the destina-tion. It is not easy to think of any unknown James who would have included such a pretentious address in his letter. To overcome the difficulty of this, it is suggested that the phrase was introduced into the letter later, in order to make it sound appropriate to James of Jer-usalem, after the letter came to be thought of as his.

One wonders if any later editor would have thought of using this particular form of address. Almost certainly he would have added some descriptive words to make clear beyond any doubt the particular James to whom he was ascribing the letter.

## *Character, Purpose and Value of the Epistle*

Several books in the New Testament appear in the form of letters, and are commonly known as "epistles", when in reality they are not letters at all. If the name "epistle" or the formal epistolary opening and conclusion were removed, there would be nothing left to suggest that the writing was a letter. This is true of Hebrews, 1 John and James. Curiously enough even the book of the Revelation is set within this letter-form.

In James, if the first verse were removed, one would never think of the writing as a letter. It would appear as a collection of wise instruc-tions from a highly competent Christian teacher. The letter form had, however, come to be accorded a special veneration in the early Church, and it seemed almost to be required of a Christian writing to be published in the form of a letter, even when what was written was in fact more like a carefully written sermon, or an urgent tract. It is possible that the real letters of Paul made such an impact on the churches which first received them that a kind of convention grew up that effective Christian writings should be in the form of letters.

The literary convention of writing and publishing "letters" as a

---

[1] Marty: *L'Épître de Jacques*, p. 241: "The exhortations in the Epistle do not always envisage a distinctive and precise situation. They visualise in turn various types of recipient".

means of communicating one's thoughts to a wide audience was earlier than the time of the New Testament. Cicero, Horace, and Seneca, for instance, all made extensive use of this literary form. It is indeed a literary device resorted to also in modern times, as a convenient way of giving expression to the deep convictions of one's heart (cf. for instance, *My Dear Timothy*, by Victor Gollancz).

The prevalence of the epistle among the New Testament writings may be due partly to this widespread literary convention, which was given a new lease of life by the effectiveness of the genuine letters of the apostle Paul.

James, therefore, is a letter in form rather than in fact. Indeed the epistolary convention is observed only in the opening verse, and is not even followed up in the conclusion. Certainly there is nothing in the body of the writing to make it sound like a real letter. It is rather a book (or pamphlet) of precise Christian instruction, with the name of the author given at the beginning and also the description of the people for whom it was particularly prepared and published. Blackman correctly describes it as "in the main a collection of paraenetic material", and Tasker quotes, though with something less than full approval, a comment that "The Epistle of James is a collection of sermon notes" (p. 9). Marty writes: "James is a sort of compendium of practical Christian teaching" (p. 238). The contents are not long sections of carefully integrated argument and progressive thought. They rather consist, in the main, of short paragraphs or even single sentences on independent themes, sometimes grouped together around a similar topic. Ropes speaks of the "aphoristic form" of the epistle and writes that individual sentences often have their "meaning complete in themselves, and gain comparatively little illumination from the context" (p. 3). He notes the skilful use of the same or of a cognate word by which these independent sayings are associated with each other. Many of these units of teachings are best expounded as individual utterances, originally unrelated to other sentences in the same context. If an attempt is made to link them with what precedes and follows in one coherent whole, the result is often artificial and strained.

Perhaps the writing most reminiscent of James is the much longer apocryphal book "Ecclesiasticus", from which many parallels to sayings in James can be cited. Blackman also points out a close similarity of structure, if not in content, between James and such passages in Tobit as 4: 5–19 and 12: 6–10, where many disconnected counsels and exhortations are linked together as if in one continuous statement. A similar collection of largely unrelated units of ethical counsel appear in Hebrews 13. Carrington also comments: "In James we are in a rabbinic school of the type of Ecclesiasticus, transfigured by the torah of the Sermon on the Mount".[1] There are also points of similarity with the book of Proverbs.

Though it is among Jewish writings that the closest parallels to James can be found, this does not mean that there are not Hellenistic features in it too. We have already had occasion to note the good quality of Greek which is used. James also adopts from time to time a feature of Hellenistic style much favoured by popular moralistic writers. This is the diatribe, where the writer constructs as it were an imaginary debate between himself and an opponent. This pattern of writing can be found in James 2: 18f, and 5: 13f. This oratorical device would, of course, be by this time well known in Greek-speaking communities in Palestine. Certainly Paul knew it and used it, as in 1 Cor. 7: 27 and Rom. 2: 17–29.

The contents of the epistle suggest that the author was a deeply sincere Jew before he became a Christian. Hort, in the introduction to his unfinished commentary, writes: "In some obvious aspects it is like a piece of the Old Testament appearing in the midst of the New Testament, and yet not out of place, for it is most truly of the New Testament too" (p. x). But it is the prophetic (or "wisdom") emphasis, not the priestly, which James represents. It is on moral obedience to the will of God that he insists, not on matters of ritual or cult or sacred institutions. There is no word to bolster Jewish national pride, and no note of the emphases associated with the Pharisees either—such as observance of the rules governing the Sabbath, and proper and improper food, or belief in angels. Nor do we hear any mention of circumcision.

On the other hand, there is a surprising lack of specifically Christian material in James. The name of Christ is mentioned only twice (though "the Lord" occurs more frequently). There is nothing whatever about the Cross or the Resurrection or the Holy Spirit (unless 4: 5 can be interpreted as referring to the Holy Spirit). There is nothing about the Kingdom of God, or of the two Church sacraments of the Lord's Supper and Baptism. In consequence some have asked whether perhaps the writing was originally a Jewish moral tract which was taken over by Christians, and adapted for Christian use by the addition of one or two Christian features.

The Christian note, however, throughout the epistle is too strong and constant for such an explanation to be satisfactory. As Ropes asserts: "The Christian references are not numerous but unmistakable". James describes himself as "a servant of the Lord Jesus Christ" (1: 1). He confesses "our Lord Jesus Christ" as "the Lord of Glory" (2: 1). He warns his readers of the need always to remember that "the coming of the Lord is at hand" (5: 8). "The honourable

[1] *Primitive Christian Catechism*, p. 28.

name by which you are called" must be the name of Christ (2: 7).
"The name of the Lord" in which the sick are to be anointed with oil
must be the name of Jesus (5: 14). For the writer, therefore, Jesus is
the Messiah and Lord, who dwells in God's glory, who is to come as
Judge of all men, and who will save those who love God (Ropes, p. 32).
Christians too are thought of as "the first fruits of God's creatures".
Moreover, throughout the epistle there are recurring echoes of the
teaching of Jesus, especially those parts of it recorded in the Sermon on
the Mount. And even when the words of Jesus are not precisely recognizable, the mind of Christ is felt to be the controlling influence in all
that is written.

James is basically a moral teacher, insisting on ethical conduct
of Christian character. But it should not be overlooked, however, that
James is also a teacher of spiritual truth. In fact, when we are dealing
with the contents of the New Testament, it is not easy to draw a sharp
distinction between what is "moral" and what is "spiritual". What
James understands by moral conduct is that conduct which God
requires of us, and at the same time that conduct which, because it is
an expression of love, aims to bring benefit to others. When acts of
goodness are carried out in obedience to God's will, they are worthy to
be thought of as spiritual acts, rather than as merely ethical behaviour.
But beyond this James has important guidance to give on such indis-
putably spiritual issues as faith (1: 3, 6; 2: 14–26), humble acknowledgement of God and our utter dependence on Him (1: 17; 4: 6–15), conversion and spiritual rebirth (1: 18), prayer (1: 5–6; 5: 13–18), and
the zeal of the evangelist to win men for God (5: 20). In all his
references to the religious life there is the same hatred of sham and
unreality as our Lord showed when He denounced the Pharisees as
"hypocrites". Ropes characterizes the epistle and its writer as "direct,
earnest, plain and sensible". All the contents are marked by "sincerity,
good sense, and true piety" (p. 15). "The epistle is a masterpiece of
robust and devout simplicity" (Marty).


*Purpose*

We touched on the purpose of the epistle when we discussed its
authorship and destination. It was suggested that it was not an epistle
written for one special occasion and one group of readers, but a
collection of important but diverse elements from the teaching of
James. They had been heard first by Christians in Jerusalem and the
many Christian visitors who came to the city. These people felt his
words to be so important and so relevant to Christian people everywhere that they had an anthology of his teaching material made and
written down so that copies of it could be taken back to their home

churches. Such a suggestion would explain many of the peculiarities of the epistle.

Brief reference should be made to alternative theories of the origin and purpose of this epistle, even though they cannot be commended.

(a). In 1896 Spitta (and others have agreed with him)[1] argued that the original document behind the epistle was a Jewish collection of moral instructions, and that this was taken over for use among Christians and given a Christian flavour by adding such verses as 1:1 and 2:1. He found support for his argument in the lack of specifically Christian teaching in the epistle.

In reply to this it may be pointed out that, although there is a Jewish flavour about the epistle, there is not a single sentence which a Christian could not have written. Moreover the Christian elements in the epistle are more numerous than the two references given, and indeed the influence of the words of Jesus is evident throughout the epistle.

Further, in the form in which Spitta put forward the theory, it implied that the original document was in Aramaic. This epistle is not, however, written in translation Greek. There are very few signs of direct Semitic influence on its style. Moreover, there are instances of word play which depend entirely on the similarity of sound between two different words in Greek, which loses its effect when translated back into Aramaic (e.g. *chairein* to mean "greeting", and *chara* meaning "joy" in 1:1–2). Greek was certainly the original language of the epistle.

(b). In 1930 A. Meyer, in *Das Ratsel des Jacobus Briefes*, put forward what appears to be a fantastic theory about the origin of the epistle. It treats the epistle as a highly elaborated allegory. He too accepts a Jewish original as lying behind the epistle in its present form, and believes this Jewish original to have been an allegory on Genesis 49, where Jacob addresses his twelve sons in turn. He sees this epistle as intended to be understood as a similar address by "Jacob" (the Hebrew form of the name "James") to his twelve sons (the "twelve tribes" of 1:1). The sons are addressed under symbols. For instance, "joy" in 1:2 represents Isaac, because in Gen. 17:19 his name is given to mean "Laughter". "Patient endurance" (R.S.V. steadfastness) in 1:3–4 is taken as a reference to Rebecca who was barren for twenty years after marriage. Simeon is repre-

---

[1] F.C. Burkitt's theory in *Christian Beginnings* (1924) assumes an Aramaic original, translated into Greek and enlarged.

sented in 1: 19–20 as "anger", and Gad in 4: 1–2 as "wars and
fightings", and so on. Meyer's book has not been translated into
English, but a careful and lengthy summary of it is included by B. S.
Easton in his introduction to the Epistle of James in Volume 12 of
the *Interpreter's Bible*. Meyer's exegesis of the epistle as an allegory
is a feature of a current revival of interest in allegorical methods of
interpreting Scripture. The same approach has been applied to other
books in the New Testament. As a method of determining the
meaning of what James writes it seems to be quite misplaced.
Tasker's comment is not unfair: "It is one of the surprising features
of contemporary biblical criticism that such a method of exegesis
should be regarded as a serious contribution to the problem of the
origin of the Epistle of James" (p. 35).


## *Kerygma and Didache*

The New Testament studies of the last thirty years have led to
new understanding of the original forms of the Christian message,
which enables us to gain a clearer picture of the part played by such an
epistle as James in the life of the early Church. The distinction between
Kerygma and Didache has become familiar to all students of the New
Testament. By Kerygma is meant that basic proclamation of the
Christian Faith with which the early missionaries went out into the
world; it was this that arrested the attention of hearers, awakened in
them a sense of the reality of God's act in Christ, and evoked faith and
also further enquiry. The substance of this proclamation was that the
God who had spoken through the prophets, promising salvation to His
people, had now fulfilled that promise in Jesus of Nazareth, who carried
out a ministry of mercy and healing, who was crucified for men's sins
and raised from the dead and given His place at God's right hand.
From there He is sending to men His gift of the Holy Spirit, and in God's
appointed time will come again in final triumph to be the judge of all
men. Thereafter men should repent and accept this offer in Christ of
God's salvation.

The main features of this proclamation can be discerned in several
of the early sermons in Acts, and also at various places in Paul's
epistles. It was the great achievement of C. H. Dodd to make this
clear in his book, *The Apostolic Preaching and Its Developments* (1936).
This was the substance of the message with which the early Christians
confronted an unbelieving world.

Once, however, this proclamation had been accepted and believed,
the believers found further questions springing up and requiring an
answer. One question concerned the life and ministry of Jesus, through
which God had worked such a signal achievement. What was He like?

What had He done? What words had He spoken? Why did He die on a Roman Cross? What happened after His death, since that seemed to be a new beginning rather than an end? The second question concerned the conduct of those who now believed in Christ and had accepted the salvation that God had offered in Him. Their lives now belonged to God. What difference should this make in the way they behaved? What changes had to take place in them? What old ways must be abandoned, and what new ways taken up?

The first of these two needs was met by such writings as the Synoptic gospels, and the second by various forms of practical instruction in matters of conduct and practical devotion. If the original proclamation was Kerygma, the teaching which followed in response to the further questions was called Didache (the Greek word meaning "teaching"). Some writers[1] have argued that before any of our present New Testament writings existed in their present form, standard patterns of moral instruction had developed within the Church. It is pointed out that when Paul, Peter and James give moral instruction there are noticeable similarities in both content and wording, and it is argued that this is due to their common use of these earlier codes of conduct.

Paul's letters tend to follow a recognizable pattern. He usually deals first with matters of faith, questions arising out of the kerygma, its further elucidation or the correction of misunderstanding. Then at the end, when the basis in faith has been established, he turns to the outworking of this faith in conduct and gives instruction in conduct— Didache. In Paul's letters this will be found in Romans 12ff., Galatians 5–6, Colossians 3–4, 1 Thessalonians 4–5—all chapters at the end of their respective epistles. In James, however, the whole epistle is Didache. He takes for granted the Kerygma. The difficulties he faces do not apparently arise from that. He concentrates entirely on the Didache, and expounds the kind of conduct in which the Christian faith should find expression, and the kind of conduct which is incongruous with it. He does not proclaim the Kingdom of God but he insists on the Royal Law (2: 8) which is the rule of life followed by those who yield themselves in obedience to the King.

Paul in his letters combines Kerygma and Didache, and this is a happy way of keeping together two elements of the Christian faith which ought never to be separated. James, however, seems to have

---

[1] A careful study of these was made by P. Carrington in *A Primitive Christian Catechism* (1940) and in great detail by E. G. Selwyn in Appendix II in his commentary on I Peter (1946). A. M. Hunter had a chapter on "The Paraenetic Tradition" in his first edition of *Paul and his Predecessors* (1940). This is repeated in the revised edition of 1961, and a further section added on the same subject, which takes account of books published since 1940. In the revised edition the two sections are at pages 52–57, and 128–131.

preferred to deal with them not concurrently but consecutively. No doubt, in dealing with newcomers, he would proclaim the kergyma as others did. When, however, he is dealing with instruction to those already believers, he concentrates entirely on the Didache.

Just as C. H. Dodd introduced English readers to the thought of the Kerygma, so his book on "Gospel and Law" expounds what is meant by Didache, and its use in the early Church.

## The Value of the Epistle

The great value of James lies in his uncompromising insistence on the moral contents of the Christian faith. If faith is living faith, and the Holy Spirit is really active in a human life, there will be inevitable "fruit" in good conduct, that is, in Christian love. If ever Christians become unduly preoccupied with the other aspects of the Christian faith, its dogma, its theological explanations, its mystical experiences, as if these were the sum total of the Faith, there is always James to remind them that the real test of Christian faith is found in the conduct it produces. Perhaps it is partly because he represents this uncomfortable reminder of an uncongenial truth that some are content to leave him a little neglected and even despised.

It is not that James is unique in this. He is not. Paul and John are just as emphatic, but James seems more emphatic because, in effect, it is the only thing he says. He is, we must concede it, less balanced than Paul or John, and less comprehensive, but this very lack of balance, this concentrated attention on one aspect of the faith makes what he has to say inescapable.

There is a difference in emphasis between James and the others. This is a good thing. It reminds us that Christian people have their differences of temperament and emphasis, and that these differences should not be allowed to separate them off into different churches looking askance at each other. The New Testament is "catholic" enough to include James as well as Paul and John, and the Christian Church should learn to practise a similar all-inclusive faith.

The fact that in James there are so many reminders of the teaching of Jesus should assure us that he is not dealing with matters of secondary importance, but something integral to our faith.

We cannot do better in conclusion than quote some wise words written by Hort in the introduction to his commentary on James (pp. ix–x): "Its very unlikeness to other books in the New Testament is of the greatest value to us, as showing . . . the manysidedness of Christian truth. . . . It was needed that various modes of apprehending the one Truth should be sanctioned for ever as contributing to the completeness of the faith. And that mode of apprehending it which we find in St.

James stamped the comprehensiveness of Apostolic Christianity in marked manner, being the furthest removed from that of the Apostle of largest influence, St. Paul. . . . The combination of St. James with St. Paul is a safeguard against much error."

# BIBLIOGRAPHY

ABBOTT-SMITH: *Manual Greek Lexicon of the New Testament* (T. & T. Clark, Edinburgh, 1923).

ARNDT, W. F., and GINGRICH, F. W.: *A Greek-English Lexicon of the New Testament and other Early Christian Literature* (Cambridge University Press and University of Chicago Press, 1957). Based on W. Bauer's famous book.

BAILLIE, J.: *The Sense of the Presence of God* (Gifford Lectures, Oxford, 1962).

BARCLAY, W.: *The Letter of James* (Church of Scotland, 1957).

BAUER, W.: *Griechisch-deutsches Wörterbuch zu den Schriften des Neuen Testaments und der übrigen Urchristlichen Literatur* (Berlin, 1949–52).

Bible in Basic English (Cambridge, 1949).

BLACKMAN, E. C.: *The Epistle of James* (Torch Bible Commentaries, S.C.M. Press, London, 1957).

BRANDON, S. G. F.: *The Fall of Jerusalem and the Christian Church* (S.P.C.K., London, 1951).

CALVIN, J.: *Commentaries on the Catholic Epistles,* translated and edited by J. Owen (Calvin Translation Society, Edinburgh, 1855).

CARPENTER, H. J.: Article on "Minister" in *A Theological Word Book of the Bible* (S.C.M. Press, London, 1950).

CARRINGTON, P.: *Primitive Christian Catechism* (Cambridge, 1940).

CHAINE, J.: *L'Épître de S. Jacques* (Paris, 1927).

DIBELIUS, M.: *Der Brief des Jakobus* (Vandenhoeck und Ruprecht, Göttingen, 1956).

DODD, C. H.: *The Apostolic Preaching and Its Development* (Hodder and Stoughton, London, 1936).

ELLIOTT-BINNS, L. E.: *Galilean Christianity* (S.C.M. Press, London, 1956).

*Expository Times:* monthly publication (T. & T. Clark, Edinburgh).

FUNK, R. W.: *A Greek Grammar of the New Testament and Early Christian Literature* (Cambridge University Press and Chicago University Press, 1961). A revision of Blass and Debrunner: *Grammatik der neutestamentichen Griechisch*).

GINGRICH, F. W.: See Arndt and Gingrich.

GOLLANCZ, V.: *My Dear Timothy* (Gollancz).

HENSHAW, T.: *New Testament Literature* (Allen & Unwin, London, 1952).

HORT, F. J. A.: *The Epistle of James* (Macmillan, London, 1909).

HUNTER, A. M.: *Paul and His Predecessors* (S.C.M. Press, London, 1940; revised edition 1961).

KNOX, J.: *The Ethic of Jesus in the Teaching of the Church* (Epworth, London, 1962).

MARTY: *L'Épître de Jacques.*

MAYOR, J. B.: *The Epistle of James* (Macmillan, London, 1892).

McNEILE, A. H.: *An Introduction to the Study of the New Testament* (Oxford, Second Edition, 1953).

*Message and Mission of Methodism*: Methodist Conference of Great Britain (1946).

MEYER, A.: *Das Ratsel des Jacobus Briefes* (1930).

MITTON, C. L.: *The Formation of the Pauline Corpus of Letters* (Epworth, London, 1955).

MOFFATT, J.: *The General Epistles* (Hodder and Stoughton, London, 1945).

MOFFATT, J.: *A New Translation of the Bible* (Hodder and Stoughton, London, 1928).

MOULE, C. F. D.: *The Birth of the New Testament* (A. & C. Black, London, 1962).

MOULTON, J. H.: *A Grammar of New Testament Greek*, Vol. I *Prolegomena* (T. & T. Clark, Edinburgh, 1906).

"New Testament Studies", *Journal of Studiorum Novi Testamenti Societas* (Cambridge University Press).

PARRY, R. S. J.: *A Discussion of the General Epistle of St. James* (Cambridge University Press, 1903).

PHILLIPS, J. B.: *The New Testament in Modern English* (Bles, London, 1959).

PLUMTRE, E. H.: *The General Epistle of St. James* (Cambridge, 1890).

RICHARDSON, A. (editor): *A Theological Word Book of the Bible* (S.C.M. Press, London, 1950).

ROPES, J. H.: *A Critical and Exegetical Commentary on the Epistle of St. James* (*International Critical Commentary*, T. & T. Clark, Edinburgh, 1954).

SANGSTER, P.: *Dr. Sangster* (Epworth Press, London, 1962).

SCHMITHALS, W.: *Paul and James* (S.C.M. Press, London, 1965).

SCOTT, E. F.: *Literature of the New Testament* (Columbia University Press, 1932).

SELWYN, E. G.: *The First Epistle of St. Peter* (Macmillan, London, 1946).

STAFFORD-CLARK, D.: *Psychiatry Today* (Penguin Books, London, 1952).

STRACK, H. L., and BILLERBECK, P.: *Kommentar zum Neuen Testament aus Talmud und Midrasch* (Beck, München, 1926).

TASKER, R. V. G.: *The General Epistle of James* (Tyndale Press, London, 1956).

WEATHERHEAD, L. D.: *Psychology and Life* (Hodder and Stoughton, London, 1934).

WESLEY, J.: *The New Testament with Explanatory Notes* (1754).

WESLEY, J.: *Collected Works*, Volumes I–XIV (Wesleyan Conference Office, London).

WEYMOUTH, R. F.: *The New Testament in Modern Speech* (James Clarke, London, 1924).

WILLIAMS, C. K.: *The New Testament: A New Translation in Plain English* (S.P.C.K., London, 1952).

# SELECTED INDEX OF AUTHORS AND SUBJECTS

# INDEX OF SCRIPTURE REFERENCES

## OLD TESTAMENT AND APOCRYPHA

## NEW TESTAMENT

# Marshalls Study Library

**J. Sidlow Baxter**
THE STRATEGIC GRASP OF THE BIBLE

**James Black**
THE MYSTERY OF PREACHING

**Ralph P. Martin**
WORSHIP IN THE EARLY CHURCH

**C. Leslie Mitton**
THE EPISTLE OF JAMES

**G. Campbell Morgan**
THE GOSPEL ACCORDING TO MATTHEW
THE GOSPEL ACCORDING TO MARK
THE GOSPEL ACCORDING TO LUKE
THE GOSPEL ACCORDING TO JOHN
GREAT CHAPTERS OF THE BIBLE
THE GREAT PHYSICIAN
STUDIES IN THE PROPHECY OF JEREMIAH
SEARCHLIGHTS FROM THE WORD

**Andrew Murray**
THE HOLIEST OF ALL
THE SPIRIT OF CHRIST

**Rene Pache**
THE FUTURE LIFE

**C. H. Spurgeon**
LECTURES TO MY STUDENTS

**R. A. Torrey**
WHAT THE BIBLE TEACHES

**W. E. Vine**
THE EPISTLE TO THE ROMANS

**Alexander Whyte**
BIBLE CHARACTERS
Vol. 1 OLD TESTAMENT
Vol. 2 NEW TESTAMENT